Praise for the "Kids Love" Guidebook Travel Series

On-Air Personality Comments (Television Interviews)

"The great thing about these books is that your whole family actually lives these adventures" – (**WKRC-TV**, Cincinnati)

"Very helpful to lots of families when the kids say, I'm bored...and I don't want to go to same places again!" – (**WISH-TV**, Indianapolis)

"Dividing the state into many sections, the book has something for everyone...everywhere." – (**WLVT-TV**, Pennsylvania)

"These authors know first-hand that it's important to find hands-on activities that engage your children..." (**WBNS-TV**, Columbus)

"You spent more than 1000 hours doing this research for us, that's really great – we just have to pick up the book and it's done..."
(**WTVR-TV**, Richmond)

"A family that's a great source for travel ideas..."
(**WBRA-TV**, Roanoke)

"What a great idea...this book needed to be done a long time ago!"
(**WKYT-TV**, Lexington)

"A fabulous idea...places to travel that your kids will enjoy"
(**WOOD-TV**, Grand Rapids)

"The Zavatskys call it a dream come true, running their own business while keeping the family together. Their goal, encourage other parents to create special family travel memories." - (**WLVT-TV,** Pennsylvania)

"It's a wonderful book, and as someone who has been to a lot of these places...you hit it right on the money!" – (**WKRC-TV**, Cincinnati)

Praise for the "Kids Love" Guidebook Travel Series
Customer Comments (actual letters on file)

"I wanted to tell you how helpful all your books have been to my family of 6. I rarely find books that cater to families with kids. I have your Indiana, Ohio, Kentucky, Michigan, and Pennsylvania books. I don't want to miss any of the new books that come out. Keep up the great ideas. The books are fantastic. I have shown them to tons of my friends. They love them, too." – H.M.

"I bought the Ohio and Indiana books yesterday and what a blessing these are for us!!! We love taking our grandsons on Grammie & Papaw trips thru the year and these books are making it soooo much easier to plan. The info is complete and full of ideas. Even the layout of the book is easy to follow...I just wanted to thank you for all your work in developing these books for us..." – G.K

"I have purchased your book. My grandchildren and I have gone to many of the places listed in your book. They mark them off as we visit them. We are looking forward to seeing many more. It is their favorite thing to look at book when they come over and find new places to explore. Thank you for publishing this book!" - B.A.

"At a retail price of under $15.00, any of the books would be well worth buying even for a one-time only vacation trip. Until now, when the opportunity arose for a day or weekend trip with the kids I was often at a loss to pick a destination that I could be sure was convenient, educational, child-friendly, and above all, fun. Now I have a new problem: How in the world will we ever be able to see and do all the great ideas listed in this book? I'd better get started planning our next trip right away. At least I won't have to worry about where we're going or what to do when we get there!" – VA Homeschool Newsletter

"My family and I used this book this summer to explore Ohio! We lived here nearly our entire life and yet over half the book we never knew existed. These people really know what kids love! Highly recommended for all parents, grandparents, etc.." – Barnes and Noble website reviewer

KIDS LOVE Pennsylvania

A Family Travel Guide to Exploring "Kid-Tested" Places in Pennsylvania...Year Round!

George & Michele Zavatsky

Dedicated to the Families
of Pennsylvania

For the latest major updates corresponding to the pages in this book visit our website:

www.KidsLoveTravel.com

REMEMBER: *Museum exhibits change frequently. Check the site's website before you visit to note any changes. Also, HOURS and ADMISSIONS are subject to change at the owner's discretion. If you are tight on time or money, check the attraction's website or call before you visit.*

INTERNET PRECAUTION: *All websites mentioned in KIDS LOVE PENNSYLVANIA have been checked for appropriate content. However, due to the fast-changing nature of the Internet, we strongly urge parents to preview any recommended sites and to always supervise their children when on-line.*

ISBN-13: 978-0-9774434-3-7
ISBN-10: 0-9774434-3-4

KIDS ♥ PENNSYLVANIA™   Kids Love Publications, LLC

TABLE OF CONTENTS

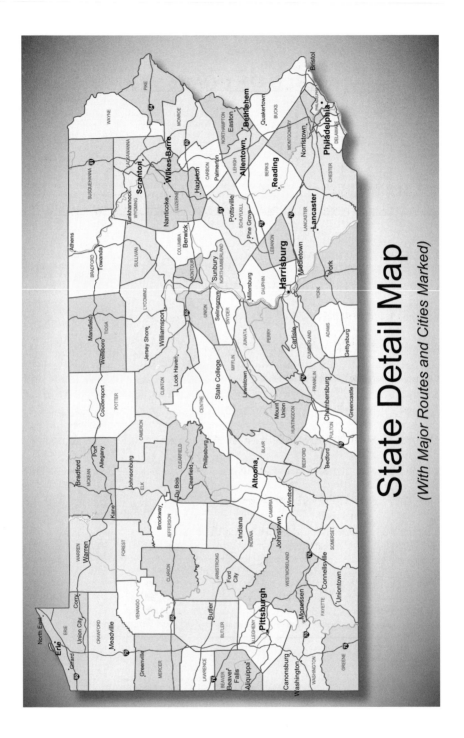

State Detail Map

(With Major Routes and Cities Marked)

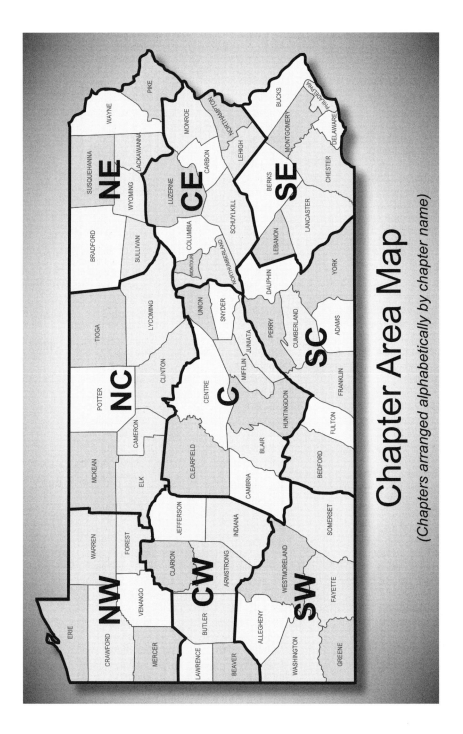

Chapter Area Map

(Chapters arranged alphabetically by chapter name)

CITY INDEX (Listed by City & Area)

CITY INDEX (Listed by City & Area)

> Note: Listings in *italics* appear only in the Seasonal Chapter

Acknowledgements

We are most thankful to be blessed with our parents, Barbara (Darrall) and Adrian Callahan & George and Catherine Zavatsky who help us every way they can – researching, proofing and baby-sitting. More importantly, they are great sounding boards and offer unconditional support. So many places around Pennsylvania remind us of family vacations years ago…

We also want to express our thanks to the many Convention & Visitor Bureaus' staff for providing the attention to detail that helps to complete a project. We felt very welcome during our travels in Pennsylvania and would be proud to call it home!

Our own kids, Jenny and Daniel, were delightful and fun children during our trips across the state. What a joy it is to be their parents…we couldn't do it without them as our "kid-testers"!

We both sincerely thank each other – our partnership has created an even greater business/personal "marriage" with lots of exciting moments, laughs, and new adventures in life woven throughout. Above all, we praise the Lord for His so many blessings through the last few years.

We think Pennsylvania is a wonderful, friendly area of the country with more activities than you could imagine. Our sincere wish is that this book will help everyone "fall in love" with all of Pennsylvania.

In a Hundred Years…
It will not matter, The size of my bank account…
The kind of house that I lived in, the kind of car that I drove…
But what will matter is…
That the world may be different
Because I was important in the life of a child.
- author unknown

HOW TO USE THIS BOOK

If you are excited about discovering Pennsylvania, this is the book for you and your family! We've spent over a thousand hours doing all the scouting, collecting and compiling (*and most often visiting!*) so that you could spend less time searching and more time having fun.

Here are a few hints to make your adventures run smoothly:

☐ Consider the **child's age** before deciding to take a visit.

☐ Know **directions** and parking. Call ahead (or visit the company's website) if you have questions *and* bring this book. Also, don't forget your camera! *(please honor rules regarding use).*

☐ **Estimate the duration** of the trip. Bring small surprises (favorite juice boxes) travel books, and toys.

☐ Call ahead for **reservations** or details, if necessary.

☐ Most listings are **closed major holidays** unless noted.

☐ Make a **family "treasure chest"**. Decorate a big box or use an old popcorn tin. Store memorabilia from a fun outing, journals, pictures, brochures and souvenirs. Once a year, look through the "treasure chest" and reminisce. "Kids Love Travel Memories!" is an excellent travel journal & scrapbook that your family can create. *(See the order form in back of this book).*

☐ Plan **picnics** along the way. Many state history sites and state parks are scattered throughout Pennsylvania. Allow time for a rural /scenic route to take advantage of these free picnic facilities.

☐ Some activities, especially tours, require **groups** of 10 or more. To participate, you may either ask to be part of another tour group or get a group together yourself (neighbors, friends, organizations). If you arrange a group outing, most places offer discounts.

☐ For the latest **updates** corresponding to the pages in this book, visit our website: **www.KidsLoveTravel.com.**

☐ Each chapter represents an area of the state. Each listing is further identified by city, zip code, and place/event name. Our popular **Activity Index** in the back of the book **lists places by Activity Heading** (i.e. State History, Tours, Outdoors, Museums, etc.).

MISSION STATEMENT

At first glance, you may think that this is a book that just lists hundreds of places to travel. While it is true that we've invested thousands of hours of exhaustive research (*and drove over 4000 miles in Pennsylvania*) to prepare this travel resource…just listing places to travel is not the mission statement of these projects.

As children, Michele and I were able to travel extensively throughout the United States. We consider these family times some of the greatest memories we cherish today. We, quite frankly, felt that most children had this opportunity to travel with their family as we did. However, as we became adults and started our own family, we found that this wasn't necessarily the case. We continually heard friends express several concerns when deciding how to spend "quality" and "quantity" family time. 1) What to do? 2) Where to do it? 3) How much will it cost? 4) How do I know that my kids will enjoy it?

Interestingly enough, as we compare our experiences with our families when we were kids, many of our fondest memories were not made at an expensive attraction, but rather when it was least expected.

It is our belief and mission statement that if you as a family will study and use the contained information to create family memories, these memories will grow a stronger, tighter family. Our ultimate mission statement is, that your children will develop a love and a passion for quality family experiences that they can pass to another generation of family travelers.

We thank you for purchasing this book, and we hope to see you on the road (*and hear your travel stories!*) God bless your journeys and happy exploring!

George, Michele, Jenny and Daniel

General State Agency & Recreational Information

Call *(or visit websites)* for the services of interest. Request to be added to their mailing lists.

- Biking Directory of PA. (717) 787-6746. Free through Penn Dot.
- **www.ExplorePAHistory.com**
- PA State Association of County Fairs. **www.pafairs.org/FairsAlpha.htm**. (717) 365-3922
- PA Tourism. (800) VISIT-PA or **www.experiencepa.com**
- PCOA. PA Campground Owners Association. **www.pacamping.com** (888) 660-7262.
- PA Fish and Boat Commission. (717) 657-4518 or **www.fish.state.pa.us**. Information on Fish Farms/Hatcheries is here. Fun place to tour.
- PA Snowmobile Hotline. (717) 787-5651.
- PA State Forests. (717) 783-7941 or **www.dcnr.state.pa.us/forestry/stateforests/**
- PA State Parks. (888) PA-PARKS or **www.dcnr.state.pa.us/stateparks/index.htm**. Junior Naturalist Program and Cabin/Camping Rentals.
- Statewide Fall Foliage Hotline. (800) FALL-IN PA or **www.fallinpa.com**

Listed by Area:

- **C** - Cambria County Conservation District. (814) 472-2120. **cccd@twd.net**
- **C** - Penn State Athletics, State College. Nittany Lions. (800) 833-5533 or (800) 863-1000 tickets or **www.gopsusports.com**. Baseball, basketball, fencing, field hockey, football, golf, gymnastics, soccer, softball, swimming, tennis, track, volleyball and wrestling.
- **CE** - Dam Releases. LeHigh River Area. (717) 424-6050. Releases create whitewater and rapids. Call for rafting outfitters. Late Spring and Early Fall.
- **NC** - PA Canyon Country. Wellsboro. (717) 724-1926.
- **NE** - POCONOs Tourist Information. (800)-POCONOS or **www.800poconos.com**. Ask about selection of whitewater rafting, canoeing and riding stables.
- **NW** - Erie Area CVB. **www.visiteriepa.com** or (800) 524-3743.
- **SE** - Berk's County Parks and Recreation Department. Wyomissing. (610) 372-8939 or **www.berksparkandrec.org**
- **SE** – Philadelphia, PA, **www.gophila.com** or Visitors Center at Independence Historical Park Center. Check out their FAMILY PHILADELPHIA packages that are truly an economical way to explore some of Philly's best sites while staying at "kid-friendly" hotels in town.
- **SW** - Laurel Highlands River Tours. **www.laurelhighlands.org**
- **SW** - Pittsburgh CVB. (888) 849-4753 or **www.visitpittsburgh.com**.
- **SW** - University of Pittsburgh Athletics. **www.pittsburghpanthers.com**. (412) 648-PITT, (800) 643-PITT.

Check out these businesses / services in your area for tour ideas:

AIRPORTS

All children love to visit the airport! Why not take a tour and understand all the jobs it takes to run an airport? Tour the terminal, baggage claim, gates and security / currency exchange. Maybe you'll even get to board a plane.

ANIMAL SHELTERS

Great for the would-be pet owner. Not only will you see many cats and dogs available for adoption, but a guide will show you the clinic and explain the needs of a pet. Be prepared to have the children "fall in love" with one of the animals while they are there!

BANKS

Take a "behind the scenes" look at automated teller machines, bank vaults and drive-thru window chutes. You may want to take this tour and then open a savings account for your child.

CITY HALLS

Halls of Fame, City Council Chambers & Meeting Room, Mayor's Office and famous statues.

ELECTRIC COMPANY / POWER PLANTS

Modern science has created many ways to generate electricity today, but what really goes on with the "flip of a switch". Because coal can be dirty, wear old, comfortable clothes. Coal furnaces heat water, which produces steam, that propels turbines, that drives generators, that make electricity.

FIRE STATIONS

Many Open Houses in October, Fire Prevention Month. Take a look into the life of the firefighters servicing your area and try on their gear. See where they hang out, sleep and eat. Hop aboard a real-life fire engine truck and learn fire safety too.

HOSPITALS

Some Children's Hospitals offer pre-surgery and general tours.

NEWSPAPERS

You'll be amazed at all the new technology. See monster printers and robotics. See samples in the layout department and maybe try to put together your own page. After seeing a newspaper made, most companies give you a free copy (dated that day) as your souvenir. National Newspaper Week is in October.

PETCO

Various stores. Contact each store manager to see if they participate. The Fur, Feathers & Fins™ program allows children to learn about the characteristics and habitats of fish, reptiles, birds, and small animals. At your local Petco, lessons in science, math and geography come to life through this hands-on field trip. As students develop a respect for animals, they will also develop a greater sense of responsibility.

RESTAURANTS

PIZZA HUT & PAPA JOHN'S

Participating locations. Telephone the store manager. Best days are Monday, Tuesday and Wednesday mid-afternoon. Minimum of 10 people. Small charge per person. All children love pizza – especially when they can create their own! As the children tour the kitchen, they learn how to make a pizza, bake it, and then eat it. The admission charge generally includes lots of creatively made pizzas, beverage and coloring book.

KRISPY KREME DONUTS

Participating locations. Get an "inside look" and learn the techniques that make these donuts some of our favorites! Watch the dough being made in "giant" mixers, being formed into donuts and taking a "trip" through the fryer. Seeing them being iced and topped with colorful sprinkles is always a favorite with the kids. Contact your local store manager. They prefer Monday or Tuesday. Free.

SUPERMARKETS

Kids are fascinated to go behind the scenes of the same store where Mom and Dad shop. Usually you will see them grind meat, walk into large freezer rooms, watch cakes and bread bake and receive free samples along the way. Maybe you'll even get to pet a live lobster!

TV / RADIO STATIONS

Studios, newsrooms, Fox kids clubs. Why do weathermen never wear blue/green clothes on TV? What makes a "DJ's" voice sound so deep and smooth?

WATER TREATMENT PLANTS

A giant science experiment! You can watch seven stages of water treatment. The favorite is usually the wall of bright buttons flashing as workers monitor the different processes.

U.S. MAIN POST OFFICES

Did you know Ben Franklin was the first Postmaster General (over 200 years ago)? Most interesting is the high-speed automated mail processing equipment. Learn how to address envelopes so they will be sent quicker (there are secrets). To make your tour more interesting, have your children write a letter to themselves and address it with colorful markers. Mail it earlier that day and they will stay interested trying to locate their letter in all the high-speed machinery.

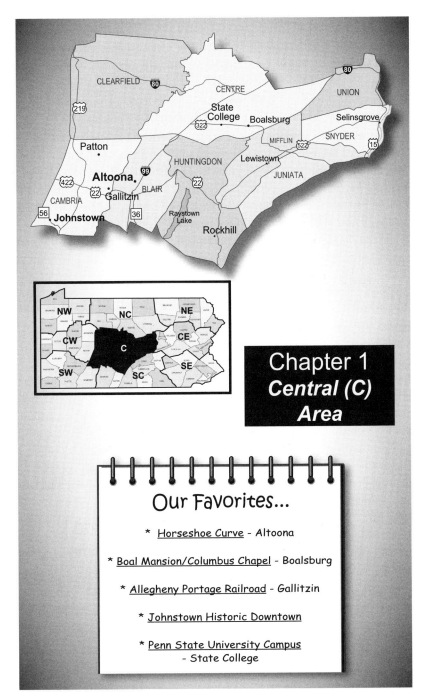

Chapter 1
Central (C)
Area

Our Favorites...

* <u>Horseshoe Curve</u> - Altoona

* <u>Boal Mansion/Columbus Chapel</u> - Boalsburg

* <u>Allegheny Portage Railroad</u> - Gallitzin

* <u>Johnstown Historic Downtown</u>

* <u>Penn State University Campus</u>
   - State College

FORT ROBERDEAU HISTORIC SITE

Altoona - RD #3 Box 391 (I-99, Bellwood Exit) 16601. Phone: (814) 946-0048.
Web: www.fortroberdeau.org Hours: Tuesday-Saturday 11:00am-5:00pm, Sunday
1:00-5:00pm (May-October). Admission: $1.00-$3.00.

A reconstructed 1778 fort with exhibits. Original site of a Revolutionary War
fort established to mine lead for the army. The rural 230-acre tract features
a reconstructed Revolutionary War stockade surrounding six log cabins. It
also includes an 1858 barn containing exhibits and a museum shop, and an
education center in an 1860 farmhouse. Includes miners quarters, officers
quarters, barracks and blacksmith. Includes 47 acres with 3 nature trails and
various habitats. Environmental education programs are available to groups
from schools, community organizations, etc. Topics include "Discovery
Trail Walk", birds, trees, wild edible plants, reading the landscape, and
stream study. Living history re-enactments. (Summer)

QUAINT CORNER CHILDREN'S MUSEUM

Altoona - 2000 Union Avenue (Downtown SR36) 16601. Phone: (814) 944-6830.
Hours: Thursday-Saturday 1:00-5:00pm. Admission: $3.00 general.

This is a real Victorian home that kids are allowed to explore - in fact, they're
encouraged to snoop around. Probably the cutest and most popular areas are
the closets and climbing the ladder into Grandma's Attic at the very top of the
house. "Gus Guts" is the highlight of the Medical Room - pick him up, pull
out his "guts" and look at a chart to see what the organs are and what they
do for the body. Draw on the wall in the Craft Kitchen or dig in the sand and
pretend you're an archeologist in the Dinosaur Dig. Visit the International
Closet to see displays from other countries, examine the Pirates Treasure or
the Amish Closet, explore nature in the Audubon Room, and see doll houses
and antiques.

ALTOONA CURVE BASEBALL CLUB

Altoona - 1000 Park Avenue (games played at Blair County Ballpark) 16602. Phone:
(814) 943-5400 or (877) 99-CURVE. Web: www.altoonacurve.com

Enjoy AA Baseball in a beautiful ballpark. A Pittsburgh Pirate's Affiliate.

HORSESHOE CURVE NATIONAL HISTORIC LANDMARK

Altoona - Horseshoe Curve Road (6 miles West of Altoona) 16602. Phone: (888) 4-ALTOONA. **Web: www.railroadcity.com** *Hours: Monday-Saturday 10:00am-6:00pm, Sunday Noon-6:00pm (April-October).* *Admission: $3.00 general admission. Miscellaneous: Large Gift shop.*

Developed in 1854, the Penn Railroad needed to expand west, but through the mountainous terrain. This curve was developed because, even if a bridge could be built, no locomotive could climb the steep grade. To solve this crossing problem, they built a track around the inside curves of the large mountain range. Inside the Interpretive Center, you can view a video of the curve's history and see a model of what the land looked like before the railroad changed the landscape. Kids like the push button display of train sounds as they make the turn (gaining

Built with just hand tools and dynamite - wow!

speed, upgrade and downgrade). The highlight is the funicular ride up to the elevation area (or you can walk up - 200 steps) where you can look out onto the horseshoe track. There's a good chance a train (the railroad still uses this curve) will pass through while you are visiting.

LAKEMONT PARK

Altoona - 700 Park Avenue (I-99 to Frankstown Road) 16602. Phone: (814) 949-PARK or (800) 434-8006. **Web: www.lakemontparkfun.com** *Hours: Daily 11:00am-dark (Summers). Weekends only in May and September, Noon-8:00pm. Admission: Buy individual ($0.50) or package ($7.95) tickets.*

One of Lakemont's most prized possessions is the world's oldest roller coaster, Leap-the-Dips. Over 30 rides and attractions. Island Waterpark. Go-Kart tracks, mini-golf, picnic areas and arcade. Kids Mini-Indy and Kiddie Lane.

RAILROADER'S MEMORIAL MUSEUM

Altoona - 1300 Ninth Avenue (off 17th Street on I-99) 16602. Phone: (814) 946-0834.
Web: www.railroadcity.com   Hours: Monday-Saturday 9:00am-5:00pm, Sunday,
11:00am-5:00pm (April-October). Weekends only (November-December). Admission:
$7.50 adult, $6.00 senior (62+), $5.00 child (3-12). Includes Memorial Museum and
Horseshoe Curve admission. Miscellaneous: Museum store.

"Here in Altoona an army of railroaders designed, built, maintained, and
moved the Pennsylvania Railroad, the largest railroad in the world…in

so doing, they changed the face
of America…this is their story!"
Why was Altoona chosen to be
the heart of construction? (watch a
27 minute film to find out). Listen
to the folks talk about their life
at local scenes depicting a home,
church, newsstand, and clubs. The
"News Boy" is funny to listen to.
Learn how railroad workers laid the tracks, worked in shops (the test lab is
pretty eye opening) and designed and built locomotives. This museum has
less focus on displays of trains and more on the lives and work habits of
people involved. Nice change.

ALTOONA SYMPHONY ORCHESTRA

Altoona - 1331 - 12th Avenue (Office) #107, 16603. Web: www.altoonasymphony.org
Phone: (814) 943-2500.

Features classical, pops and family concerts. Each spring and fall, the Altoona
Symphony Orchestra invites students from the surrounding area to attend a
concert. $10.00-$30.00 tickets, discounted for student concerts.

BOAL MANSION MUSEUM / COLUMBUS CHAPEL

Boalsburg - 300 Old Boalsburg Road (US322 -
Business Route) 16827. Phone: (814) 466-6210.
Web: www.boalmuseum.com Hours: Tuesday-
Saturday 10:00am-5:00pm, Sunday Noon-5:00pm
(Summer). Tuesday-Sunday 1:30-5:00pm (May,
September, October). Admission: $10.00
adult, $8.00 senior (59+), $6.00 child (7-16).
Miscellaneous: Still privately owned.

Columbus' actual sea desk...

The view from the loft

Want to see a real part of Christopher Columbus? On the grounds of the originally furnished mansion is the Columbus Chapel that was brought here from Spain in 1909. They actually have a sea desk once owned by Columbus and many Columbus family heirlooms dating back to the 1400s. The highlight of this place begins with your first step inside the chapel. If you're like us…your mouth will drop wide open in disbelief as you begin to notice the centuries-old heirloom pieces. Many of the artifacts look like movie props (the natural way they have aged makes it hard to believe they are real!) Actual parchment family documents, the family cross, a copy of the family tree and 2 actual pieces of the "true" cross are awesome to see up close. It's just incredible that all of this history is in a small town museum! Also on the grounds are the mansion and several exhibit rooms. The Boal Mansion Museum contains the original furnishings, papers, portraits, tools and weapons of nine generations of this American

Two pieces from Jesus' cross...amazing!

family. The first exhibit room contains medieval armor, a scale model of the Santa Maria and other family memorabilia. The "Country Life" room contains a beautifully restored 1850s stage coach, a buckboard buggy, farm tools, the 1816 accounts book from David Boal's tavern and many more farm and kitchen implements. The Weapons Room contains a large collection of swords, rifles and pistols from the Revolutionary War through World War I, including David Boal's Pennsylvania long rifle from the 1790's and Captain John Boal's officer's sword from the Civil War. Hearing stories about the Boal family and their home can be interesting, too.

PENNSYLVANIA MILITARY MUSEUM

*Boalsburg - South Atherton Street (Business Route 322) (US322) 16827. Phone: (814) 466-6263. **Web: www.psu.edu/dept/aerospace/museum** Hours: Tuesday-Saturday 9:00am-5:00pm, Sunday Noon-5:00pm (April-October). Open Friday and Weekends only (Winter).*

Honoring Pennsylvania's soldiers from Benjamin Franklin's first volunteer unit to Operation Desert Storm. Younger children enjoy climbing on tanks and cannons outside in the park, but it takes older kids to enjoy the museum. As they study American History, this place brings it to life, especially the World War I trench scene, complete with sound and light effects. The museum only focuses on citizen soldiers – "the men and women of Pennsylvania who served their country in time of war."

TUSSEY MOUNTAIN SKI AREA

Boalsburg - 301 Bear Meadow Road - Route 322 16827. Phone: (814) 466-6266 or (800) 733-2754. **Web: *www.tusseymountain.com***

Longest Run: 2700 ft.; 8 Slopes & Trails plus snowboarding in winter. Skatepark, driving range, batting cages and par 3 golf in the fall.

PENN'S CAVES

Centre Hall - 222 Penns Cave Road (SR 192 East, Near I-80, Exit 14) 16828. Phone: (814) 364-1664. **Web: *www.pennscave.com*** *Hours: Generally daily 9:00am-5:00pm. Open later summers. Closed January. Weekends Only 11:00am-5:00pm (December & February). Closed Thanksgiving and Christmas Day. Admission: CAVERN: $12.95 adult, $11.95 senior, $5.95 child (2-12). WILDLIFE, FARM AND NATURE TOURS: $17.95 adult, $16.95 senior, $9.95 child (2-12).*

America's only all-water cavern and wildlife (1000 acre) sanctuary. Colored lights enhance "The Statue of Liberty", "The Garden of Gods" and "Niagara

 Falls". The farm and wildlife tour is a guided 90-minute motorized tour over the thousand acres of Penn's Cave forests and fields and a natural habitat for birds, plants, and animals. North American animals, such as deer, elk, wolves, bears, bison, and mustangs are seen, as well as longhorn cattle. Come to Penn's Cave and enjoy both tours. You will be educated about the geology, biology, and geography of Central Pennsylvania.

BLUE KNOB ALL SEASONS RESORT/ SKI AREA

Claysburg - PO Box 247 (between Altoona & Johnstown, in north corner of Bedford County) 16625. Phone: (814) 239-5111. **Web: *www.blueknob.com***

Activities include skiing/snowboarding, a tubing park, and cross country skiing. In the warmer months, golfing, hiking and trail biking are big attractions. All condos are furnished with fully equipped kitchens and fireplaces. Longest Run: 2 miles; 34 Slopes & Trails.

ALLEGHENY PORTAGE RAILROAD & NATIONAL HISTORIC SITE

Gallitzin - 110 Federal Park Road (US22, Gallitzin exit - follow signs) 16641. Phone: (814) 886-6150. Web: www.nps.gov/alpo/ Hours: Daily 9:00am-6:00pm (Summer), Daily 9:00am-5:00pm (rest of year). Closed winter holidays. Admission: $4.00 adult (age 16+). FREE for children and park pass holders. Miscellaneous: Visitor Center with 20 minute film. Costumed presentations during the summer. Lemon House - restored tavern and business office on premises along with the Engine House and walking trails to the incline site.

You'll be amazed at the ingenuity of railroad engineers back then! The problem was the Allegheny Mountains. No trains or canals could get through them before the idea of the "incline" was introduced. Called "an engineering marvel" at its opening, travel that took three weeks by wagon took only four days by railroad and canal. It used a combination of 10 inclines and horses or steam locomotives pulling cars on levels in between. It's difficult to visualize until you see the working small-scale model in the center of the

It's just like
"The Little Engine that Could"

museum - then it all makes sense (still in amazement of course!). With a hands-on demonstration, you can personally try turning a wheel hooked to balanced and unbalanced weights. This clearly demonstrates the need for balanced (one car up - one car down at the same time) inclines.

GALLITZIN TUNNELS PARK, CABOOSE AND MUSEUM

Gallitzin - 702 Jackson Street (off Route 22 - Follow signs) 16641. Phone: (814) 886-8871. Web: www.visitjohnstownpa.com/attractions.html Hours: Daily, daylight hours. Museum open daily 11:00am-5:00pm, weather permitting. Admission: FREE.

See and feel the awesome power of the trains passing through the Allegheny Tunnel (modified 1854). View the tunnels that were built with picks and shovels using over 300 immigrants to complete it. Twin tunnels, the Allegheny and Gallitzin Tunnels, are the highest and longest on what once was the Pennsylvania Railroad. Because of their integral role in the transportation system, these tunnels were guarded during times of war. Also on site is a PRR walkway and railroad signal and a restored PRR caboose - climb aboard to see the sleeping quarters and pot-bellied stove. This is a cute side trip between visits to the Allegheny Portage Railroad and Horseshoe Curve.

CANOE CREEK STATE PARK

Hollidaysburg - RR 2, Box 560 (US 22) 16648. Phone: (814) 695-6807. Web: www.dcnr.state.pa.us/stateparks/parks/canoecreek.aspx

The park boasts one of the largest bat colonies in the Eastern US. The visitor center has natural and historical exhibits and information. Modern Cabins: Eight modern cabins overlook the lake. They are within walking distance of the swimming area and are available for year-round rental. Beach, Boat Rentals, Horseback Riding, Sledding, Limestone kilns, Trails, and Cross-Country Skiing.

BALD EAGLE STATE PARK

Howard - 149 Main Park Road (off PA Route 150, midway between Milesburg and Lock Haven, it is accessible by I- 80) 16841. Phone: (814) 625-2775. Web: www.dcnr.state.pa.us/stateparks/parks/baldeagle.aspx

The 5,900-acre park lies in the broad Bald Eagle Valley of North Central Pennsylvania. Two geologic provinces create Bald Eagle's scenic beauty. The Allegheny Plateau to the north and west holds smooth uplands. The Ridge and Valley Province to the south and east contains numerous long, narrow mountain ridges separated by valleys. The rugged Bald Eagle Mountain and Allegheny Plateau of the 1,730-acre lake features unlimited horsepower boating, hiking and butterfly trails. Swimming is available at the sand beach. Boat Rentals, Year-round Education & Interpretation Center, Sledding, Campsites, Hiking, and Fishing.

JOHNSTOWN CHIEFS HOCKEY

Johnstown - 326 Napoleon St (Cambria County War Memorial Arena) 15901. Phone: (800) 243-8499. Web: www.johnstownchiefs.com

ECHL Hockey (October-April). Tickets $9.50-$14.50 for single games.

JOHNSTOWN RIVERHAWKS

Johnstown - 326 Napoleon Street (Cambria County War Memorial Arena) 15901. Phone: (814) 361-3460 or (814) 536-3670. Web: www.johnstownriverhawks.com

Johnstown Riverhawks of the American Indoor Football Association are continuing to build a cornerstone franchise.

JOHNSTOWN SYMPHONY ORCHESTRA

Johnstown - 227 Franklin Street, Suite 302 (University of Pittsburgh at Johnstown's Pasquerilla Performing Arts Center) 15901. Web: www.johnstownsymphony.org Phone: (814) 535-6738.

Young Peoples Concerts for grade school students and a Christmas concert.

JOHNSTOWN INCLINED PLANE

Johnstown - 711 Edgehill Drive (off SR56, 403 or 271 & Johns St.) 15905. Phone: (814) 536-1816. Web: www.inclinedplane.com Hours: Daily 9:00am-11:00pm (May-September). Daily 11:00am-10:00pm (October-April). Closed Christmas and New Years. Admission: $4.00 adult, FREE senior (65+), $2.50 child (2-12). Round Trip. Miscellaneous: Gift shop. Visitor's center. Observation deck on top.

Brightly lit, it is the world's steepest vehicular inclined plane (71 % grade) with a panoramic view of the city through viewing windows. After the flood, many residents wanted to live up on the hill…but they needed a way to commute. It was also used as an escape route during subsequent floods. A  viewing window looking into the motor room explains the "physics" behind the scenes. Hang on tight to those little ones! Ride on the incline and then dine at the top. Spectacular views of the valley and see the largest American flag in the county (814-536-1816). The JAMES WOLFE SCULPTURE TRAIL is the first nature trail with sculptures made from steel. It honors the city's steel heritage with ten pieces, eight on the trail. Most photographed and visible is "Steel Floats" (Bottom of the incline).

JOHNSTOWN FLOOD MUSEUM

Johnstown - 304 Washington Street (off SR56 West to Walnut Street Exit) 15907. Phone: (814) 539-1889. Web: www.jaha.org Hours: Daily 10:00am-5:00pm. Admission: $4.00-$6.00 (age 6+). Your ticket includes admission to the Heritage Discovery Center. Miscellaneous: Museum store. Film shown hourly (25 minutes long). Film has some shrill screaming that may frighten young children.

On May 31, 1889, a neglected dam and a phenomenal storm led to a catastrophe in which 2,209 people died, tens of thousands were left homeless, and a prospering city became a wasteland. Hear and see the story of the

3D Wall of Wreckage

infamous disaster of 1889 focusing on both the tragedy and triumph of the human spirit. View the Academy Award Winning "The Johnstown Flood" documentary film (shown hourly) with multi-media exhibits including an animated map with sound and light effects showing water movement. … "it was a roar and a crash and a smash…". Other exhibits include: A Quilt - used as a rescue rope, A Wall of Wreckage in 3-D (17 feet tall - flood wall was actually 40 feet tall). It really captures the horror of the moment, yet is subtle enough to not scare school-aged children.

JOHNSTOWN HERITAGE DISCOVERY CENTER

Johnstown - *(Route 56, at the corner of Broad Street and Seventh Ave.) 15907. Phone: (814) 539-1889. Web: www.jaha.org Hours: Daily 10:00am-5:00pm. Closed Thanksgiving, Christmas, Easter and New Years. Admission: $4.00-$6.00 (age 6+). ticket includes admission to the Johnstown Flood Museum.*

All Johnstown's immigrants were history-makers - ordinary men, women, and children who made a contribution to the rise of industrial America. And, as they kept traditions and values alive for their families and communities, they enriched the life and culture of a changing city and nation. When you visit the museum, you will be able to assume the persona of such immigrants as Josef and Maria (as well as Prokop, Katerina, Andrej, and Stefan) as you journey through the exhibit that examines the world the immigrants made in Johnstown, Pennsylvania. The visitor will be able to see and touch the environments - you will feel the sharpness of the coal mine walls and smell the scent of incense in the church. You will hear the thoughts of a young immigrant girl as she sells eggs and butter on the street to help the family's finances. Play "History Jukeboxes" -You sit down in front of the computer and tell your story. The "jukebox" records your voice and image.

JOHNSTOWN FLOOD NATIONAL MEMORIAL

Johnstown (South Fork) - *733 Lake Road (US219 to St. Michael Exit - SR869east) 15956. Phone: (814) 495-4643. Web: www.nps.gov/jofl Hours: Daily 9:00am-5:00pm. Closed winter holidays. Admission: $4.00 adult (16+).*

The flood began here - see what little is left of South Fork Dam. It is operated by the National Park Service and features exhibits an actual size "debris wall" which dramatically illustrates the wall of water that devastated Johnstown. The film Black Friday chillingly recreates that day in 1889 - a little frightening for youngsters. Remember over 2200 people died in  about 10 minutes. In addition, visitors can enjoy a picnic area, hike nearby trails around the dam's remains, take part in the park's interpretive program or view exhibits created by the South Fork Fishing and Hunting Club. Other recreational activities available: bird watching and cross country skiing.

BALD EAGLE STATE FOREST

Laurelton - PO Box 147 (mostly between I-80 and US 22) 17835. Phone: (570) 922-3344. Web: www.dcnr.state.pa.us/forestry/stateforests/baldeagle.aspx

There are thirteen streams within the Bald Eagle District totaling 47 miles that are stocked and fishable. The District has 340 miles of drivable roads and about the same number of miles of trails. There are five designated scenic drives. ATV Trails. (7 miles), Winter Sports, and Camping.

R.B. WINTER STATE PARK

Mifflinburg - RR 2, Box 314 (on PA Route 192, 18 miles west of Lewisburg) 17844. Phone: (717) 966-1455. Web: www.dcnr.state.pa.us/stateparks/parks/rbwinter.aspx

This park is situated in a narrow valley surrounded by oak forests on steep mountain ridges. A spring-fed mountain stream flows through the valley. Beach, Visitor Center, Year-round Education & Interpretation Center, Campsites, Camping Cabins, Trails, and Winter Sports.

RAVENSBURG STATE PARK: This pretty valley is especially beautiful when the mountain laurel blooms in late June and during the fall foliage of early October.

REEDS GAP STATE PARK

Milroy - 1405 New Lancaster Valley Road (U.S. Route 322 from Milroy by following park signs for seven miles) 17063. Phone: (717) 667-3622. Web: www.dcnr.state.pa.us/stateparks/parks/reeds.htm

The Self-guiding Interpretive Trail is a 1.1-mile trail following the scenic banks of Honey Creek. Interpretive waysides focus on the various ecological communities. This green-blazed trail starts at the kiosk beside the snack bar and follows parts of Blue Jay and Honey Creek trails between the swimming pool complex and Picnic Pavilion #3. Two, free, guarded swimming pools offer about 4,000 square feet of water for swimming. Also offered: Sledding, Campsites, Fishing, Winter Sports.

POE PADDY STATE PARK is located at the confluence of Big Poe Creek and Penns Creek, a trout angler's paradise featuring the nationally recognized green drake mayfly hatch in June. You can hike through the 250-foot long Paddy Mountain Railroad Tunnel on the Mid State Trail by following the trail upstream along Penns Creek, crossing a pedestrian bridge and then going to the tunnel.

POE VALLEY STATE PARK's hiking trail system connects to the extensive trail network of Bald Eagle State Forest. The hiking trails vary from easy hiking to very rugged, steep trails. Boating, Fishing, Swimming with beach, Hiking, and Winter Sports.

PRINCE GALLITZIN STATE PARK

Patton - 966 Marina Road (SR 1021) (reached by PA Routes 36 and 53 and U.S. Route 219) 16668. Web: www.dcnr.state.pa.us/stateparks/parks/princegallitzin.aspx Phone: (814) 674-1000.

The major attractions to the park are the 1,600-acre Lake Glendale and the large campground. Beach, Visitor Center, Boat Rentals, Horseback Riding, Sledding, Campsites, Modern Cabins, Fishing, Trails, and Cross-Country Skiing.

SELDOM SEEN TOURIST COAL MINE

Patton - PO Box 83 (I-76 to US219 to US22 East to Patton - Route 36) 16668. Phone: (814) 247-6305. Web: www.seldomseenmine.com Hours: Open 11:00am-5:00pm, Memorial Day weekend, July 4th, and Labor Day weekend. Open Saturday & Sunday in June, Thursday through Sunday in July and August, and for scheduled tours only in April, May, and September. Admission: $7.00 adult, $4.00 child (3-12).

a 3-ton hunk of coal...

Go underground to learn first hand the lives and working conditions of coal miners from the past to the present. Family run operations, so tours are given by miners or descendants. You'll learn that coal was dug by hand, loaded on cars and hauled from the mine by mules - for as little as 25 cents per ton!

PARKER DAM STATE PARK

Penfield - RD 1, Box 165 (I- 80, take Exit 18 onto Route 153 North, Turn right onto Mud Run Road) 15849. Web: www.dcnr.state.pa.us/stateparks/parks/parkerdam.aspx Phone: (814) 765-0630.

This rustic, remote park in the heart of MOSHANNAN STATE FOREST is almost entirely wooded and offers picturesque areas of forest and swamp meadows, pine plantations and mixed hardwoods. The CCC Interpretive Center interprets the Civilian Conservation Corps. Parker Dam is a good base to explore the surrounding state forest. Beach, Visitor Center, Boat Rentals, Sledding, Campsites, Rustic Cabins, Hiking Trails, and Cross-Country Skiing.

S.B. ELLIOTT STATE PARK is a quiet, rustic, mountaintop recreational area just off of I-80 near the mid-point of the state. This 318-acre park, in the heart of the Moshannon State Forest, is entirely wooded and offers picturesque areas of forest and swamp meadows and typical second growth mixed hardwood and oak timber. Camping, Rustic Cabins and Winter Sports.

BLACK MOSHANNON STATE PARK

Philipsburg - RR 1, Box 185 (PA Route 504) 16866. Phone: (814) 342-5960. Web: www.dcnr.state.pa.us/stateparks/parks/blackmoshannon.aspx

Black Moshannon State Park features the Black Moshannon Bog Natural Area. Trails and a boardwalk help people explore the birds and plants of the bog and surrounding forests. According to local tradition, American Indians called this watershed "Moss-Hanne," meaning "moose stream," thus the origin of the park's name. Appropriately, the "black" in the park name describes the tea-colored waters. Beach, Mountain Biking, Boat Rentals, Campsites, Modern Cabins, Trails, and Cross-Country Skiing.

LAKE RAYSTOWN RESORT

Raystown Lake (Entriken) - 100 Chipmunk Crossing (Route 994) 16638. Phone: (814) 658-3500. Web: www.raystownresort.com

The Resort is located between Harrisburg and Pittsburgh in Entriken on Pennsylvania's largest inland lake with 118 miles of scenic shoreline and thousands of acres of pristine woodlands and streams. Lodge rooms, boating and boat rentals, Hiking, Biking and Fitness Trails, Camping and Cottages, Swimming and Beach Areas. Other attractions:

PROUD MARY TOURBOAT: Sightseeing cruises. Food available. Scheduled departures by season (April - October). Admission: Adults $7.50+, Children

50% off Adult pricing (under 12), (for most cruises).

<u>WILDRIVER WATER PARK</u>: Speed slides, twisting slides, whitewater tubing slides, Children's splash pool and mini-golf. $4.00-$13.00 depending on activity.

SEVEN POINTS CRUISES

Raystown Lake (Hesston) - RD #1, Route 26 (Seven Points Marina) 16647. Phone: (814) 658-3074. Web: www.7pointsmarina.com Hours: May - mid-October. Summers usually have 3 cruises. Admission: $10.00 adult, $9.00 senior, $3.00 child (2-8). (15 passenger minimum on all cruises).

Public sightseeing boat cruises where you can view wooded shoreline (esp. cedar trees), wild turkey, deer, beaver, bald eagles, and ravens. Close to Lake Raystown Resort (waterpark and activities). Ask for the "Kids Kruz" that includes tour, box lunch, fish feeding, and demonstration of "rack storage" of 200+ boats in a warehouse (real neat if you're not a boater and already familiar with this).

GREENWOOD FURNACE STATE PARK

Raystown Lake (Huntingdon) - RR 2, Box 118 (SR 305 North) 16652. Phone: (814) 667-1800. Web: www.dcnr.state.pa.us/stateparks/parks/greenwoodfurnace.aspx

Relive the 1800s by visiting this 423-acre park, site of an active iron furnace community. Greenwood Furnace was the site of an active iron furnace community from 1834 to 1904. The visitor center is a restored blacksmith shop and provides historical programming. Along the Mid-State Trail to the Greenwood Forest Fire Lookout Tower, you can view charcoal hearths where wood was made into charcoal.

Greenwood Historic Walking Tour: Greenwood Furnace was once a thriving ironmaking village. Today, only a handful of its 127 buildings remain. This walking tour explores a portion of the historic district and includes parts of the town, tramway, historic roads and charcoal hearths. A free guide to the historic district is available at the park office and visitor center.

Blacksmith Shop: This historic building has displays on the history of the park and offers blacksmithing demonstrations in the summer. It is open Wednesday, Friday, Saturday and Sunday through the summer months and weekends in May, September and October.

Visitor Center/Park Office: The Visitor Center/Park Office is open 8:00am-4:00pm, Monday through Friday and seven days a week from Memorial Day to Labor Day. There are temporary exhibits on display. Beach and Campsites.

LINCOLN CAVERNS & WHISPER ROCKS

Raystown Lake (Huntingdon) - *RR1 Box 280 (I-76 to US 522 north to US 22 west) 16652. Phone: (814) 643-0268. Web: www.lincolncaverns.com Hours: Daily open at 9:00am until dark. Daily 9:00am-4:00pm (March and November, December - Weekends only). Admission: $10.50 adult, $9.50 senior (65+), $6.50 child (4-12). Miscellaneous: Gift shop, nature trails, gem panning.*

Nature's handiwork has been protected and preserved for your visit since they were first discovered in 1930 and 1941. Two crystal caverns - Lincoln and Whisper Rock have winding passages, large "rooms" with massive and delicate flowstones, pure white calcite and crystals. Ask about seasonal "Kids' Cave Crawls".

SWIGART ANTIQUE AUTO MUSEUM

Raystown Lake (Huntingdon) - *PO Box 214 (US22 East) 16652. Phone: (814) 643-0885. Web: www.swigartmuseum.com Hours: Daily 9:00am-5:00pm (May-November). Admission: $3.00-$6.00 (age 6+).*

See over 40 cars on display and the world's largest collection of cars, toys, license plates, bicycles and clothing. The 1908 Studebaker Electric sits in mint condition. It is one of two that belonged to the United States government and were used to transport people in the tunnel between the House and the Senate in Washington, D. C. The 12-passenger vehicle was designed with two front ends so it could reverse direction without turning around.

ROTHROCK STATE FOREST

Raystown Lake (Huntington) - *Rothrock Lane - Box 403 16652. Phone: (814) 643-2340. Web: www.dcnr.state.pa.us/forestry/stateforests/rothrock.aspx*

Vistas or scenic overlooks are a major attraction for many forest visitors. The best known and most easily accessible is the well-known overlook atop Tussey Mountain along PA Route 26 at the Centre/Huntingdon County line. 93,349 acres of Fishing, Camping, Hiking, Cross-Country Skiing, Snowmobile and Bike Trails, and Picnic Areas.

TROUGH CREEK STATE PARK

Raystown Lake (James Creek) - *RR 1, Box 211 (PA Route 994) 16657. Phone: (814) 658-3847. Web: www.dcnr.state.pa.us/stateparks/parks/troughcreek.aspx*

Located along a scenic gorge where Great Trough Creek cuts through Terrace Mountain and empties into Raystown Lake. Rugged hiking trails lead to wonders like Balanced Rock and Rainbow Falls. Rothrock State Forest and

Raystown Lake Recreation Area border the park, making a large, contiguous area of public land for recreation Campsites, Modern Cabins, Fishing and Hiking. WARRIORS PATH STATE PARK Natural cliffs, boating, and part of Raystown Lake area.

EAST BROAD TOP RAILROAD

Rockhill Furnace - PO Box 158 (I-76, exit 13 to US522 North, Orbsonia Station) 17249. Phone: (814) 447-3011. Web: www.spikesys.com/EBT/ Hours: Weekends at 11:00am, 1:00 & 3:00pm. (June-October). Admission: $10.00 adult, $7.00 child (2-12).

Excursions are usually pulled by one of four mikado steam locomotives, built for the EBT by Baldwin between 1911 and 1918. Vintage diesel locomotives operate as backup power. The train passes through wooded areas and farmland and passes through cuts and over fills and bridges. As you ride an authentic steam powered train through a valley, you'll learn railroad history. Station gift shop.

ROCKHILL TROLLEY MUSEUM

Rockhill Furnace - PO Box 203 (PA Turnpike, exit 13 to US522 North to Route 994 - Meadow Street) 17249. Phone: (814) 447-9576 (weekends only) (610) 437-0448. Web: www.rockhilltrolley.org Hours: Weekends and Holidays 11:00am-4:00pm (Memorial Day-October). Admission: $5.00 adult, $2.00 child (2-12). Miscellaneous: Pennsylvania Transportation Museum and restoration shop where volunteers are always working on new projects.

a fun way to travel...wish more cities still used them!

Take the 2 1/2 mile trolley rides along with a motorman on an antique streetcar - unlimited rides on many different varieties of streetcars. Even though they run on a standard railroad track, streetcars or "interurbans" (city to city) are powered by electricity. Wires running along the length of main streets were connected to rods moving along a set track. The grandparents will remember this form of transport and have fun memories to share of the friendships that freely developed on the way to work or to the movies.

INDIAN CAVERNS

Spruce Creek - *(take Rt. 22 west to Waterstreet then Rt. 45) 16683. Phone: (814) 632-7578.* **Web: www.indiancaverns.com** *Hours: Daily 10:00am-6:00pm (Summers). Daily 10:00am-4:00pm (May, September, October). Admission: $4.95-$9.95.*

Pennsylvania's largest limestone cavern is known for its massive formations. The tour is conducted by a knowledgeable guide who explains the complete history of the caverns and points out various rock formations. Learn a bit of geology as the guide takes you through nearly a mile of lighted walkways - including a one-of-a-kind "Star Room" grotto and the "Frozen Niagara". Concrete and gravel walkways enable even elderly visitors to tour the cave with ease. Authentic Indian history - 400 relics and a tablet of picture writing were found in the cave. A photogenic Indian totem pole and teepee grace the grounds and there is a free picnic area.

PENN STATE UNIVERSITY PARK CAMPUS

State College - *(Hetzel Union Building) (off US322) 16801. Phone: (800) PSU-TODAY.* **Web: www.alumni.psu.edu/VRPennState/VirtualAmbassador/links.html** *Hours: Mostly weekdays. Some museums also open Saturday & Sundays - Call first.*

Things you can see:

NITTANY LION SHRINE - The 13 ton block of Indiana limestone shaped like the mascot, Nittany Lion.

FOOTBALL HALL OF FAME - Greensburg Sports Complex, (814) 865-0411. Nittany Lion football greats.

MUSEUM OF ANTHROPOLOGY - (814) 865-3853. Ethnographic and archeological collection.

FROST ENTOMOLOGICAL MUSEUM - (814) 865-2865. 250,000 insects!

EARTH & MINERAL SCIENCES MUSEUM - (814) 865-6427. Minerals and paintings depicting Pennsylvania's mineral industries.

PALSNER MUSEUM OF ART - (814) 865-7672.

PENN STATE BOOKSTORE - (814) 863-0205.

COLLEGE OF AGRICULTURAL SCIENCES - Dairy, beef and sheep research center, deer pens. Look for Coaly the mule.

THE CREAMERY - **www.creamery.psu.edu**. west on Bigler Road (814-865-7535). Approximately 500,000 cones of ice cream are sold here each year. Most visitors to the Creamery at Penn State know only of its famous

**Always something
yummy here...**

ice cream, sherbet, and cheeses sold at the store or over the Internet, but what they don't know is that it is the largest university creamery in the nation. Each year, approximately 4.5 million pounds of milk pass through the Creamery's stainless steel holding tanks.These dairy products are produced in the Food Science Lab, located directly behind the Creamery. These products are used throughout the campus. Ben and Jerry actually took a correspondence course through Penn State to learn about ice cream production.

STONE VALLEY RECREATION AREA

State College - *(CR1029 - off SR26 South) 16801. Phone: (814) 863-1164. Center - (814) 863-2000. Web: www.psu.edu/dept/Stone_Valley/ Hours: Dawn - Dusk (AREA). Daily 10:00am-5:00pm (CENTER). Closed mid-December through January. Admission: FREE*

Boating, fishing, hayrides, ice skating, sledding, cross-country skiing, hiking (equipment rental), and cabins.

SHAVER'S CREEK ENVIRONMENTAL CENTER - Raptor Center (rehabilitate injured large birds) and Day Camps. FREE Admission. Fees for rentals. Shaver's Creek Environmental Center is nestled in the ridge-and-valley area of central Pennsylvania, between State College and Huntingdon, in the Stone Valley Recreation Area of the Penn State Experimental Forest. Explore discovery rooms, tour the raptor center, walk the network of trails, and visit the gardens and the Pennsylvania nature book and gift shop. Explore animal tracks, constellations, and other cultural and natural history games. Under the Children's Loft, you will find live Pennsylvania frogs, toads, turtles, and snakes, just waiting for your visit.

SHIKELLAMY STATE PARK

Sunbury - *Bridge Avenue (Blue Hill is reached from the town of Shamokin Dam on US 11 north. Marina off of PA 147) 17801. Phone: (717) 988-5557. Web: www.dcnr.state.pa.us/stateparks/parks/shikellamy.aspx*

The marina provides access to unlimited horsepower boating on Lake Augusta that is formed by an inflatable dam on the Susquehanna River. The Blue Hill area is across the river from the Marina and provides panoramic views of the confluence of two branches of the Susquehanna River. Paved paths encircle Shikellamy Marina. A walk around the one-mile nature trail on Shikellamy Overlook can reveal the wildlife that abounds in the park, like deer, songbirds and wildflowers. Different forest stages can be seen from scrub forest to mature hardwood forest. Unique geologic formations can be studied in the park and on the eastern boundary cliff trail extension. Bicycling: A one-mile, paved hiking and biking path encircles Shikellamy Marina. Bicycle rentals are available at the boat rental during the summer.

DELGROSSO'S AMUSEMENT PARK

Tipton - Old Route 220 (I-99 North, Exit Grazierville or Bellwood) 16684. Phone: (814) 684-3538. Web: www.delgrossos.com Hours: Daily (Summer). Weekends in May and September. Open at 11:00am. Admission: FREE. (All-day passes, ~$12.95+ and individual ride prices, ~50 cents each available).

Today, more than six decades after they started a spaghetti sauce company, Mafalda's and Fred's seven sons and daughters, 22 grandchildren and 20 great-grandchildren make millions of jars of spaghetti sauce and host hundreds of thousands of guests at their amusement park. 30 rides and attractions. Most of the rides are old-fashioned spinning rides and roller coaster. Mini-golf - (18 holes with lakes and waterfalls), Go-Karts, mini-train rides and an Interactive water park. Free concert series during the summer.

GARDNER'S CANDY MUSEUM

Tyrone - 30 West 10th Street (I-99 to SR453 or SR220) 16686. Phone: (814) 684-0857. Web: www.gardnerscandies.com Hours: Monday-Saturday 9:30am-9:00pm, Sunday 1:00-9:00pm. Admission: FREE

Gardners is famous for the Original Peanut Butter Melt-away, a creamy, smooth peanut butter dipped in rich chocolate. Many have tried, but none can duplicate the Gardner's family recipe. Take a Nostalgic walk through a penny candy store. Big candy counters with large jars of candy. Also stop in the Candy Kitchen where old-time (mostly brass) equipment is displayed. Take a look at their giant Taffy Hook. Mr. Gardner started "the sweetest place in town" in 1897 and still has licorice whips and candy buttons for sale.

WINDBER COAL HERITAGE CENTER

Windber - 501 15th Street (off SR56) 15963. Phone: (877) 826-3933. Hours: Tuesday-Saturday 10:00am-5:00pm (May-October). Admission: $6.00 adult, $1.50 child, $3.00 student, $4.50 senior. Web: http://www.progressfund.org/windber

Travel back to a turn-of-the-century coal town and experience the everyday life of a coal miner and his family. State-of-the-art exhibits, media presentations and archives also chronicle the evolution of coal mining technology, the struggle for unionization and the impact of the Berwind-White Co. and the

coal industry has on small, rural areas. Mine #40 Scenic Overlook has 3 floors of exhibits, videos, and interactive maps. A working mine seam exhibit is interesting and other exhibits help you to experience the life of a miner and his family. See working and living conditions - "The Underground Farmer" as they were called. Cities were created overnight by mining companies - Windber being a model town. Unique coal gift shop.

QUECREEK MINE EXHIBIT: The nightshift of Black Wolf Coal Company in the Quecreek Mine started out at 3:00pm on July 24th 2002. The day began like any other day, but at 8:50pm "All hell broke loose." A nine man mining crew breached a wall at entry No. 6, 245 feet underground. The abandoned Saxman Mine No. 2 instantly flooded their workplace with 150 million gallons of water. The rescue efforts took place over a 78 hour period, with hundreds of individuals, agencies, and organizations contributing to the rescue itself and the support efforts. Photos and artifacts displayed try to personally tell the rescue story.

WOODWARD CAVE

Woodward - SR 45 (US 22 east to Water Street, then SR 45 east) 16882. Phone: (814) 349-9800. Web: www.woodwardcave.com Hours: Daily 9:00am-7:00pm (Summer). Friday-Sunday 10:00am-4:00pm (Spring, Fall). Admission: $5.00-$10.50 (age 2+).

Experience spectacular Woodward Cave, nicknamed "The Big One". One of the largest caverns in Pennsylvania, its nickname reflects its five spacious rooms, one of which, "The Hall of Statues" is 200 feet long. Experienced guides conduct a well explained, easily walked tour. Five big, well-lit rooms include the "Ball Room", "Square Room". "Hanging Forest", "Tower of Babel" (largest stalagmites in U.S.) and "Upper Room" (cathedral ceiling). Indian burial room and the passageways are wide and flat.

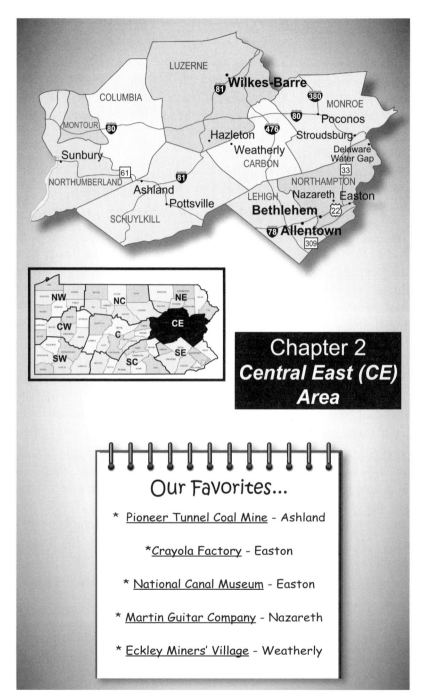

Chapter 2
Central East (CE) Area

Our Favorites...

* <u>Pioneer Tunnel Coal Mine</u> - Ashland

* <u>Crayola Factory</u> - Easton

* <u>National Canal Museum</u> - Easton

* <u>Martin Guitar Company</u> - Nazareth

* <u>Eckley Miners' Village</u> - Weatherly

ALLENTOWN ART MUSEUM

Allentown - 31 North Fifth Street (5th & Court Streets) 18101. Phone: (610) 432-4333. Web: www.allentownartmuseum.org Hours: Tuesday-Saturday 11:00am-5:00pm, Sunday Noon-5:00pm. Admission: $3.00-$6.00 (over age 6). Admission includes audio tour. Children under 6 are admitted at no charge. Free Museum admission every Sunday. Art Ways is always open during regular Museum hours, free with Museum admission.

European to architecture of Frank Lloyd Wright to American art. Gem Collection, photography, textiles, museum shop. Art Ways with hands-on and touchable art & Family Fun Days or ArtVentures.

LEHIGH VALLEY HERITAGE CENTER MUSEUM

Allentown - 432 West Walnut Street (US-22 take PA 145 south 1.8 mi. to Walnut St. Turn left on Walnut .2 miles to 5th St.) 18101. Web: www.lchs.museum Phone: (610) 435-1074. Hours: Monday-Saturday 10:00am-4:00pm. Admission: $3.00-$5.00 per person. Miscellaneous: Original Indian inhabitants, Pennsylvania German and local historians. Geology Garden adjacent.

Here you can trace the main lines of the county's story: from the region's indigenous peoples, through the rural life of early Pennsylvania German immigrants, to the developments that made Lehigh County a birthplace of the American Industrial Revolution. From the Lenni Lenape, through the settlement of the Pennsylvania Germans, to the development of nationally important industries such as iron, cement and silk, and into the present. Take a trip into the world of the Pennsylvania Dutch rural community and tour the:

TROXELL-STECKEL HOUSE (PA-German farmhouse), Claussville One-Room School, and Haines Mill. Or learn how Lehigh County served as a birthplace of the American Industrial Revolution as you view the soaring remains of the Lock Ridge Iron Furnace and Saylor Cement Kilns. Other properties worth a look in this county are: (small adult fee required to tour)

CLARISVILLE ONE-ROOM SCHOOLHOUSE- 2917 Rte. 100. (May - September weekends)

SAYLOR CEMENT INDUSTRY MUSEUM - 245 N. 2nd. On site, 9 cement kilns from beginnings of cement industry (May - September weekends)

HAINES MILL MUSEUM - 3600 Dornay Park Road. Operating gristmill built in 1760 shows milling techniques (May - September weekends)

LOCH RIDGE FURNACE MUSEUM (Alburtis) - 525 Franklin. Iron furnaces, industry park (May - September)

DA VINCI SCIENCE CENTER

Allentown - 3145 Hamilton Blvd. Bypass, Cedar Crest College (corner of the Hamilton Blvd. Bypass and Cedar Crest Blvd.) 18103. **Web: www.davinci-center.org** *Phone: (484) 664-1002. Hours: Monday-Saturday 9:30am-5:00pm, Sunday Noon-5:00pm. Closed only Christmas Day and New Years Day. Admission: $8.95 adult; $6.95 children, seniors, military members and veterans; children under 3 are free.*

This new center is based on the understanding that each young person, like Leonardo da Vinci, is insatiably curious about the world around them, uses multiple modes of investigation, embraces creativity, and seeks to make connections among all the things they are learning. Learn what makes the Earth work and become a real weather forecaster. Investigate forces and discover how machines make work easier. Can you lift 1,000 pounds? Other Family favorites include:

WHAT HURTS? You are the doctor, and Justin needs your help! When your body is hurt or sick, it provides clues to what is wrong. You can use these clues to figure out the problem and how to fix it.

WATTS UP? Experiment with energy as you explore light, electricity, and magnetism. Enjoy images from deep space and dance in the Shadow Room.

WHAT'S THE MATTER? Atoms can join together in many unique, but predictable, ways to form new materials with new properties. Have

...watch water freeze you ever rearranged some atoms?

MUSEUM OF INDIAN CULTURE

Allentown - 2825 Fish Hatchery Road (I-78 exit Cedar Crest Blvd. Take Rte. 29 south and then left on Fish Hatchery) 18103. **Web: www.museumofindianculture.org** *Phone: (610) 797-2121. Hours: Friday-Tuesday Noon-4:00pm. Admission: $3.00-$4.00 (over age 12).*

Hands-on exhibits enhance the learning of the Native American culture. Pretend you're walking in an Indian's moccasins and head dress as you look at exhibits of their crafts and tools. Special events include corn planting in May and Time of Thanksgiving in October.

DORNEY PARK AND WILDWATER KINGDOM

*Allentown - 3830 Dorney Park Road (I-78 West to Exit 16 B) 18104. Phone: (610) 395-3724. **Web:** www.dorneypark.com Hours: Daily (Memorial Day-Labor Day), Weekends (May and September). Admission: $18.00 (starlight) - $40.00 (ages 4+) (includes wet and dry park rides). Parking $7.00.*

THRILL RIDES — Dorney Park & Wildwater Kingdom is home to more than 100 rides and attractions, including eight roller coasters and dozens of state-of-the-art thrill machines. Steel Force is the longest, tallest, fastest coaster in the East. Hang Time - "hang out" thrill ride and Water Works interactive aquatic play ride. Also, high energy live shows.

CAMP SNOOPY — Dorney Park & Wildwater Kingdom is the only place on the East Coast where families can visit Snoopy, Charlie Brown and the PEANUTS™ gang.

WILDWATER KINGDOM — Dorney Park & Wildwater Kingdom offers two great parks for the price of one. Splash around and beat the heat in one of the country's best-ranked water parks. . . Includes 18 water slides, a giant wavepool and Lollipop Lagoon for little kids. Aquablast is the longest elevated water slide (701ft.) in the world.

LEHIGH VALLEY ZOO

*Allentown (Schnecksville) - 5150 Game Preserve Road (off SR309) 18078. Phone: (610) 799-4171. **Web:** www.lvzoo.org Hours: Daily 9:30am-5:00pm (Late April - October). Admission: $5.50-$7.25 (age 2+). Off Season (November - March) offers discounted admission and operating hours are daily, 9:30am-4:00pm.*

For more than 90 years, the Game Preserve - located north of Allentown/ Lehigh Valley, PA - has entertained and educated more than five million people inside and outside Pennsylvania. Founded by General Harry C. Trexler, a local industrialist, the Game Preserve played a significant role in saving the North American Bison from extinction.

Native, exotic birds, and petting zoo inhabit a 25 acre zoo. Investigation Station: Become an Investigative Agent and solve eco-crimes or solve the earth's dilemmas. Catch live animal presentations daily (look on the announcement board). Conserving species of endangered animals is a specialty. Look for their mascot bison, Wooly Bully.

ALPINE MOUNTAIN

Analomink - Route 447 18320. Phone: (717) 595-2150. (800) 233-8240 (Lodging).
Snow Report: (800) 233-8100. **Web: www.alpinemountain.com**

Alpine's Snowtubing Park has been expanded and now includes a new "Kiddie Park" area. Longest Run: 2640 ft.; 20 Slopes & Trails.

PIONEER TUNNEL COAL MINE

Ashland - 19th & Oak Streets (SR61 North to Downtown Area - Follow signs off Center Street SR61) 17921. Phone: (570) 875-3850. **Web: www.pioneertunnel.com** *Hours: Daily 10:00am-6:00pm (Summer). Weekdays 11:00am, 12:30pm, 2:00pm and Weekends 10:00am-6:00pm (May, September, October). Weekdays only in April. Some reserved group tours in November. Admission: $6.50-$8.50 adult, $5.00-$6.00 child (each activity). Save money by purchasing the combo of both tours. Miscellaneous: Snack bar, Gift shop where most novelties are made from coal. Wooden "train" playground.*

Two tour options are available and we highly recommend both. (Pre-schoolers may find the mine tour frightening due to darkness, dampness, and confined areas...but will love the lokie train tour).

COAL MINE TOUR - Watch you children's eyes light up with fascination as you enter and travel 400' deep into a real working coal mine! Though closed in 1931 (because of the Great Depression), you will see and have explained all the features of a real mine. Learn how and why tunnels were built to access the coal. See the Mammoth Vein (the largest in Pennsylvania) and learn why all miners carried a safety lamp (not for light, but for safety from dangerous gases). Our guide was a real miner who carefully explained what we were seeing. He even turned out all of the lights to show how dark a real mine is! If you're concerned, the mine is inspected regularly by the state to insure its safety. If your parents or grandparents were miners, this will surely bring their stories to life. A top 10 Pennsylvania tour and we definitely agree!

TRAIN RIDE - OPEN COAL FIELD TOUR - A "lokie" (steam locomotive) called the "Henry Clay" takes real mine cars to show you strip mining - where a "vein" of coal is discovered and dug out of the side of a mountain. Also stop by a relic "bootleg" coal mine where men risked life and the law during the Great Depression. They used these small illegal mines to get bags of coal to sell and heat their homes.

TUSCARORA STATE PARK

Barnesville - RD 1, Box 1051 (Off I-81, exit 131A, Hometown) 18214. Phone: (717) 467-2404. Web: www.dcnr.state.pa.us/stateparks/parks/tuscarora.aspx

This popular camping spot is heavily forested and the only cleared area is the 52-acre lake. Nestled against Locust Mountain, visitors will find many year-round recreational opportunities like boating and fishing, and opportunities to see wildlife. The hiking trails are short enough (most well under one mile) for younger ones to follow. A seasonal beach, swimming and boat rentals are available, too.

LOCUST LAKE STATE PARK is six miles upstream from Tuscarora. The park was developed as a family tent and trailer campground and has 282 campsites. Additional camper facilities include modern restrooms, swimming beach, boat rental, campstore, bicycle trail, hiking trails, fishing, playgrounds, and nature programs.

RICKETTS GLEN STATE PARK

Benton - RR 2, Box 130 (PA Route 487) 17814. Phone: (717) 477-5675. Web: www.dcnr.state.pa.us/stateparks/parks/rickettsglen.aspx

A series of trails, covering a total of five miles, parallel the streams as they course down the Glens. A shorter hike of ½ mile, the Evergreen Trail, offers an excellent view of the final series of falls as it meanders through a majestic stand of giant hemlocks and white pine. Twenty-one waterfalls are along the Falls Trail within the Glens Natural Area, while one (Adams) is only a few hundred feet from the Evergreen Parking Lot off of PA 118. Take the Falls Trail and explore the Glens which boasts a series of wild, free-flowing waterfalls, each cascading through rock-strewn clefts in this ancient hillside. The 94-foot Ganoga Falls is the highest of 22 named waterfalls. Beach/ Swimming, Boat Rentals, Horseback Riding, Campsites, Modern Cabins.

PENNSYLVANIA YOUTH THEATRE

Bethlehem - 211 Plymouth Street 18015. Web: www.123pyt.org Phone: (610) 332-1400. Pennsylvania Youth Theatre (PYT) is a nonprofit performing arts organization with the mission of educating, entertaining, and enriching the lives of young people and their families through the art of theatre. Productions for/by youth like Cinderella, Babes in Toyland and Charlie and the Chocolate Factory.

BETHLEHEM HISTORIC AREA

Bethlehem - 459 Old York Road (off SR378 - Historic area) 18018. Phone: (800) 360-8687. **Web: www.historicbethlehem.org** *Hours: Daily, except Christmas Admission: FREE (Walking self-guided tours). Guided, scheduled tours are $4.00-7.00/person. Miscellaneous: Best to visit during re-enacted history festivals around Christmas, Bach Festival in May, Celtic Festival in September or Musicfest in August.*

Points of interest include:

VISITORS CENTER - Learn about Moravian Missionaries who first developed this town using pre-Revolutionary German architecture. Watch a video before you take a self-guided walking tour. Open daily until 5:00pm.

MORAVIAN MUSEUM - 66 West Church Street. Can you imagine a 5 story log cabin, built without nails? Once used as a church, dorm and workshop, now it's a Moravian historical museum. (open Thursday-Sunday)

INDUSTRIAL QUARTER - Start at the Luchenbach Mill (HistoryWorks! Children's interactive gallery located on the first floor), stop at a 1761 tannery or 1762 waterworks - the first pumped municipal water system in the colonies.

WATER GAP TROLLEY

Delaware Water Gap - Main Street, Rte. 611 (I-80, exit 310) 18327. Phone: (570) 476-9766. **Web: www.watergaptrolley.com** *Hours: Daily 10:00am-4:00pm (April-November). Admission: $8.00 adult, $3.50 child (2-11). Miscellaneous: Picnic areas and miniature golf on premises.*

Replica streetcars take a relaxed tour of the Water Gap - Shawnee area where you can learn about Indians, early settlers, and some history. The first half of tour may be boring to kids but the second half stops at Chief Taminy's face formed from rough edges in the mountain rocks (like a natural profile - Mt. Rushmore).
Also stop at the Cold Air Cave (regardless of the outside temperature; the air rushing out of the entrance to the small cave is always 38 degrees F. – your kids will say – really cool!)

BUSHKILL PARK

Easton - *2100 Bushkill Park Drive (from Rte. 22 east take the 25th Street exit (Rte. 248), head left, make a RIGHT TURN at the Palmer Park Mall onto Park Drive, behind the Mall) 18040. Phone: (610) 258-6941.* **Web:** *www.bushkillpark.com Hours: Weekends Noon-6:00pm (Memorial Day - Mid-June), Wednesday-Sunday Noon-6:00pm, Friday-Saturday until 9:00pm (Mid-June - Labor Day). Admission: FREE (weekdays). $3.00 Weekends and Holidays. Individual Ride Tickets. Miscellaneous: Picnic. Concessions. Mini-golf.*

This is the same kind of park your parents went to. Most rides are 30-50 years old. A 1926 Allan Herschell Carousel with Grand Wurlitzer organ. 9 Kiddie rides and 8 large rides. Carousel Candy Factory - chocolate handmade before your eyes. Fascination Station 3-level indoor soft play area and Skateland open each winter.

CRAYOLA FACTORY

Easton - *30 Centre Square. Two Rivers Landing (Look for giant box of crayons on top at Two Rivers Landing) 18042.* **Web:** *www.crayola.com/factory Phone: (610) 515-8000. Hours: Tuesday-Saturday 9:30am-5:00pm (earlier winter closing times),*

Sunday Noon- 5:00pm. Also open holiday and summer break Mondays. Closed Christmastime, New Years, Easter and Thanksgiving & first two weeks of January. Admission: $9.50 general (3+), $9.00 senior (65+), $8.50 military. Includes admission to the National Canal Museum. Miscellaneous: The Crayola Store - Colorful collection of anything using color to create is sold. Also area to try new products. To get the most benefit from the full admission price, be prepared to participate in most/all of the activities (that includes you Mom & Dad - you get to be kids...again!)

...it's fun just walking through the front door...

No, The Crayola Factory is not the real manufacturing plant. Instead, it is a family hands-on discovery center that not only provides live demonstrations on how Crayola Crayons and Markers are made but also has more than a dozen hands-on art activities for guests to create momentos of their visit. Each person is asked to learn and think "Outside the Lines" here. Do you know what celebrity molded the 100 billionth crayon? "Color on the Wall" - Go ahead, it's glass and is wiped clean easily. You can color, draw and create with the latest Crayola® product without the worry of cleanup afterwards. Hurry kids, this may be your only chance to break the rules! Everyone creates "their own souvenirs to take home". Especially great is the Factory Floor exhibit where a worker mixes melted wax and colors to help you

Creative fun at every station

make your own souvenir crayons to take home. The most favorite color is red

Jenny gets her freshly made souvenier box to take home!

and our kids got to help put the wrappers on real (just manufactured) crayons. The Wax Works area allows you to actually paint with melted crayons or re-create Folk Art in another exhibit. Older kids will like the Light Zone area where you experiment with color and light combinations. The Crayola Factory went through a $1.5 million redesign, adding two Animation Stations, a manufacturing theatre and new

exhibits to give visitors an improved experience. Parents, it does get crazy in here, but if you go with the flow and start creating yourself…you CAN survive and have FUN!

EASTON MUSEUM OF PEZ

*Easton - 15019 Bank Street (Interstate 476 north. Exit onto Route 22 east toward Allentown. Follow for about 22 miles and exit onto Fourth Street in Easton) 18042. Phone: (888) 843-7391. **Web: www.eastonmuseumofpez.com** Hours: Tuesday-Saturday 10:00am-5:00pm, Sunday 11:00am-5:00pm. Admission: $4.00 adult, $2.00 child. FREE for ages 4 and younger.*

Some 1,500 PEZ dispensers, all nestled in creative landscapes and dioramas, fill the Easton Museum Of Pez Dispensers. Disney PEZ sit in a 10-foot-high castle. Psychedelic PEZ are set beside a real Volkswagen Beetle that appears to be crashing through the wall. Look for circus and zoo scenes, the Beatles and

popular old-and-new children's TV shows and movie characters. There are NFL PEZ and superheroes, Star Wars and Charlie Brown and holiday dispensers. There is also a "Where in the World Is Waldo" game set up on a wall display containing more than 500 dispensers. The owners (brothers) created the PEZ shrine to appeal to the spiked interest in the past decade, fueled by a nostalgia for childhood toys and the Internet collecting. It's something everyone can relate to - most everyone's got a PEZ dispenser lying around in a drawer somewhere.

HUGH MOORE CANAL RIDE PARK

Easton - Hugh Moore Park (off I-78 or off US22 to Lehigh Drive) 18042. Phone: (610) 559-6613. Web: www.canals.org/hmp/index.html Hours: Monday-Saturday 10:30am-5:00pm, Sunday 12:45-5:00pm (mid-June - Labor Day). Weekends only (Friday- Sunday, May & September) Admission: $6.00 adult, $4.00 child (3-15). Miscellaneous: Canoes and pedal boats can be rented at the canal boat boarding area for use on the canal. Trails, picnic, boat rentals, gift shop.

The mule-drawn canal boat Josiah White II rides is on a restored section of the LeHigh Canal. The large boat and costumed drivers are carried by a mule or two (Dixie and Daisy). Why are mules better to use than horses or

donkeys? Visit the Loctender's House Museum - lifestyle of his family and also a great view of the dam, lock, and bridge. You can also view the piers and cables of the Change Bridge, including the oldest machine-made wire rope in America.

NATIONAL CANAL MUSEUM

Easton - 30 Centre Square (I-78, Easton exit & US22 - 3rd floor - Two Rivers Landing) 18042. Phone: (610) 559-6613. Web: www.canals.org/ncm/index.html Hours: Tuesday-Saturday 9:30am-5:00pm, Sunday Noon-5:00pm (Closed Mondays except school holidays). Admission: Included in the purchase price of Crayola Factory tickets. (not available separately) Miscellaneous: Admissions are limited based on building capacity. Call ahead if you're traveling from out of town.

Visit a short time in history before railroads, highways, and airplanes. Follow the story lines of immigrants and locals who built and ran the canals. Hear the boatman tell stories and sing canal songs. Walk through the middle of a full size replica boat. Hands-on exhibits help kids understand this mode of transport. Actually operate a lock model and pilot your play boat through it. Don't miss the miniature train display and the interactive water table. Then dress up as socialites traveling the canal in luxury with Mr. Tiffany (of Tiffany glass in 1886). The Molly Polly Chunker

Waterworks lock
experiments

was a luxury liner canal boat decorated in Victorian fashion. This is the best interactive way to truly understand canals and this brief era of time.

WELLER CENTER

Easton - 325 Northampton Street 18042. Web: www.wellercenter.org Phone: (610) 258-8500. Admission: Varies by group size and program chosen. Only group pricing is available. The center is not open to the public for admission.

Take an exciting trip in one ear and out the other in the World of the Brain. The only exhibit of its kind in the world, this 672 square-foot walk-through brain teaches kids about the many functions of the amazing human brain. An interactive extravaganza of video, light and sound. Shop the aisles of the kid-sized Wegman's grocery store and learn to make healthy food choices. Complete with computerized scanners and check-out stations, this market is filled with simulated breads, vegetables and other foods that look good enough to eat. In filling their miniature shopping carts, kids learn how to choose foods for a balanced meal. Peddling the Wheels of Energy, kids learn just how much energy it takes to eat an M&M and other popular foods. Why should we cover our mouths and noses when we sneeze? You'll find out when you experience the Germ Blaster, their larger-than-life sneezing nose. Take the balance-maze challenge and learn how the inner ear controls balance or try the Impaired Driving Simulator.

KNOEBEL'S AMUSEMENT RESORT

Elysburg - PO Box 317 (I-80 West to Bloomsburg exits 232, 236, 241. Rte. 232, PA 42 South to Catawissa & SR 487) 17824. Web: www.knoebels.com Phone: (800) ITS-4-FUN. Hours: Daily 11:00am-10:00pm (Summer). Weekends only (May & September). Admission: FREE. Pay-One-Price Plans are available Monday-Friday during the in-season ($23.00-$34.50). Weekends are pay-as-you-go. $1.00-$3.00 per *ride. Miscellaneous: Pool and water slides. Games, entertainment. Restaurants. Gift shops. Mini-golf. Swimming and Camping.*

41 rides including the "Phoenix" - rated one of America's 10 best roller coasters. Knoebels just built their own version of a "Classic" wooden ride called Flying Turns. This is a roller coaster like ride where you sit in a train and roll down a wood track much like a bobsled run. Just as many family rides as thrill or kiddie rides. Ride in the Antique Cars or get a birds-eye view from the Giant Wheel. Want a little more action? Try the Whipper or shriek in the Haunted Mansion. Compose yourself with a nice quiet ride on the Pioneer Train before you return home from a fun filled day at Knoebels. An extremely family-friendly, old-fashioned attraction!

LOST RIVER CAVERNS

Hellertown - 726 Durham Street (I-78, Exit 21, Rt. 412 South) 18055. Phone: (610) 838-8767. Web: www.lostcave.com Hours: Year-round. 9:00am-6:00pm (Memorial Day-Labor Day), Rest of year closes at 5:00pm. Closed Thanksgiving, Christmas, and New Year's Day. Admission: $9.50 adult, $5.50 child (3-12).

Guided walking tours through beautiful crystal formations. Limestone cavern with five chambers and underground stream. Indoor tropical garden, rock museum.

SPLIT ROCK RESORT SKI AREA

Lake Harmony - 1 Lake Drive (I-80 East to Exit 277 or I-476 to exit 95, follow Rte.940 East 18624. Phone: (717) 722-9111. (800) 255-ROCK (Lodge). Snow Report: (717) 722-9111. Web: www.splitrockresort.com

Lodge with 2 indoor pools, whirlpools or sauna, 18 hole championship golf course, sail on beautiful Lake Harmony, mountain bike or hike to Hickory-Run State Park, or do some skiing. Longest Run: 1700 ft.; 7 Slopes & Trails.

BELTZVILLE STATE PARK

Lehighton - 2950 Pohopoco Drive (US 209) 18235. Phone: (215) 377-0045. Web: www.dcnr.state.pa.us/stateparks/parks/beltzville.aspx

Beltzville Lake is seven miles long and features fishing, swimming, water sports and unlimited horsepower boating. Along the shore, you can sometimes find fossils. A hike along Wild Creek Trail leads to waterfalls and Sawmill Trail wanders through forests and by a creek. Beach, Boat Rentals, & Cross-Country Skiing.

BIG DIAMOND RACEWAY

*Minersville - (Near Forestville, off Rt. 901) 17901. Phone: (570) 544-6434. **Web:** www.bigdiamondraceway.com   Hours: Fridays at 8:00pm (April-Labor Day). Nationals end of September weekend.*

NASCAR - Winston Series Stock Car Racing.

MARTIN GUITAR COMPANY

*Nazareth - 510 Sycamore Street (I-80 to SR33 South to SR191 South to North Broad to Beil St - Follow Signs) 18064. Phone: (610) 759-2837. **Web: www.martinguitar.com** Hours: Monday-Friday 8:30am-5:00pm (shop and museum). Closed Holidays and week of Christmas. Miscellaneous: 1833 shop memorabilia, strings, books and accessories.*

Founded in 1833, Martin guitars are known as "America's guitar". Used by many legendary performers, you'll start your tour in the museum shop of vintage guitars. Children are encouraged to "gently play" several guitars in the waiting area. If any of your children play the guitar, they will be especially interested in all the posters of famous performers who use Martins. Follow a guitar from rough lumber to a finished product which requires more than 300 steps to complete. The tour shows step-by-step production and is very educational. See the types of wood (cured for 4 months prior to production) used - from the usual to the exotic. Watch how each piece is computer-routed or bent in special  jigs. Martin even makes their own strings to insure that "one of a kind" Martin sound. They've even produced a $50,000 custom order guitar with diamonds in the guitar neck! Sometimes famous performers (or their band members) stop by the Martin plant...maybe even on your tour!

BLUE MOUNTAIN SKI AREA

*Palmerton - 1600 Blue Mountain Drive 18071. Phone: (610) 826-7700. Snow report: (800) 235- 2226. **Web: www.skibluemt.com***

1,082-foot vertical, plenty of trails for ALL abilities plus a half-pipe and two terrain parks. Longest Run: 6400 ft.; 29 Slopes & Trails plus snowboarding.

JACK FROST MOUNTAIN & BIG BOULDER SKI AREAS

*Poconos (Blakeslee) - PO Box 707 (I-476 exit 95 or I-80 exit 284, head north to Jack Frost, head south to Big Boulder) 18610. Phone: (800) 468-2442. **Web: www.jfbb.com** Admission: per activity Miscellaneous: Baby sitting provided. Choose from Poconos resorts' townhouses, condominiums, cabins, or campsites. SnowMonsters skiing and snowboarding programs are geared towards kids to teach them basic techniques and important safety tips in a fun environment! Chair lifts and SkiCarpets (make it easier for younger skiers to move up the mountains).*

BIG BOULDER SKI AREA - Longest Run: 2900 ft.; 14 Slopes & Trails. Five family and seven single tubing chutes.

JACK FROST SKI AREA - Longest Run: 2700 ft.; 21 Slopes & Trails.

RIDE ATV PARK - 4 wheeler vehicle park with curves, hill, whoop-de-doos, mud pits. Smaller course and ATV's for youngsters. Fee includes rentals.

SPLATTER - 2500 acres of paintball fields (with special themes). Year round.

WHEELS SKATE PARK - In-line skate and board park with half pipes, quarter pipes, rail slides and pyramids. Kids area. Rentals. Daily (April - October).

POCONO SNAKE AND ANIMAL FARM

Poconos (Marshalls Creek) - Route 209 (US209 Northeast) 18335. Phone: (570) 223-8653. Hours: Daily Noon-5:00pm, weather permitting. Admission: $4.00-$5.00 (age 2+).

Visit the "Great Little Zoo". They have over 100 animals including a giant Anaconda, Alligators, Emus, and Mountain Lions. Some of the most popular attractions include a 160 year old snapping turtle, a giant python, Grey Wolves, and the beloved Siberian Tiger whose best friend for over 13 years is a bear - watching them play is an unforgettable experience. The antics of the monkeys, or more engaging pot belly pigs, may make your kids "squeal". Petting and feeding areas, too.

GREAT WOLF LODGE RESORT & INDOOR WATERPARK

*Poconos (Scotrun) - 1 Great Wolf Drive (just off I-80, Scotrun exit, Route 611 north) 18355. Phone: (800) 905-WOLF. **Web: www.greatwolflodge.com** Admission: Rates (include admission to waterpark) for lodging run $169-$300 per night depending on package.*

The Poconos first new family destination resort in nearly three decades. The 401-suite Great Wolf Lodge has an array of amenities including: a huge indoor Waterpark, an Arcade, Cub Club activity/crafts room, Spa, Fitness Room, the Camp Critter Bar & Grille, The Loose Moose Cottage gourmet buffet and food court, Claw Café confectionery and an animated Great Clock Tower to greet you. The Pocono Great Wolf indoor waterpark is the largest of any in the chain. They have a new, state-of-the-art water roller coaster ride that defies the law of gravity, winding up and down hill, and the cannon bowl tube ride, which offers a whirling water ride.

SHAWNEE MOUNTAIN SKI AREA

Poconos (Shawnee-on-Delaware) - PO Box 339 (Exit 309, Off I-80) 18356. **Web:** *www.shawneemt.com Phone: (570) 421-7231. (800) VILLA-4-U. (Lodge). Snow Report: (800) 233-4218.*

SKIwee Bowl Teaching Area: This exclusive contoured teaching terrain, located between lower Bushkill Trail and Little Chief Slope, features new extended carpet lifts, colorful teaching aides, permanent fencing and automated snow-making.

INCUBATOR TERRAIN PARK: Complementing Shawnee's huge 3000' Bushkill Super Park, this new terrain park will be located on the Country Club Slope and will offer beginner/novice skill level rails, boxes and snow features. The Incubator Park will serve as a learning area for those Riders and Skiers not yet at a comfortable skill level to challenge the Bushkill Park.

TANDEM SNOW TUBES: Shawnee's Pocono Plunge Snow Tubing Park will be adding a limited number of two person snow tubes able to accommodate one adult and one small child in the same snow tube.

22 Trails, Terrain Park, Snowboarding, "Pocono Plunge" Snow Tubing Park & Half-Pipe. Open Day & Night. Longest Run: 5100 ft. Comfortable rooms, dining, indoor pool/jacuzzi, & the only full-size indoor ice rink in the region.

SHAWNEE PLACE CHILDREN'S PLAY AND WATER PARK

Poconos (Shawnee-on-Delaware) - PO Box 339 (I-80, Exit 309, US 209 North, Follow signs) 18356. Phone: (570) 421-7231. **Web: www.shawneemt.com** *Hours: Daily 10:00am-5:00pm (Mid-June - Labor Day). Admission: Participants $15.00, Spectators $10.00.*

"Kids Rule" at Shawnee Place where families splash and play all day for one low admission price (geared towards kids ages 2-12). COOL ACTIVITY

POOL with Rain Drop & Lemon Drop Fountains. Two great Waterslides & Splash-Down Pools. Ball Crawls, Cloud Bounces, Cable Glide, Toddlers Area and Kids Venture River Ride. Daily Magic Shows and Activities, Video Games, Snack Bar, Gift Shop and Picnic Area.

QUIET VALLEY LIVING HISTORICAL FARM

*Stroudsburg - 1000 Turkey Hill Road (I-80 to exit 304, US209 SW (Bus Rte), right at Shafer's School House Road, left on Business Route 209. 18360. Phone: (570) 992-6161. **Web:** www.quietvalley.org Hours: Tuesday-Saturday 10:00am-5:30pm, Sunday 1:00-5:30pm (June 20 - Labor Day). Admission: $6.00 adult, $4.00 child (3-12).*

Meet a Pennsylvania Dutch family as they go about their numerous daily chores – pretend the time is the early 1800s. Daily activities include spinning, weaving, smoking and drying meats, vegetables and fruits; cooking, gardening, and tending to animals. Kids can touch barnyard animals and jump in a giant haystack! Usually one craft is highlighted weekly - ex. quilting, butter churning, candle dips, basket making, natural wool dying (how do they get color naturally?) and blacksmithing. Actual aunts, uncles, cousins, and siblings escort you around the farm & treat you like visiting relatives.

DELAWARE STATE FOREST

*Swiftwater - HC 1, Box 95A 18370. Phone: (570) 895-4000. **www.dcnr.state.pa.us/ forestry/stateforests/delaware.aspx***

Messing Nature Center lead to Trails, Horse Trails, ATV Trails (35 miles), Fishing, Cross-Country Skiing.

CAMEL BEACH WATER PARK (CAMELBACK SKI AREA)

*Tannersville - PO Box 168 (I -80, Exit 299) 18372. Phone: (570) 629-1661. **Web:** www.camelbeach.com or http://skicamelback.com/ Hours: Waterpark open Daily at 10:00am (Summers). Weekends only (early Fall and late Spring). Skiing (December-March). Admission: Avg. $15.00 (twilight) to $30.00 (adult day rate). See website for skiing.*

WATERPARK: New for 2006, The Flow Rider, the ultimate surfing ride! 22 Water-slides- The most in the region featuring Checkered Flag Challenge with Kahuna Lagoon wave pool, two kids play zone, the Blue Nile Adventure River, bumper boats, mini golf, swimming pool, scenic chairlift & more. 3200 foot long Alpine Slide, bumper boats, go-carts, mini-golf, chairlift rides, Cameltop Restaurant (lunch only).

SKI AREA: Skiing, snowboarding and tubing. You'll find 33 trails, 13 lifts including 2 high-speed detachable quads, halfpipe, 2 terrain parks, night skiing and 100% snowmaking. PA Ski & Winter Sports Museum is located here.

ECKLEY MINERS' VILLAGE

Weatherly - Route #2, Box 236 (I-80 West to Exit 40 - SR940 West - then follow signs) 18255. Phone: (570) 636-2070. **Web: www.eckleyminers.org** *Hours: Monday-Saturday 9:00am-5:00pm, Sunday Noon-5:00pm. Closed State Holidays except summer holidays. Admission: $4.00 adult, $3.50 senior, $2.00 child (6-12). Miscellaneous: Great supplement to a nearby tour of a coal mine.*

What is a Patch Town? A patch was a cluster of a few dozen company houses along a crooked, unpaved street built within the shadow of black silt ponds and strip mining pits. See an actual town (only slightly restored) just as it appeared in a movie (in the 1970s). Retired miners, miner's widows, and children still live here. Watch a 15 minute video at the Visitor's Center first, then walk by audio displays of a typical miner's day or week (including church

A large "breaker" tower. built as a movie prop, but it looks so real...

on Sunday). School-aged kids will want to take the tour which includes going inside a house (1870s - 1890s - notice all of the updates!), a company store, and a doctor's office. Just imagine having to be a young boy then, helping to support the family by being a "breaker boy" in the smoky, dangerous mill. Boy, can you feel the coal miner ancestry here!

HICKORY RUN STATE PARK

White Haven - RD 1, Box 81 (PA Route 534, I-80 exit 274) 18661. Phone: (717) 443-0400. Web: www.dcnr.state.pa.us/stateparks/parks/hickoryrun.aspx

The Boulder Field, a striking boulder-strewn area, is a National Natural Landmark. This large park has over 40 miles of hiking trails, three natural areas and miles of trout streams. While at the park, learn about lumbering history at the Visitors Center, observe wildlife or see Hawk Falls. Beach & Swimming, Sledding, and numerous Campsites. Mountain biking is prohibited on all trails at Hickory Run State Park, but is permitted at nearby Lehigh Gorge State Park.

JACOBSBURG ENVIRONMENTAL EDUCATION PARK

Wind Gap - *835 Jacobsburg Road (PA 33) 18091. Phone: (610) 746-2801.* **Web:** *www.dcnr.state.pa.us/stateparks/parks/jacobsburg.aspx Hours: The center office is open 8:00am-4:00pm, Monday through Friday. The center's main parking area on Belfast Road is open from sunrise to sunset, seven days a week for your enjoyment. Miscellaneous: Heritage programming includes displays and demonstrations of early gunmaking at the Pennsylvania Longrifle Heritage Museum currently in the Henry Homestead. Living history programs include mid-1840s rendezvous and period military encampments. Gunmaking and blacksmithing classes are offered and historic buildings are open for tours. Please contact the center office for a schedule and reservation information.*

Environmental Education Center offers many programs. Once the site where the famous Henry Rifle was made, the Jacobsburg National Historic District lies almost entirely within the park. Henrys Woods offers scenic hikes and the rest of the center grounds have multi-use trails. Horseback Riding and Mountain Biking are most popular here.

FRANCES SLOCUM STATE PARK

Wyoming - *565 Mt. Olivet Road (exit 170B of I- 81, take Rte. 309 North) 18644.* **Web:** *www.dcnr.state.pa.us/stateparks/parks/francesslocum.aspx Phone: (717) 696-3525.*

The horseshoe-shaped lake provides 165 acres for boating and fishing. An environmental interpretive center located in the day use area features exhibits on American Indians and ecological topics. The park is named for a young girl who was kidnapped by a Lenni Lenape raiding party in 1778. Frances Slocum spent her first night of captivity in a rock shelter in the park. Pool, Campsites, Boat Rentals, and Sledding.

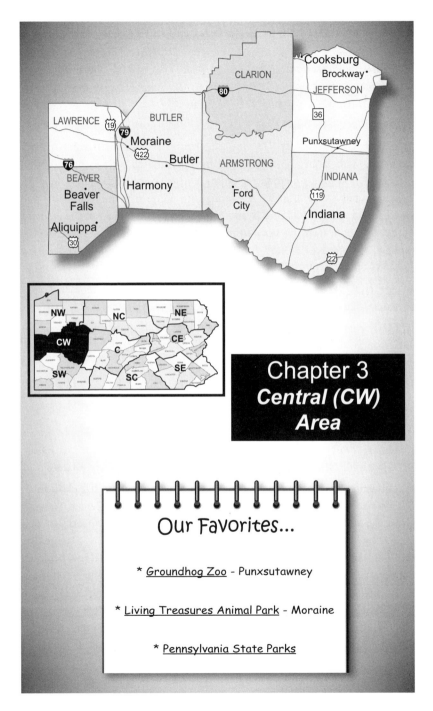

Chapter 3
*Central (CW)
Area*

Our Favorites...

* <u>Groundhog Zoo</u> - Punxsutawney

* <u>Living Treasures Animal Park</u> - Moraine

* <u>Pennsylvania State Parks</u>

BUTLER COUNTY MUSEUMS

Butler - 119 West New Castle Street, downtown 16003. Phone: (724) 283-8116. Web: www.butlercountyhistoricalsociety-pa.org Hours: open to the public Sundays, 1:00 pm-3:00pm and Wednesdays 11:00am-1:30pm, May through August and for special events. Admission: $3.00 adult, $1.00 youth ages 5-17.

Country life at 4 different sites:

COOPER CABIN - (off Rte. 356, Cooper Rd.). The 1810 cabin is still furnished with family heirlooms and memorabilia as well as other period pieces. Out buildings include a spinning house, spring house and tool shed. A self-guided nature trail winds through the more than four acres of land surrounding the cabin. There is also a model oil well and an extensive herb garden. Cooper Cabin is open to the public for tours and a program on the 2nd and 4th Sundays of June, July, and August, 1:00pm-4:00pm. Admission fees: $3.00 per adult, $1.00 for youth ages 5-17.

SHAW HOUSE - a summer residence for Butler's only U.S. Senator, Walter Lowrie (1828).

LITTLE RED SCHOOLHOUSE - (1838) living history museum on 200 Jefferson St. which recreates the one-room school experience for visitors and school classes.

HERITAGE CENTER - 119 West New Castle Street. Industry in the area including tin shop, Bantam Jeep, and Franklin glassworks.

COOK FOREST STATE PARK

Cooksburg - River Road - PO Box 120 (I-80 exit 78, PA 36 north) 16217. Phone: (814) 744-8407. Web: www.dcnr.state.pa.us/stateparks/parks/cookforest.aspx

Virgin white pine and hemlock timber stands nick-named the "Black Forest". Highlights are the Forest Cathedral, Log Cabin Inn Visitor Center, Sawmill Craft Center and Theater, the Fire Tower and Seneca Point Overlook. Log Cabin Inn: Cook Forest's environmental learning center is a large log building built in 1934 by the CCC. It is at one end of Longfellow Trail and contains a variety of displays, taxidermy animals and logging tools from early lumbering days. Near the entrance on Route 36 is Double Diamond Deer Ranch, where deer are raised from birth. Children can bottle-feed fawns June -August. Pool, Horseback Riding, Campsites, Rustic Cabins, Boating, Fishing, Skiing, and Snowmobiling. Several private canoe rentals are in the Cooksburg area.

DOUBLE DIAMOND DEER RANCH

Cooksburg - *(I-80, Brookville exit north on SR36, South of Cook Forest) 16217. Phone: (814) 752-6334.* **Web: www.doublediamonddeerranch.com** *Hours: Daily 10:00am-Dusk (May-November), Weekends Only (December-April). Admission: $4.00+ (age 5+).*

Photograph or watch white tail deer in natural habitats. Covered walkways, scenic trails, and a Museum & gift shop. Fawns are born early June. Come see how tiny they are. "Bottle times" and "Treat Times" are scheduled in June, July and August. The deer do not drop their antlers until February, March and April. The last buck always sheds his antlers around April 15th.

RACCOON CREEK STATE PARK

Hookstown - *RD 1, Box 900 (3000 SR 18, or enter from US 22 or US 30) 15050. Phone: (724) 899-2200.* **Web: www.dcnr.state.pa.us/stateparks/parks/raccooncreek.aspx** *Hours: 8:00am-Sunset*

A centrally located 100-acre lake provides opportunities for outdoor recreation like fishing, boating, and photographing and viewing waterfowl and other wildlife. Wild Flower Reserve (899-3611, Rte 30.) A 315 acre tract of land with over 500 species of wildflowers and wildlife. Frankfurt Mineral Springs - explore the reported "medicinal" properties of the water. Beach/Swimming, Visitor Center, Boat Rentals, Horseback Riding, Sledding, Winter Sports, Campsites, and Modern Cabins.

JIMMY STEWART MUSEUM

Indiana - *845 Philadelphia St (Indiana Public Library - 3rd Floor, corner of 9th) 15701. Phone: (724) 349-6112 or (800) 83-JIMMY.* **Web: www.jimmy.org** *Hours: Monday-Saturday 10:00am-5:00pm, Sunday & Holidays Noon-5:00pm. Closed Christmastime and New Years time. Admission: $5.00 adult, $4.00 senior, $3.00 child (7-17).*

A legendary actor (every Christmas we still all watch "It's a Wonderful Life") who had accomplishments in film, radio and television plus civic and family roles. Displays of his great grandfather's uniform, baby photographs, furniture from the family hardware store, original movie posters, props and costumes. Watch films that are shown in a small 1930s vintage movie theatre most weekends.

LIVING TREASURES ANIMAL PARK

*Moraine - US422 16101. Phone: (724) 924-9571. Web: www.ltanimalpark.com
Hours: Daily 10:00am-8:00pm (Summer). Daily 10:00am-6:00pm (April and May,
September, October). Admission: $7.50 adult, $7.00 senior, $5.50 child (3-11).*

Watch kangaroos, tigers and wolves and ride the miniature horses. Kids
love the petting area (babies, reindeer, and camels) and feeding areas (bears,
otters, monkeys, goats, sheep, and llamas). Cups of animal feed are available
in the gift shop or at coin-operated food dispensers throughout the park.

HARLANSBURG STATION'S MUSEUM OF TRANSPORTATION

*New Castle - West Pittsburgh Road (US19 & SR108) 16101. Phone: (724) 652-9002.
Hours: Tuesday-Saturday 10:00am-5:00pm, Sunday Noon-5:00pm. Weekends Only
(March, April, May, November, December) Admission: $2.00-$3.00.*

Olde time railroad station with display of real Pennsylvania railroad
cars outside and memorabilia displayed inside the cars. Meet the mascot
conductor and see lots of railroad uniforms. In the station are trains, cars,
planes, trucks, and trolleys. The scale train layout depicts four scenes of
Western Pennsylvania. Tours of silver-sided passenger cars are available.

YELLOW CREEK STATE PARK

*Penn Run - 170 Route 259 Highway (PA 422 or PA 259) 15765. Phone: (724) 357-
7913. Web: www.dcnr.state.pa.us/stateparks/parks/yellowcreek.aspx*

Yellow Creek State Park is in Indiana County along one of the first "highways"
in the state, the Kittanning Path. This trail was used by the Delaware and
Shawnee nations and by early settlers. Today, US 422 roughly follows the old
Kittanning Path, and provides the main access to the park from Indiana and
Ebensburg. The park is named for Yellow and Little Yellow creeks, which
create the lake. The creeks have lots of yellow clay in the banks and bottoms.
Beach, Visitor Center, Boat Rentals, Sledding, Fishing, and Trails.

MCCONNELL'S MILL STATE PARK

*Portersville - RD 2, Box 16 (near the intersection of PA 19 and U.S. 422) 16051.
Web: www.dcnr.state.pa.us/stateparks/parks/mcconnellsmill.aspx Phone: (724)
368-8091.*

A 400 ft. deep gorge with giant boulders and unique eco-system. Slippery
Rock Creek flows through the gorge. The steep-sided gorge contains
numerous rocky outcrops, boulders, old growth forest, waterfalls and rare

plants. Cleland Rock Vista is a great place to view the gorge. You can tour the restored rolling gristmill or the covered bridge. There is also scenic hiking, whitewater boating and two rock climbing and rappelling areas. Historical Center, sledding, boating, fishing, swimming, biking, camping, skiing, and snowmobiling.

MORAINE STATE PARK

Portersville - 225 Pleasant Valley Road (bisected by PA Route 422 running east/ west and PA 528 running north/south) 16051. Phone: (724) 368-8811. **Web:** *www.dcnr.state.pa.us/stateparks/parks/moraine.aspx*

Moraine State Park features 3,225-acre Lake Arthur, an outstanding warm water fishery that is also great for sailing and boating. Visitors sometimes see osprey that were reintroduced to the park. Of special interest is the Frank Preston Conservation Area and a 7-mile paved bike trail that winds around the north shore of the lake. Beach, Visitor Center, Horseback Riding, Mountain Biking, Modern Cabins, Fishing, Trails, and Winter Sports.

PUNXSUTAWNEY GROUNDHOG ZOO

Punxsutawney - East Mahoning Street, Civic Center Complex (I-80 to exit 97, US119) 15767. Phone: (800) 752-PHIL. **Web:** *www.groundhog.org Hours: Museum: Tuesday-Saturday 1:00-4:00pm, Sunday 2:00-4:00pm. Zoo: (Dawn to Dusk. Call first to confirm hours of museum. Admission: FREE Miscellaneous: At 401 West Mahoning Street, (814) 938-2555 is the Punxsutawney Museum devoted to groundhog history and legend. All around the town, colorful, whimsical, 6-foot tall fiberglass Phantastic Phils! adorn the public spaces of the Weather Capital of the World. Each of the large fiberglass groundhogs is an individual work of art created by artists from across the state and the country.*

On Groundhog Day (February 2), the world looks for "Punxsutawney Phil" each year to peek out of his burrow on Gobbler's Knob and see if his shadow appears. His prediction indicates how much of the winter season is left. The legend was brought to this country by German immigrants. Phil and his descendants have been popping out every year since February 2, 1887.

"Now Phil, you gotta help me out", says Jenny. "Daniel likes summer, but I like winter...shadow please!"

...gotta love me!

He and his family reside at this zoo. We might suggest you watch the movie "Groundhog Day" starring Bill Murray prior to your visit to get into the spirit of things! By the way, Phil gets almost as much mail as Santa Claus and on Groundhog Day up to 35,000 people come to see him each year! (they have pictures to prove it). It's worth a trip anytime of the year to meet a live groundhog up close ... your family may be surprised how they can change their shape to fit around the landscape.

CLEAR CREEK STATE PARK

*Sigel - RR 1, Box 82 (1-80 to exit 73) 15860. Phone: (814) 752-2368. **Web:** www.dcnr.state.pa.us/stateparks/parks/clearcreek.aspx*

Set along the Clarion River, Clear Creek is a cozy getaway and a canoeist's paradise. Whether you bring your own canoe or rent one, a popular activity is the 11-mile trip from Clear Creek to Cook Forest State Park. Rustic log and stone cabins are nestled among ancient pines and hemlocks, making this park the perfect place to spend a secluded, rustic vacation. Beach, Visitor Center, Historical Center, Boat Rentals, Sledding, Campsites, Fishing, Winter Sports, and Trails.

JENNINGS ENVIRONMENTAL EDUCATION CENTER

*Slippery Rock - 2951 Prospect Road 16057. Phone: (724) 794-6011. **Web:** www.dcnr.state.pa.us/stateparks/parks/jennings.aspx Hours: Daily, Dawn - Dusk. Educational Center Monday-Friday 8:00am-4:00pm. Admission: FREE. Miscellaneous: Hiking trails. Picnic areas.*

Surviving remnants of a Midwest Prairie. A unique attraction at the center is its relict prairie, which includes the spectacular and well-known prairie flower, the blazing star. The relict prairie ecosystem is rare in Pennsylvania. In late July, blooms of blazing star (wild prairie flowers) along with other assorted wildflowers of all varieties are full peak color. Due to the glacial activity, the ground is mostly clay and only supports growth of thin grasses and plants.

SUGGESTED LODGING AND DINING

<u>**LOG CABIN INN**</u> - **Harmony/Zelienople**. 430 Perry Highway. Phone: (724) 452-4155 or **www.springfields.com/lci_files/logcabininn.html**. The Log Cabin Inn is just north of the hustle and bustle of Cranberry. Rural and rustic, it is built around a 160 year old cabin. The original dining room area floor is tilted and the logs are huge. Casual Dress. Relaxing atmosphere. Showing all Steeler football games and a great outdoor (heated) deck overlooking the 'Backwoods'.... you'll love it. All American fare with children's menu complete with coloring and crayons. Daily, Lunch & Dinner.

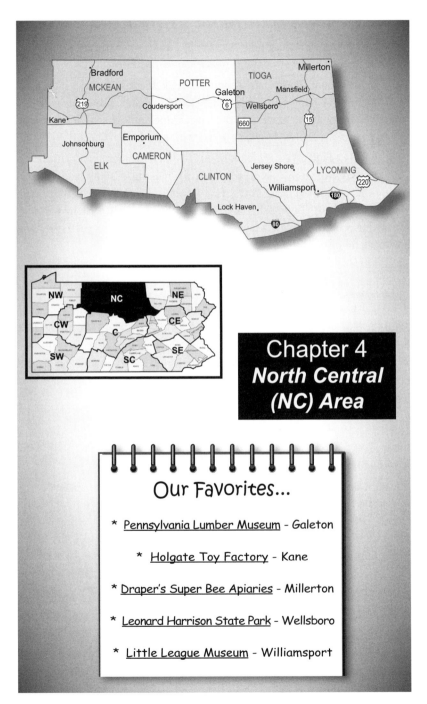

Chapter 4
North Central (NC) Area

Our Favorites...

* <u>Pennsylvania Lumber Museum</u> - Galeton

* <u>Holgate Toy Factory</u> - Kane

* <u>Draper's Super Bee Apiaries</u> - Millerton

* <u>Leonard Harrison State Park</u> - Wellsboro

* <u>Little League Museum</u> - Williamsport

SINNEMAHONING STATE PARK

Austin - 8288 First Fork Road (junction of PA 872 and US 6 or PA 120) 16720. **Web:** *www.dcnr.state.pa.us/stateparks/parks/sinnemahoning.aspx Phone: (814) 647-8401.*

The diverse habitat supports the American eagle, black bear and white-tailed deer. Interpretive pontoon boat rides on George B. Stevenson Reservoir are available during the summer to allow a closer look at lake wildlife. Boating, Fishing, some Trails, Modern Campsites, and one Modern Cabin.

ELK STATE FOREST: Principally in Elk and Cameron Counties, the 200,000 acres of forest land are open to hunting, fishing and general recreation. Within Elk State Forest is a portion of the Quehanna Wild Area, which is south of Sinnemahoning. The Quehanna Trail System provides access for primitive-type forest recreation limited to day use activities and backpack hiking. 814-486-3353

SKI DENTON

Coudersport - PO Box 367 (on US 6) 16915. **Web:** *www.skidenton.com Phone: (814) 435-2115.* With slopes ranging from the steepest in the Eastern states to long, gentle beginner trails, Ski Denton draws skiers of all levels. Addition of a lighted Snowboard Park and new tube slide. Longest Run: 1 mile; 20 Slopes & Trails. Located in Denton Hill State Park. There are five cabin chalets and hostel-style group lodging located on the Ski Denton grounds. They now have mountain-biking, too.

OLE BULL STATE PARK

Cross Fork - Box 9 (PA Route 144) 17729. Phone: (814) 435-5000. **Web:** *www.dcnr.state.pa.us/stateparks/parks/olebull.aspx*

The park area is referred to as the Black Forest of Pennsylvania. Its dense tree cover and mountainous terrain attracts thousands of campers along Kettle Creek. The park is named after Ole Bornemann Bull, the famous Norwegian violinist who toured this country in the 1850s. Ole Bull Trail leads to the historic foundation remains of Ole Bull's "home site" and a panoramic view of the park area. The Beaver Dam Nature Trail provides an introduction to the habitats along Kettle Creek. This 0.75-mile trail starts at the concrete fordway and has a flat trail surface. The 85-mile Susquehannock Trail System passes through Ole Bull State Park. Beach, Modern Cabin rental, Fishing, Trails, and Cross-Country Skiing.

BUCKTAIL STATE PARK

Emporium - *RD 1, Box 1-A (Route 120) 15834. Phone: (814) 486-3365.* **Web:** *www.dcnr.state.pa.us/stateparks/parks/bucktail.aspx*

Hemmed in by mountains, this state park scenic drive follows PA Route 120 as it winds from Lock Haven to Emporium along the West Branch of the Susquehanna River and the Sinnemahoning Creek. It stretches through a narrow valley which has for years been called the Bucktail Trail, named after the famous American Civil War regiment of Woodsmen, the Bucktails or Bucktail Rangers. This is the old Sinnemahoning Trail used by American Indians on their way to and from the eastern continental divide between the Susquehanna and Allegheny rivers. Aside from the three towns named above, the valley is mostly forested land with an occasional small village or isolated farm. The scenic drive has no recreational facilities. In June, the mountain laurel is in bloom and in early October the fall colors are breathtaking. Boating permitted, Fishing, and some Trails.

SIZERVILLE STATE PARK

Emporium - *RD 1, Box 238-A (PA Route 155) 15834. Phone: (814) 486-5605.* **Web:** *www.dcnr.state.pa.us/stateparks/parks/sizerville.aspx*

The Bottomlands, Campground and North Slope trails take the visitor through a variety of lowland habitats and are relatively easy to walk making them ideal for hikers of any age. The Sizerville Nature Trail is a three-mile loop that nearly everyone can enjoy. It has educational stopping points. Maps are available in the park office. Nady Hollow Trail is a 1.5-mile loop that ascends a 1,900-foot mountain. The "Cutback" section takes the hiker halfway up the mountain and then, gradually runs down along the mountainside. Due to the slope of this trail, it is more challenging. Sizerville State Park is also a trailhead for the Bucktail Path Trail, which is part of an extensive trail system throughout the northern tier region of central Pennsylvania. Within the park, you will find beautiful white pines, hemlocks, spring wild flowers, a butterfly garden and flaming fall foliage in early October. Pool, Visitor Center, and Campsites.

CHERRY SPRINGS STATE PARK

Galeton - *RD 1, Box 136 (PA Route 44 - Potter County) 16922. Phone: (814) 435-5010.* **Web:** *www.dcnr.state.pa.us/stateparks/parks/cherrysprings.aspx*

Cherry Springs State Park is nearly as remote and wild today as it was two centuries ago, a haven for campers who like to rough it and who can appreciate one of the finest scenic drives in Pennsylvania. Its dark skies make it a haven for astronomers. Named for the large stands of black cherry trees in the park, the 48-acre state park is surrounded by the 262,000-acre Susquehannock State Forest. The Susquehanna Trail passes nearby and offers 85 miles of backpacking and hiking. Public Stargazing Saturdays.

LYMAN RUN STATE PARK

Galeton - 545 Lyman Run Road   16922. Phone: (814) 435-5010.   Web: www.dcnr.state.pa.us/stateparks/parks/lymanrun.aspx

Lyman Run State Park has been carved from the Susquehannock State Forest. The shaded picnic area is popular for picnicking and hiking, and the lake is a fishing hot spot. Beach, Campsites, Fishing, Trails.

Hiking is available on many trails in the SUSQUEHANNOCK STATE FOREST, though the main trail is the Susquehannock Trail System, an 85-mile loop through the forested hills and valleys of the region. During the summer months, a 43-mile-ATV trail is available within Susquehannock State Forest. The trail passes through Lyman Run State Park, where parking and sanitary facilities are located. 261,784 acres of Fishing, Trails, Winter Sports, and ATV Trails.

PENNSYLVANIA LUMBER MUSEUM

Galeton (Coudersport) - 5660 US 6 West (just west of PA 449) 16922. Phone: (814) 435-2652. Web: www.lumbermuseum.org Hours: Wednesday-Sunday 9:00am-5:00pm (April-November). Closed fall state holidays.   Admission: $2.00-$4.00 (age 5+). Miscellaneous: The museum is set in the heart of the Susquehannock State Forest, where an abundance of State Parks, campgrounds, rental cabins and motels are available for an overnight stay.

Pennsylvania once had a prosperous lumber heritage with its wealth of white pine and hemlock trees. Now on display, are 3000+ objects including old-fashioned logging tools and a logging locomotive. The best part of the visit is the short walk to the preserved remains of, a once very busy, logging camp. See the huge sawmill (buzzing logs that have floated down river), mess hall, dormitories, rails, and engines used for transport. The well kept operational facility is extremely interesting and educational.

CRYSTAL LAKE SKI CENTER

Hughesville - 1716 Crystal Lake Rd (off US 220) 17737. Phone: (570) 584-2698. Snow Report: (570) 584-4209. **Web: www.crystallakeskicenter.com**

The facilities include an unusual natural setting of 960 acres of mountain woodlands at elevations from 1550 to 2100 feet, several lakes and ponds, dining facilities for up to 200 in a modern, fully winterized dining hall, lodging for up to 180 in the winter months and recreational facilities. Cross-country skiing, ice skating and snowshoeing.

HYNER RUN STATE PARK

Hyner - Box 46 (Hyner Run Road, PA 1014) 17738. Phone: (717) 923-6000. **Web: www.dcnr.state.pa.us/stateparks/parks/hynerrun.aspx**

The terrain of the park is generally level and occupies the small valley created by Hyner Run, with steep mountains on both sides. The park is entirely surrounded by SPROUL STATE FOREST. Hyner Run State Park and Hyner View State Park are in the heart of the 276,764-acre Sproul State Forest. There are many miles of scenic state forest roads, foot trails, snowmobile trails and scenic overlooks. The very first purchase of public lands by the Commonwealth is not far from the park on the Young Womans Creek at Bull Run, where a monument commemorates this event. 717-923-6011. Pool, Campsites, one Modern Cabin, Fishing, Winter Sports, and Trails. Horse Trails, ATV Trails (32 miles).

BENDIGO STATE PARK

Johnsonburg - 533 State Park Road (four miles northeast of Johnsonburg on SR 1004) 15845. **Web: www.dcnr.state.pa.us/stateparks/parks/bendigo.aspx** *Phone: (814) 965-2646.*

Located in a valley on a bank of the East Branch of the Clarion River, a charming streamside picnic area sits amidst a mixture of hardwood trees. A trout stream provides ample opportunities for anglers and the swimming pool is a big hit in summer. Sledding. Kinzua Bridge (very high railroad bridge).

HOLGATE TOY FACTORY

*Kane - One Holgate Drive (US6 to Kane, follow signs - west of downtown) 16735. Phone: (800) 499-1929 or (814) 837-7600. **Web:** www.holgatetoy.com Hours: Monday-Friday 9:00am-5:00pm, Saturday 10:00am-4:00pm, Sunday Noon-4:00pm (May-December). Closed Sundays (January-April). Miscellaneous: Toy Store with discounted seconds at great prices. Bring your infant/preschool kid's gift list.*

This is where they make "Mr. Roger's Neighborhood" trolleys! What a fun, cute place to visit and learn! The colorful shop draws kids and parents

in to explore. Grandparents will love the old pull toys in the museum. All the toys are made from wood - no plastic to break or batteries to replace - We like that! While the young kids may gravitate to the play areas with toys galore (try before you buy), the older kids and adults will want to watch the operations. During some weekdays, you can see actual operators make the different pieces of a toy. The giant computerized routers are the most fun to watch. Other times, the factory is silent, but you can watch a 25 minute video of the manufacturing process. Our favorite was watching the wood shapes "dance" for the paint sprayers. Although old-fashioned toys are their namesake, they are still progressive. Their toy, the G-Yo is a geometric wood Yo Yo shaped very differently. We thought the one shaped like Mr. Roger's trolley was the coolest - and it really works!

...durable wood, no batteries required!

DRAPER'S SUPER BEE APIARIES

*Millerton - RR #1, Box 96 (SR15 & SR238. Follow signs. Close to NY border) 16936. Phone: (570) 537-2381 or (800) 233-4273. **Web:** www.draperbee.com Hours: Monday-Friday 8:00am-5:00pm, Saturday 8:00am-1:00pm. Admission: FREE Miscellaneous: Gift shop with honey products galore and bee keeping equipment for sale. They even sell "bee" theme "knick knacks" which the owner said is also found in her house.*

Every visit warrants a view of the observation hive (don't worry, it's enclosed in safety glass). On tour, you'll learn about different products produced from bee hives. Hopefully, you'll be able to get to a bee site, help extract some honey, and then take a taste test. If you call ahead, Mrs. Draper might make some baked goods and beverages (Kool-Aid with honey) for you to sample. TIDBITS YOU MIGHT LEARN - Wildflower honey has the most nutrients (why? - Find out!); the Queen Bee lays 2000 eggs per day (the larva are what bears really love!). Speaking of bears, can you guess how they keep the "locals" away

a bee...hard at work making honey...

from their outdoor hives? Learn why honey is liquefied in a "hot room" and not boiled. Learn how to identify the difference between worker bees, male drones, and the Queen. This is an extremely family-oriented, educational, and helpful (health-wise) tour given by people who care deeply about what they do. Well worth the trip into the "Endless Mountains".

SKI SAWMILL MOUNTAIN RESORT

Morris - *P.O. Box 5 (Rte. 220 to Rte. 287) 19963. Phone: (570) 353-7521. Snow Report: (800) 532-SNOW. **Web: www.skisawmill.com***

They have 12 slopes and 3 lifts. Peak elevation is 2,215 feet and base elevation is 1,770 feet - giving a vertical drop of 515 feet. There is also a terrain park adjacent to our double chairlift. Beginner area and tubing area. New in summer/ fall season for groups will be: Paintball Rentals, Mountain Bike Rentals, and Canoe Trips down the pine creek. Also ask about hay rides, bonfires, archery classes and more off-peak season.

KETTLE CREEK STATE PARK

*Renovo - Box 96 (SR 4001) 17764. Phone: (717) 923-6004. **Web: www.dcnr.state.pa.us/ stateparks/parks/kettlecreek.aspx***

A 250-foot sandy beach area is open from late-May to mid-September, 8 a.m. to sunset. Horseback Riding, Sledding, Campsites, Fishing, Trails, Winter Sports.

HILLS CREEK STATE PARK

Wellsboro - RD 2, Box 328 (US Route 6 or PA Route 287) 16901. Phone: (717) 724-4246. Web: www.dcnr.state.pa.us/stateparks/parks/hillscreek.aspx

Osprey, loon and waterfowl visit the lake that boasts a variety of warm water fish species. A sand beach is open from late-May to mid-September, 8:00am-to sunset. Lake Side Trail - 1.5-mile - This trail begins at the entrance to the camping area and follows the lake shore in a westerly direction for about one mile, finally arriving at the Beaver Hut Boating Area. A beaver house plus many signs of beaver activity may be seen in this area. Camping, modern cabins, and picnicking. Visitor Center and Boat Rentals.

LEONARD HARRISON STATE PARK

Wellsboro - RR 6, Box 199 (take PA Route 660 west from Wellsboro for 10 miles) 16901. Web: www.dcnr.state.pa.us/stateparks/parks/leonardharrison.aspx Phone: (717) 724-3061. Miscellaneous: The environmental interpretive center, at the Leonard Harrison main overlook entrance, is open during the summer season through the fall foliage season. A video and educational displays interpret the area and its wildlife.

The "Grand Canyon" of Pennsylvania begins just south of Ansonia, along U.S. Route 6 and continues south for about 47 miles. At Leonard Harrison and Colton Point State Parks, the depth of the canyon is about 800 feet and these park locations have the most spectacular scenic overlooks. Well worth the drive off the beaten path for the scenic views! If your children are able, we suggest hiking one of the trails up or down the gorge. There is no bridge across Pine Creek at the bottom. A beautiful vista, one-half mile down the Turkey Path Trail, was constructed by the Youth Conservation Corps in 1978. Shortly after the vista, there is a scenic waterfall along the path on Little Four-Mile Run. Major improvements on the Turkey Path

...a walk with a view!

Trail, including steps, observation decks and hand rails were completed in the 1990s. The Pine Creek Trail runs through the bottom of the gorge and provides great bicycling. Bring along quarters (for viewers) or binoculars to get detailed views. Rustic camping and Canoe/Raft liveries threaded throughout the park system.

TIOGA STATE FOREST

Wellsboro - One Nessmuk Lane Rte. 287 south) 16901. Phone: (570) 724-2868. Web:
www.dcnr.state.pa.us/forestry/stateforests/forests/tioga/tioga.htm

Discover the three state forest picnic areas that are maintained, along with
two Pine Creek access areas. Fishing, Camping, Trails, Winter Sports.

CHILDREN'S DISCOVERY WORKSHOP

Williamsport - 343 West 4th Street (Runs parallel to I-180. In YMCA building -
Downtown) 17701. Web: www.williamsportymca.org/cdw/ Phone: (570) 322-KIDS.
Hours: Tuesday-Saturday 10:00am-4:00pm (Summer). Tuesday-Friday 10:00am-5:00pm,
Sunday 1:00-5:00pm, Saturday 11:00am-5:00pm (September - May). Admission:
$4.00 general (over age 2). Miscellaneous: Educational Gift Shop.

This hands-on children's museum is designed for kids ages 3-11. There are
many rooms of exhibits but our favorite, most unique areas were the Kids'
Clinic, Human Habitrail, Ice Cream Parlor, and Funnel. The Kids' Clinic was
full of actual size equipment that got the kids into the act by pretending to

be nurses, doctors, or x-ray technicians (with real
x-rays to review - a real hospital bed too!). The
Ice Cream Parlor featured life-size equipment
that taught children how to be "soda jerks". The
Human Habitrail and Funnel are giant-sized
environments where you would usually find
small animals - but now they're re-sized for
human kids! The habitrail is like the one that your

...giant block fun!

hamster might play in, and the FUN-nel is like a pipe a rodent might wander
through underground. Giant Legos and a play castle. Both teach adaptation
to a new environment and encourage strengthening large motor skills. Well
done!

HIAWATHA RIVERBOAT TOURS

Williamsport - Susquehanna State Park (Docked at Arch Street - US220 to Reach
Road Exit - Follow signs) 17701. Web: www.ridehiawatha.com Phone: (570) 326-
2500 or (800) 248-9287. Hours: Tuesday-Sunday, 1:00, 2:30, and 4:00pm. (Summer).
Weekends Only in May, September & October Admission: $7.50 adult, $6.50 senior
(60+), $3.50 child (3-12).

An old-fashioned paddlewheel boat cruises along the river as your narrator
tells tales of the river when "lumber was king". Snacks and gifts are available on
board. Tuesday night is "Family Night" during the summer (reduced family rates).

LYCOMING COUNTY MUSEUM

Williamsport - 858 West 4th Street 17701. Web: www.lycoming.org/lchsmuseum Phone: (570) 326-3326. Hours: Tuesday-Friday 9:30am-4:00pm, Saturday 11:00am-4:00pm, Sunday 1:00-4:00pm. Closed Sundays (November-April). Admission: $5.00 adult, $4.00 senior, $1.50 child (2-12).

Over 12,000 square feet of exhibits include the history of lumbering, The LaRue Shempp model train exhibit, an American Indian gallery, and period rooms. See a one room schoolhouse and a working gristmill. A changing art gallery is on the premises, also.

WILLIAMSPORT TROLLEYS

Williamsport - 1500 West Third Street (Trolley Gazebo Downtown) 17701. Phone: (800) CITY-BUS or (570) 326-2500. Web: www.citybus.org/trolleys.html Hours: Tuesday, Thursday, Saturday 10:45am & 12:15pm or 1:45pm (Summer) . Call ahead to confirm times -Only 10:45 am on Saturdays. Admission: $3.00-$5.00 general. Tickets for the Williamsport Trolley Tour may be purchased from the Trolley Driver or at the Hiawatha House, Susquehanna State Park.

Millionaires Row (impressive mansions built by lumber barons) is the focus of this tour. Kids enjoy Memorial Park (the site of the first Little League Baseball game). For fidgety children, there are several on and off stops throughout the trip.

The Peter Herdic Transportation Museum/Williamsport Trolley Hub Project consists of renovations to the existing railroad freight station, development of a trolley turnaround area (including a gazebo), construction of two Victorian bus shelters, purchase of a railway passenger "parlor" car, historic bus stop signs.

REPTILAND, CLYDE PEELING'S

Williamsport (Allenwood) - RR 1, Box 388, US 15 (I-80 exit 210B head north 6 miles) 17810. Phone: (570) 538-1869 or (800) REPTILAND. Web: www.reptiland.com Hours: Daily 9:00am-7:00pm (Summer). Daily 10:00am-5:00 or 6:00pm (September-May). Admission: $10.00 adult, $8.00 child (4-11) Miscellaneous: Enjoy a healthy selection of hot and cold sandwiches and salads at Crocodile Creek Café

A visit to Reptiland explodes common myths and inspires scientific curiosity. The newly renovated indoor exhibit complex allows comfortable viewing of more than 40 species in recreated natural habitats. During summer months, Cobras, alligators, pythons, vipers, are all slithering around in a tropical garden setting. You even get to touch a real snake! Meet "Big Boy" the alligator or poison dart frogs. A multi-media show reveals the close-up world of reptiles and there's often live lecture demonstrations or viewing of daily feedings.

LITTLE PINE STATE PARK

Williamsport (Waterville) - Box 100 (four miles north of PA 44 at Waterville and eight miles south of PA 287) 17776. Phone: (570) 753-6000. Web: www.dcnr.state.pa.us/ stateparks/parks/littlepine.aspx

Little Pine State Park is located in one of the most beautiful sections of the TIADAGNTON STATE FOREST in the Appalachian Mountains. A sand beach with grass turf is open from late-May to mid-September, 8:00am-to sunset. Boat Rentals, Sledding, Campsites, Fishing, Trails, and Winter Sports.

LITTLE LEAGUE MUSEUM

Williamsport, South - US 15 17701. Web: www.littleleague.org/museum/ Phone: (570) 326-1921. Hours: Monday-Saturday 10:00am-7:00pm, Sunday Noon-7:00pm (Memorial Day-September). Monday, Thursday, Friday 10:00am-5:00pm, Saturday Noon-5:00pm, Sunday Noon-4:00pm (October-Memorial Day). Admission: $5.00 adult, $3.00 senior (62+), $1.50 child (5-13). Miscellaneous: The museum is next to the Little League International Headquarters and overlooking the Howard J. Lamade Little League World Series Stadium.

The birthplace of Little League is host to the world championship (nationally televised-last weekend in August). From its humble beginnings in 1939  through today and its 3 million participants in over 90 countries, the museum is a tribute to Little League Baseball. Learn about the legends, swing the bat or test your arms. Actually "Play Ball" in the batting and pitching areas, and then watch your form on instant replay. Experience the running track, push-button quiz  panels, and the opportunity to do your own play-by-play commentary on a World Series game. Learn about nutrition that will help you play your best. Watch videotaped highlights of the most exciting moments of the Little League World Series.

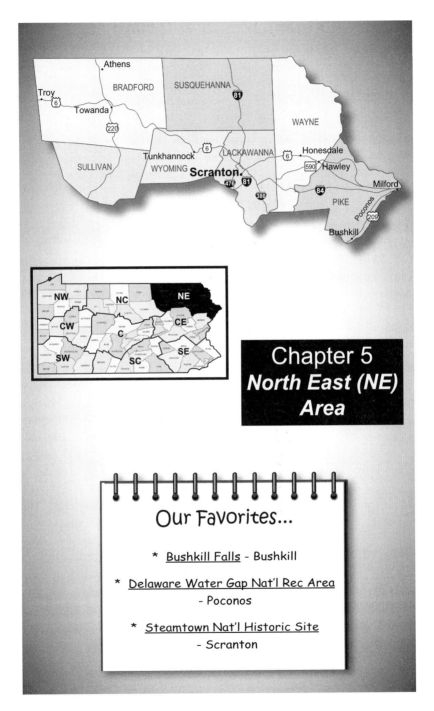

Chapter 5
North East (NE)
Area

Our Favorites...

* <u>Bushkill Falls</u> - Bushkill

* <u>Delaware Water Gap Nat'l Rec Area</u>
  - Poconos

* <u>Steamtown Nat'l Historic Site</u>
  - Scranton

CAROUSEL WATER AND FUN PARK

Beach Lake - Box 134 (Rte 6 East to Honesdale, then Rte 652 East) 18405. Phone: (570) 729-7532. **Web:** *www.carousel-park.com Hours: Daily 11:00am-10:00pm (Summers) Weekends 11:00am-6:00pm (late spring/late summer). Waterslides close at 6:00pm. Admission: Free Parking, Free Admission. Pay one price ticket ($12.00-$18.00) or pay per activity ($2.00-$4.00).*

Water slides (regular and juvenile), Go-karts, bumper boats, water slides, kiddie-kars and mini-golf all included in our pay-one price ticket. Also available: hardball and softball batting range, arcade and snack bar.

BUSHKILL FALLS

Bushkill - Bushkill Falls Road (I-80 to Exit 309 - SR209 North) 18324. Phone: (888) 628-7454 or (570) 588-6682. **Web:** *www.visitbushkillfalls.com Hours: 9:00am-5:00-7:00pm (April-November). Basically closes before dusk sets in. Due to weather conditions, some trails may be restricted partly or in full. Admission: $9.00 adult, $8.00 senior, $4.00 child (4-10). Miscellaneous: Check out the Pennsylvania Wildlife Exhibit, fish Twin Lakes, visit a variety of gift shops, stop at the Fudge Kitchen for delectable sweets in the Wagon Wheel Pavilion, take a paddle-boat ride, or enjoy a round of miniature golf. Additional activities run $3.00-$5.00.*

"The Niagara of Pennsylvania," has eight waterfalls. The main falls include Upper Canyon (craggy glen), Bridle Veil Falls (long, misty), Laurel Glen (mountain laurel wildflowers), Pennell Falls and Main Falls (over 100 foot cliff). Trails and bridges lace the area. Visitors may take part in a new Map Adventure while they hike. An official trail map that is especially detailed and accurate has been developed. The map includes 20 "control points" that can be found on the trails. When five, ten, or twenty locations have been found and verified with a unique punch, the hiker becomes eligible for a monthly prize drawing. Waterfalls are just the beginning of your visit to Bushkill Falls. Step into a Native America long-house and experience the Lenni Lanape Native Americans longhouse exhibit where kids can walk into an Indian home with "beds" - pretty neat! Plan to spend at least one-half day here.

FERNWOOD RESORT

Bushkill - Route 209 North (20 Minutes from Camelback Ski Area) 18371. Phone: (888) FERNWOOD. Web: http://resortsusa.com/tubing.php

Spend the day snowtubing, horseback riding, ice skating or take a horse drawn sleigh ride. Longest Run: 1500 ft.; 2 Slopes & Trails. Lodging with gameroom and indoor/outdoor pools.

LACKAWANNA STATE PARK

Dalton - RD 1, Box 230 (I-81 exit 60, travel 3 miles west on PA Route 524) 18414. Web: www.dcnr.state.pa.us/stateparks/parks/lackawanna.aspx Phone: (570) 945-3239.

Includes Salt Spring - a 36 acre natural area with old-growth hemlocks, streams and 3 waterfalls. Also Archbold Pothole - world's largest geological pothole - 38 ft. deep, 42 ft. wide. There is a campground, organized group tenting sites and a pool. Boaters and anglers enjoy the 198-acre Lackawanna Lake, and Kennedy Creek. This park is a favorite of canoeists, hikers, nature enthusiasts and campers. Biking, skiing, and snowmobiling.

WORLD'S END STATE PARK

Forksville - PO Box 62 (PA Route 42 from 1-80, then to Rte. 184) 18616. Phone: (570) 924-3287. Web: www.dcnr.state.pa.us/stateparks/parks/worldsend.aspx

Virtually in a class by itself, this wild, rugged and rustic area seems almost untamed. Camping, rustic cabins and hiking on the Loyalsock Trail attracts many visitors. The scenery is spectacular, especially the June mountain laurel and Fall foliage. Canyon Vista, reached via Mineral Spring and Cold Run Roads, has outstanding views. Beach, Horseback Riding, Visitor's Center, Fishing, Boating, Horse Trails, and Winter Sports.

World's End State Park is adjacent to the LOYALSOCK STATE FOREST and offers hiking, hunting fishing and other outdoor recreation. 570-387-4255.

CLAWS AND PAWS ANIMAL PARK

Hamlin (Lake Ariel) - 1475 Ledgedale Road (SR590 East - then follow signs) 18436. Phone: (570) 698-6154. Web: www.clawsnpaws.com Hours: Daily 10:00am-6:00pm (May-late October). Admission: $12.95 adult, $11.95 senior, $8.95 child (2-11). Miscellaneous: Snack bar. Gift shop. Picnic Area. Large walk-in petting zoo. Dino dig and Turtle Town interactive areas. Wild West Territory-pictures on a covered wagon, mining for gemstones and "gold" at the Gemstone Mining set-up, or see *some interesting animals of the old west like buffalo (bison), prairie dog, coyote, and camel.*

"Get Close to the Animals" is their theme…and you will! Many cages have glass front enclosures - so animals can walk right up to your face and you're still protected. During posted times, you can feed giraffes using a long stick or hand-feed fruits and vegetables to Lory Parrots (colorful, small, tame parrots). The animals are comfortable with visitors and they're not bashful about getting close to get a good nibble from your snack-filled hands. During the summer months they have unique Performing Parrot shows and Wildlife Encounter shows. When was the last time you saw a parrot ride a bike or you got to pet an alligator?

LAKE WALLENPAUPACK

Hawley - US 6 18428. **Web: www.hawleywallenpaupackcc.com** *Phone: (570) 226-3191 Area Chamber.*

RITZ COMPANY PLAYHOUSE - (570) 226-9752.

BOAT TOURS - US6, Gresham Landing. **www.eastshorelodging.com** (570) 226-3293. (June - October). Daily scenic tours for one half hour. Tour boats run daily from 11:00am to 7:00pm on weekends from May 1 through October and daily from June 15 through Labor Day. Admission: $8.00-$10.00.

TRIPLE "W" RIDING STABLE RANCH - Beechmont Drive - off Owego Turnpike. (570) 226-2670 or **www.triplewstable.com**. Horse ranch and western riding trips from one hour to overnight camping ($25 - 100+). Overnight accommodations at Double "W" Bed and Breakfast. Year round except hunting season.

STOURBRIDGE RAIL EXCURSION

Honesdale - (I-84, exit 5 - SR191 north - to Main Street) 18431. Phone: (570) 253-1960. **Web: www.hawleywallenpaupackcc.com** *Hours: Sundays @ 1:00pm (Sunday before July 4th - Sunday before Labor Day), plus seasonal tours listed on their website. Admission: Start at $10.00 and up depending on excursion.*

Honesdale is the birthplace of the American railroad and the small brick building which now houses the Wayne County Historical Society was once the D&H Canal's company office. On August 8, 1829, the Delaware & Hudson operated the first commercial locomotive on rails in the western hemisphere. That locomotive left from this spot, ran three miles to Seelyville and returned. On the Great Train Robbery Run, see masked men from the "Triple W Ranch" ambush the train on a 3 hour round trip (includes a one-hour stop for sightseeing). Or, take a Fall Foliage Tour or one of the many holiday tours listed in Seasonal & Special Events chapter.

LERAYSVILLE CHEESE FACTORY

Le Raysville - RR 2 Box 71A (Off SR467 - turn on dirt road 1/2 mile from town) 18829. Phone: (800) 859-5196 or (570) 744-2554.   Hours: Daily 9:00am-5:00pm (March - December) Admission: FREE

The majority of the region's Amish community resides in the Le Raysville area. Their horse-drawn carriages are a common sight along the local roadways. This factory uses local milk from several local farms in the town. Specialize in traditional cheddar cheese. Store.

GREY TOWERS NATIONAL HISTORIC SITE

*Milford - 151 Grey Towers Drive (84 East to Exit 46, Milford. Bear right off ramp onto Highway 6 East) 18337. Phone: (570) 296-9630. **Web: www.fs.fed.us/na/gt/***

Grey Towers is the ancestral home of Gifford Pinchot, first chief of the US Forest Service and twice Governor of Pennsylvania. House and garden tours are offered every day from Memorial Day weekend through October 31. A guided tour of the mansion and grounds is an interesting and unique way to learn about how one family shaped and influenced our conservation ideals and values, while experiencing what life might have been like at Grey Towers in the early 20th century. The guided tour takes the visitor through three first-floor rooms of the mansion and several garden areas and takes about one hour. Other Grey Towers activities include short hiking trails, on-site programs, and conservation education programs for all ages.

UPPER MILL WATERWHEEL CAFÉ

*Milford - (off US6 - follow signs) 18337. Phone: **Web: www.waterwheelcafe.com** (570) 296-2383.   Hours: Daily 8:00am-5:00pm (May-October). Other times of year, by season. Weekend (Thursday-Sunday) evening dinner served by reservation.*

An early 1800s water-powered 3 story gristmill still operates and you can watch the giant water wheel turn which drives a series of shafts, gears, and pulleys. Through the glass walls of the café, you can see the stones and grain milling equipment at work. Sit down and enjoy whole grain pancakes, muffins, and scones or multi-grain bread sandwiches.

DELAWARE WATER GAP NATIONAL RECREATION AREA

Poconos (Bushkill) - *(I-80 to US209 north along the Delaware River) 18324. Phone: (570) 588-2451. Web: www.nps.gov/dewa Admission: Only for guarded beaches (per vehicle) and boat ramp access. Generally $7.00-$10.00 per vehicle.*

Stretching over 37 miles along the Delaware River, you'll find extremely scenic roads and trails to wander along. Great canoeing & rafting (some short - kid friendly), fishing, skiing, and snowmobiling. (For updated brochures or information call 1-800-POCONOS or www.800poconos.com).

DINGMAN'S FALLS - A flat boardwalk trail, accessible to wheelchair-users, leads through a hemlock ravine to the base of Dingmans Falls (1/2 mile round-trip, no climb.) From the base of the falls, a steep climb of 240 steps reaches the top of the falls. Rangers give guided walks to the falls on summer weekends at 2:00 p.m. The visitor center at Dingmans Falls is closed indefinitely for construction. Dingmans Falls is on Johnny Bee Road, which is just south of the traffic light on Route 209 in Dingmans Ferry PA (milepost 13).

BUSHKILL VISITOR'S CENTER - Daily 9:00am-5:00pm (summer). Weekends only in late spring and early autumn.

RAYMONDSKILL FALLS - A 1/4-mile round-trip hike leads through a hemlock ravine to the Upper Falls. (70 ft. climb) The Middle Falls are a 1/2-mile round-trip, using steep, uneven stairs (150 ft. climb.) Raymondskill Creek at the bottom of the ravine is a 1 mile round-trip with a steep ascent on the return (200 ft. climb.) Directions: Raymondskill Road is a sharp left turn, if northbound on Route 209, just north of milepost 18.

Both Visitor's Centers offer "ranger picked must sees" during each season. They also have a Junior Ranger program which includes a kid's self-guided exploring booklet. During the summer, rangers present programs just for kids, as well as family campfire programs and guided walks suitable for children as well as adults.

POCONO INDIAN MUSEUM

Poconos (Bushkill) - *PO Box 261 (SR209 North off I-80 exit 309) 18324. Phone: (570) 588-9338. Web: www.poconoindianmuseum.com Hours: Daily 10:00am-5:30pm. Extended summer hours. Admission: $2.50-$5.00 (age 6+).*

The museum recreates the life of the Delaware Indians from B.C. to the contact period with Europeans to post American Revolution. You will be given a cassette player which will guide you step by step through the museum in great detail. See their lifestyle through homes (some made of bark - and you thought they only lived in tee-pees!), weapons, and kitchen pottery. Most of these items were unearthed in the Delaware Water Gap. Boys like the "150 year old scalp" and buying an authentic "peace pipe".

PROMISED LAND STATE PARK

Poconos (Greentown) - RD 1, Box 96 (PA Route 390) 18426. Phone: (717) 676-3428. Web: www.dcnr.state.pa.us/stateparks/parks/promisedland.aspx

Promised Land lies in the heart of the Poconos. Two lakes, campgrounds, many hiking trails and beautiful scenery make the park popular in all seasons. There are about 50 miles of hiking trails in Promised Land State Park and the surrounding state forest, providing access to many natural scenic places. Hike Bruce Lake Road to a natural glacial lake, or see the little waterfalls along Little Falls Trail, or walk a loop around Conservation Island. A seasonal museum explores CCC contributions and area wildlife. Beach, Boat Rentals, Rustic Cabins, Fishing, Boating, Hiking, and Winter Sports.

POCONO RACEWAY

Poconos (Long Pond) - 184 Sterling Road 18344. Web: www.poconoraceway.com Phone: (800) RACEWAY.

Pocono Raceway has long been recognized as one of NASCAR's most competitive raceways. Pocono's unique 2.5 mile track features three turns, each with its own degree of banking. NASCAR 2.5 Mile super speedway - NASCAR racing, mid-June and early August.

TANGLWOOD SKI AREA

Poconos (Tafton) - PO Box 165 (Lake Wallenpaupack - on Route 390) 18464. Phone: (570) 226-SNOW. Snow Report: (888) 226-SNOW. Web: www.tanglwood.com

Longest Run: 1.25 miles; 10 Slopes & Trails

ELECTRIC CITY TROLLEY MUSEUM

Scranton - (at Cliff Street, on the grounds of the Steamtown National Historic Site, I-81 exit 185) 18503. Phone: (570) 963-6590. Web: www.ectma.org/museum.html Hours: The trolley museum is open seven days a week (Wednesday through Sunday only - during the Winter) from 9:00am-5:00pm, except Christmas, New Years and Thanksgiving Day. Special excursions for holidays. Admission: Average $3.00 museum fee. Additional avg.. $4.00 fee for trolley ride.

Electric City Trolley Museum *(cont.)*

A late 19th century mill building serves as the museum. Trolleys are exposed for viewing and rides. Interactive displays, where visitors will actually generate electricity and learn how this energy form is harnessed to serve transportation needs. The Electric City, a hands-on interactive kids exhibit, puts children in the operator's seat of a recreated open-style trolley car as they view a model trolley in operation on a suspended track.

TROLLEY EXCURSIONS: The scenic route follows a portion of the former Lackawanna & Wyoming Valley Railroad right-of-way as it parallels Roaring Brook and makes stops at the Historic Iron Furnaces and continues through the Crown Avenue Tunnel. At 4747 feet long, the tunnel is one of the longest interurban tunnels ever built.

LACKAWANNA COAL MINE

Scranton - McDade Park. (I-81, Exit 57B or 51 – follow signs) 18503. Phone: (570) 963-MINE or (800) 238-7245. Web: www.lackawannacounty.org Hours: Daily 10:00am–4:30pm (April–November). Closed Easter and Thanksgiving. Admission: $7.00 adult, $6.50 senior (65+), $5.00 child (3-12). Company Store – souvenir coal jewelry and such. Food service. Constant 55 degrees F. below so bring along a jacket. McDade Park has excellent areas for picnics and play.

"Go down in history" where you descend (by railcar) 300 feet below the ground to see how men "hand harvested" coal. Actual miners are your guides as they share personal stories about the hard life, the work, and the dangers of digging for "black diamonds". A walking tour of three veins of mine floor.

LACKAWANNA STATE FOREST

Scranton - 401 Samters Building, 101 Penn Avenue 18503. Phone: (570) 963-4561. Web: www.dcnr.state.pa.us/forestry/stateforests/lackawanna.aspx

The name Lackawanna is the English spelling of an Indian word which means "a place where the river forks". This 6,711-acre woodland offers extensive outdoor recreational opportunities such as picnicking, hiking, backpacking, hunting, snowmobiling, cross-country skiing, fishing and nature walks.

STEAMTOWN NATIONAL HISTORICAL SITE

Scranton - 150 South Washington Avenue (I-81, exit 185 - toward downtown) 18503. Phone: (888) 693-9391. (570) 340-5200. Web: www.nps.gov/stea Hours: Daily 9:00am-5:00pm. Reduced winter hours. Closed New Years Day, Thanksgiving Day, and Christmas Day. Admission: $6.00 adult. The Park Entrance Fee (all visitors *age 17 and over) includes admission to the railroad yard, History Museum, Theater, Technology Museum, Roundhouse and all walking tours and theater programs.*

"This is just like Thomas the Train" squealed our kids as we all saw the roundhouse come to life! This fully restored roundhouse and turntable are incredible to watch. As the Baldwin #26 enters the yard, it stops on the turntable and advances to the correct numbered house where it will "sleep" or receive maintenance. While you are out walking around the roundhouse,

The roundhouse...watch it come to life!

talk with the crew as they share stories about their jobs and the engines. The conductors love to wave and are good photograph opportunities. The Visitor's Center (mostly oriented for older kids) has both a Technology Center and

The Union Pacific #4012 "Big Boy" - over a million pounds of hardworking iron!

History Museum of American Steam Railroading. The theater at Steamtown shows an 18-minute film called Steel and Steam. This short film follows one man's career on the railroad, and illustrates the massive changes railroads underwent in a fairly short time during the early 20th century. Join a Park Ranger or a Volunteer for a walking tour through a portion of the former locomotive shops to see and learn what it takes to keep steam-era

railroad equipment operational. The express train ride is a short excursion best for younger children who can't endure the longer 2 hour train rides.

PENNSYLVANIA ANTHRACITE HERITAGE MUSEUM

*Scranton - RD #1 - Bald Mountain Road (I-81 - Exit 57B or Exit 51 - Follow signs to McDade Park) 18504. **Web: www.anthracitemuseum.org** Phone: (570) 963-4804 or (570) 963-4845. Hours: Monday - Saturday 9:00am-5:00pm, Sunday Noon-5:00pm (Closed holidays - except summer holidays). Admission: $4.00 adult, $3.50 senior (60+), $2.00 child (6-11).*

Explore the culture created by life and work in the coal towns. Their collections include highlights of the mines, canals, railroads, mills, and factories. This was really hard work! To see a close-up of the mills producing iron "T" rails for America's railroads, stop over to the park setting of Scranton Iron Furnaces.

MONTAGE SKI AREA

Scranton - 1000 Montage Mountain Road 18505. Phone: (570) 969-7669. Snow Report: (800) GOT-SNOW. Web: www.skimontage.com

Longest Run: 1+ miles; 21 Slopes & Trails. Ice skating and snow tubing, too.

RED BARONS BASEBALL

Scranton - 225 Montage Mountain Road (Lackawanna County Stadium) 18507. Phone: (570) 969-BALL. Web: www.redbarons.com

AAA Class affiliate of the Yankees (April-August).

HOUDINI MUSEUM

Scranton - 1433 North Main Avenue (I-81 to exit 56) 18508. Phone: (570) 342-5555. Web: http://houdini.org/ Hours: Weekends 1:00-4:00pm (Memorial Day – June), Daily 12:30-6:00pm (July, August – Labor Day Weekend). Open Holiday Weekends throughout the year. Admission: $7.95-$9.95 per person. Miscellaneous: Gift/Magic Shop. Admission includes video presentation and live magic shows (check website or call for exact times of shows). Very enthusiastic magicians answer questions and perform illusions before your eyes.

The world's only exhibit devoted entirely to Houdini. It helps to know the magic word if you want to get into the Famous Houdini Museum (Houdini Lives!). Houdini and his brother Hardeen toured through this area often. Now, nationally known magicians re-create these shows daily. Wander around and see Houdini's favorite trick props and photographs.

EVERHART MUSEUM

Scranton - 1901 Mulberry Street (Mulberry and Arthur Avenue) 18510. Phone: (570) 346-7186. Web: www.everhart-museum.org Hours: Generally, Daily Noon-5:00 pm. Closed Wednesday and Tuesday. PLEASE CALL FOR HOURS as they change each season. Admission: $5.00 adult, $3.00 senior, $2.00 child (6+).

Housing exhibits of American Folk, Native American, Oriental and primitive art. They also have fun exhibits for kids in dinosaur hall and the bees and bird collections. Children's store.

TOBYHANNA STATE PARK

Tobyhanna - PO Box 387 (accessible from I- 84 via PA Routes 507, 191 and 423) 18466.
Web: www.dcnr.state.pa.us/stateparks/parks/tobyhanna.aspx Phone: (570) 894-8336.

The 5,440-acre park includes the 170-acre Tobyhanna Lake. Tobyhanna is derived from an American Indian word meaning "a stream whose banks are fringed with alder." Beach, Boat Rentals, Campsites. Also in this location are Big Pocono and Gouldsboro State Parks. Trails and Winter Sports.

FRENCH AZILUM

Towanda - RD #2, Box 266 (Rte. 6 take SR 187 south. off SR187 - follow signs) 18848.
Phone: (570) 265-3376. Web: www.frenchazilum.com Hours: Wednesday-Sunday
11:00am-4:00pm. (late May thru late October). Weekends 11:00am-4:30pm (May)
Admission: $3.00-$5.00 (age 12+). Miscellaneous: Picnic pavilion. Nature trails.

Few sites in Pennsylvania address another country's historic events like this one does. Founded in 1793, 50 log cabins were created as a refuge for French nobility fleeing the Revolution. After Napoleon's pardon, most left the area. There are still a few log cabins standing and an 1836 LaPorte House containing period furnishings. Warm weather archeological digs occur frequently. Stand around and ask what they're finding.

MT. PISGAH STATE PARK

Troy - RD 3, Box 362 (2 miles north of US Route 6) 16947. Phone: (570) 297-2734.
Web: www.dcnr.state.pa.us/stateparks/parks/mtpisgah.aspx

At the base of Mt. Pisgah and set along Mill Creek. A dam on Mill Creek forms Stephen Foster Lake, named after the famous composer and onetime local resident. The 75-acre lake provides fishing, boating and skating. Adjacent to the park are Mt. Pisgah County Park. Also Pool, Visitor Center, Trails, and Winter Sports.

ELK MOUNTAIN SKI AREA

Union Dale - RR 2, Box 3328 (I-81 exit 206) 18470. Phone: (570) 679-4400. Snow
Report: (800) 233-4131. Web: www.elkskier.com

Skiing and Snowboarding. Longest Run: 1.75 miles; 27 Slopes & Trails.

WILKES-BARRE/SCRANTON PENGUINS HOCKEY

Wilkes-Barre - 415 Arena Hub Plaza 18702. Web: www.wbspenguins.com Phone:
(570) 208-PENS.

Kids Club activities, section and skate. AHL Hockey (October-early April).

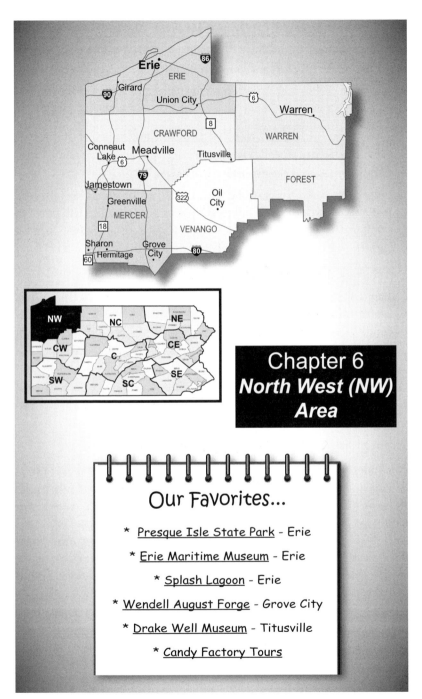

Chapter 6
North West (NW) Area

Our Favorites...

* <u>Presque Isle State Park</u> - Erie

* <u>Erie Maritime Museum</u> - Erie

* <u>Splash Lagoon</u> - Erie

* <u>Wendell August Forge</u> - Grove City

* <u>Drake Well Museum</u> - Titusville

* <u>Candy Factory Tours</u>

MOUNTAIN VIEW SKI AREA

Cambridge Springs - *14510 Mount Pleasant Road 16403. Phone: (814) 734-1641.*
Web: www.skiresortsguide.com/stats.cfm/pa16.htm

Longest Run: 2500 ft.; 9 Slopes & Trails (snowboarding, snowtubing and night skiing, too).

CHAPMAN STATE PARK

Clarendon - *RD 2 Box 1610 (off US Route 6) 16829. Phone: (814) 723-0250.* **Web:**
www.dcnr.state.pa.us/stateparks/parks/chapman.aspx

Chapman sits on the banks of the West Branch of Tionesta Creek. Among its many recreational offerings, the park boasts a 68-acre lake that provides swimming at a beach and warm and cold water fishing. Boat Rentals, Campsites, Fishing, Trails, and Winter Sports.

CLEAR CREEK STATE FOREST

Clarion - *158 South Second Avenue   16214. Phone: (814) 226-1901.* **Web:**
www.dcnr.state.pa.us/forestry/

Points of interest within the State Forest are the Clear Creek State Park with overnight camping facilities, swimming, fishing, hiking trails, and day-use areas; Bear Town Rocks, a vista with an excellent view accessible by trail or automobile; and Hays Lot Fire Tower with a panoramic view of great distances. Visitors can tour the laurel fields located on Spring Creek Road during the early June wildflower season.

CONNEAUT LAKE PARK

Conneaut Lake - *12382 Center St (I-79, exit 147B west on Rte. 322, follow signs to PA 618) 16316. Phone: (814) 382-5115.* **Web: www.conneautlakepark.com** *Hours: Wednesday-Sunday Noon-8:00 to 10:00pm (Memorial Day weekend-Labor Day weekend). Extended weekends in October for Fall Festival Admission: FREE, pay for each ride or buy combo packages. For around $13.00. All Ride-A-Rama passes include unlimited admission to all amusement rides and Splash City attractions on date issued. Ride-A-Rama does not include the Pony Track, Cascade Express Miniature Golf, or the Kaylee Belle Paddlewheel Boat.*

Old-fashioned 100 year old park with rides, water attractions, kiddie land, restaurant, Camperland and beach/boardwalk. Conneaut Lake Park has over 80 rides, including the famous Blue Streak Wooden Roller Coaster (1938).

WOODEN NICKEL BUFFALO FARM

Edinboro - 5970 Koman Road (I-79 to exit 166 - go east - follow signs) 16412. Phone: (814) 734-BUFF. Web: www.woodennickelbuffalo.com Hours: Daily 11:00am-5:00pm (Friday-Sunday only in winter). Admission: $3.50 per person ($15.00 per tour, minimum charge). Reservations required. Before leaving, every person in the group will receive a newsletter and a Wooden Nickel as a souvenir.

The owners loved the meat when they first tried it and decided to breed and sell buffalo products. The tour includes a talk on Bison as you view them in the pastures. You will learn about their history and relationship with Native Americans, see the handling facilities, and view authentic Native American art and Bison products in the Gift Shop. This is done with visuals and videos to keep the kids attention. Ribs and fur from the animals (not live animals!) can be touched. American Indian folklore and festival in July. Feel a real buffalo hide or admire cute baby bison (late July).

BICENTENNIAL OBSERVATION TOWER

Erie - Dobbins Landing 16501. Web: www.porterie.org/touring.html#tower Phone: (814) 455-6055. Hours: Open at 10:00am - closing varies seasonally between 6:00-10:00pm (April-October). November - March (open Saturday & Sunday only) 12:00pm-4:00pm. Admission: $2.00-$3.00 (age 7+). Free admission on Sundays (excluding holidays).

Enjoy an aerial view of the city and Presque Isle Bay. The 187-ft tower features two observation decks, and markers of Erie's harbor history and geography. 210 stairs to the observation deck (or, yes, there is an elevator!). If you climb the stairs, follow the 16 stations that highlight various landmarks. Souvenirs and food available in tower lobby.

ERIE COUNTY HISTORICAL MUSEUM

Erie - 417 - 422 State Street (I-79 to Bayfront Parkway) 16501. Phone: (814) 454-1813. Web: www.eriecountyhistory.org Hours: Wednesday-Saturday 11:00am-4:00pm. Extended to Tuesday and Sundays in the summer. Admission: $2.00-$4.00 (age 5+).

Local history, architecture and industry. "Voices from Erie County History" offers glimpses into Erie County's rich heritage from the days of pre-settlement to the turn of the twenty-first century. The two-building complex contains the Museum of Erie County History, which features Voices, an interactive exhibit offering selective views of Erie County's rich heritage from pre-settlement to present day, the Admiral Curtze Maritime Hall, an exhibit presenting the region's ongoing maritime legacy, the Kovacs Kids

Korner children's area filled with captivating educational, fun activities. The Cashier's House, adjacent to the History Center, is a beautifully restored 1839 Greek Revival style townhouse which features life in Erie during the Antebellum period.

ERIE OTTERS HOCKEY

Erie - 809 French Street (office) (Louis J. Tullio Civic Center) 16501. Phone: (814) 452-4857 (Box Office) or 455-7779 (office). **Web: *www.ottershockey.com*** *Admission: $6.00-$10.00.*

Ontario Hockey League (players between the age of 16-20). The Otters play a 68-game regular season schedule (34 home, 34 away), plus playoffs, in the Ontario Hockey League. Since the franchise relocated to Erie prior to the 1996-1997 season, a total of 23 players have been selected at the National Hockey League Entry Draft.

ERIE SEA WOLVES

Erie - 110 East 10th Street (office) (Jerry Uht Ballpark) 16501. Phone: (814) 456-1300. **Web: *www.seawolves.com*** *Admission: $3.00-$8.00*

AA Class affiliate of the Detroit Tigers.

PRESQUE ISLE SCENIC BOAT TOURS

Erie - (Departing from Perry Monument on Presque Isle State Park) 16505. Phone: 814-836-0201 or toll free 800-988-5780. **Web: *www.piboattours.com*** *Admission: Rates are adults: $14.00 child: $9.00 and under 5 free.*

Experience the scenic beauty of the Peninsula and Erie waterfront while viewing three historic lighthouses on the 65-foot great lakes vessel, "Lady Kate." The 14-mile, 90-minute tour ventures out onto the open waters of Lake Erie. You will view Presque Isle's shores, Erie's skyline, lighthouses, ships, the beaches, Gull Point Nature Preserve, wildlife and numerous other sights. Live narration takes place on each tour by knowledgeable guides that identify and describe points of interest while they supply enlightening information about the area's ecology, history, development, nature and more.

PRESQUE ISLE STATE PARK

Erie - PO Box 8510 (Lake Erie, reached by PA Route 832 or by boat) 16505. Phone: (814) 833-7424. **Web: *www.dcnr.state.pa.us/stateparks/parks/presqueisle.aspx***

Seven miles of sandy beaches (Top 100 swimming holes) and it has the only surf beach in the Commonwealth. Because of the many unique habitats,

Presque Isle contains a greater number of the state's endangered, threatened and rare species than any other area of comparable size in Pennsylvania. On a nice day, many locals and visitors head to Presque Isle for boating, fishing, nature walks or biking. The park is so clean, the beaches well-maintained, and the paved

A break from our 5 mile trip...

multi-purpose paths allow easy transport around most of the 14 miles of the isle. We especially recommend biking 5 miles of the trails, stopping every now and then to enjoy a beverage or dip in the water along the beaches. Stop in their nature center first to discuss your plans with a ranger...they were most helpful! Also offered: Canoe and Boat Livery. Lighthouses. Camping, Skiing, & Snowmobiling.

The beaches were beautiful...but we were dressed for biking!

WALDAMEER PARK AND WATER WORLD

Erie - 220 Peninsula Drive (Close to entrance of Presque Isle State Park) 16505. Phone: (814) 838-3591. Web: www.waldameer.com Hours: Tuesday-Sunday (Mid-May - Labor Day) Admission: General Admission ranging from $14.00-$20.00. There is no admission fee to enter the amusement park. ALL Parking is FREE! Individual ride tickets also available for everyone. (Due to ride restrictions, we recommend the use of individual ride tickets, not wrist band, for children under two years old.) Everyone must pay to enter Water World. Miscellaneous: Restaurants. Tubes and life jackets are free.

Five incredible body slides, Three fabulous double tube slides, The Wild River single tube slide, A daring free fall slide, a speed slide, A refreshing Endless River innertube ride, A heated relaxing pool, Three tad pool areas with five great kiddie slides, and Beautiful parks. Thunder River log flume ride plus many more classic amusement rides in Waldameer Park. Puppet shows and concerts, too!

ERIE MARITIME MUSEUM / U.S. BRIG NIAGARA

Erie - *150 East Front Street (I-79 North to Bayfront Parkway) 16507. Phone: (814) 452-BRIG.* **Web: www.brigniagara.org/museum.htm** *Hours: Monday-Saturday 9:00am-5:00pm, Sunday Noon-5:00pm. Closed Monday-Wednesday (January, February, March) Admission: $6.00 adult, $5.00 senior, $3.00 youth (6-17). Reduced prices when Niagara is out of port. Miscellaneous: Shipwright gift shop. First-person costumed interpreters are featured on weekends and for special events.*

U.S. Brig Niagara

New, artistic exhibits about the ship "Niagara" (including video), Lake Erie ecology, the bow of the Wolverine, bilge pumps in action, cannon fire, knots and sails. Berthed within yards of the museum, Niagara is visible from the building's bay side picture window. Tour the flagship "Niagara" (when in port) built to fight in the War of 1812 - the Battle of Lake Erie - Commodore Perry's ship. Once aboard, see over 200 oars, steered with a tiller instead of a wheel, sleeping quarters, and rows of cannons. Do you know the difference between a Brig (2 sails) and a ship (3 sails)? How do you preserve a ship? - Sink it in freshwater! (it's the air & salt that causes deterioration)

Inside, the centerpiece exhibits of the museum are a former steam-powered electricity generating station and a reconstruction of the mid-ship section of the Lawrence. The replicated Lawrence, Commodore Oliver Hazard Perry's first flagship during the Battle of Lake Erie, comes complete with mast, spars and rigging to foster hands-on learning in the ways of sail handling. Probably the most powerful display is the adjoining section of the Lawrence replica that has been blasted with live ammunition from the current Niagara's own carronades. This "live fire" exhibit of the Lawrence recreates the horrific carnage inflicted upon both ships and men during the Battle of Lake Erie and throughout the Age of Fighting Sail. Why can't cannons fire all at once on one side of the ship?

EXPERIENCE CHILDREN'S MUSEUM

Erie - *420 French Street (Discovery Square) (I-79 North to Bay Front Highway) 16507. Phone: (814) 453-3743.* **Web: www.eriechildrensmuseum.org** *Hours: Tuesday-Saturday 10:00am-4:00pm, Sunday 1:00-4:00pm. Closed Tuesday during school year. Admission: $4.50 general (ages 2+) Miscellaneous: Aimed at 2-12 year old children. The Much More Store gift shop.*

Daniel's diverting a creek

Raining or snowing in Erie? Just head downtown to the Experience Children's Museum. For a smaller museum, we were impressed how they use their space in this old building. A few of our favorites: People At Work where kids move vehicles and stones to change the way a stream flows; Owl Pellet Dissecting Table – yes, that's right, you use picks to discover what the owl ate last!; and their Market was the most colorful, realistic and well-stocked we've ever seen…check out the meat and seafood market items! The first floor is full of science - from giant bubble creations to energy, light, and motion. Check out Radar Rooster weather, a Bedrock Cave, or the Circles and Cycles (pollution - unregulated and innumerable, and its effects on the Lake Erie watershed). Children are challenged to create a safe community. The second floor is the "Gallery of the Human Experience" and has career dress up areas, Rookie Reporter newsroom, the Corner Store, Senses, Safety, Construction, and your heartbeat.

…searching for the best steak & seafood

FIREFIGHTER'S HISTORICAL MUSEUM

Erie - 428 Chestnut Street (I-79 to Route 5) 16507. Phone: (814) 456-5969. Hours: Saturday 10:00am-5:00pm, Sunday 1:00-5:00pm (May-August). Saturday - Sunday 1:00-5:00pm (September, October). Admission: $1.00-$4.00 (students+).

The #4 Erie Firehouse has 1300+ items on display. Items include antique equipment, uniforms, badges, helmets, masks, fire extinguishers, hand pumps and horse drawn carts. They have the only display of an 1889 horse drawn fire engine and an understandable demonstration of the relay system in fire call boxes.

ERIE ZOO

*Erie - 423 West 38th Street (I-90 to exit 7) 16508. **Web: www.eriezoo.org** Phone: (814) 864-4091. Hours: Daily 10:00am-5:00pm except Christmas Day and New Year's Day. Children's Zoo is open March through November. Admission: $6.50 adult, $5.50 senior (62+), $3.75 child (2-11). Slightly reduced admission in the winter. Miscellaneous: Train & Carousel rides ($1.25-$1.50 extra).*

The Erie Zoo is home to over 500 animals, representing more than 100 species, from around the world. Winding walkways take visitors through the beautifully landscaped grounds. Children's Zoo - feed and pet babies - "Critter Encounters". Monkey and otter's habitats are especially fun to watch and they even have one area with traditional lions, and

tigers and bears. Visit the Kiboka Outpost with rhinos, cheetahs and warthogs. Various gardens include the Butterfly gardens, the Greenhouse, and the great gardens at Kiboka Outpost

...the amazing entrance to "Wild Asia"...

where the rhinos roam. The animals are so-o-o close and the settings (indoor/outdoor) were well done and easy to manage. Our favorites were the gorillas and orangutans that are so endearing to watch and communicate with!

...this gorilla seemed to be in deep "thought"?

MARX TOY MUSEUM

*Erie - 50 East Bloomfield Parkway 16509. **Web: www.themarxtoymuseum.org** Phone: (814) 825-6500. Hours: Friday-Sunday 1;00-5:00pm. Admission: $1.00-$3.00 (age 5+).*

Not all the monkeys are in the Zoo. The Marx Toy Museum, Inc. has a few monkeys on display as well as other toys. Parents, remember the Johnny West action figures you played with as a kid? Remember riding the world's first three-wheeled speed cycle: the Big Wheel? Or remember having fun on the

Krazy Kar or the Rock'Em Sock'Em Robot? These toys plus hundreds more Marx Toys ranging from 1920 through 1970 are on display.

SPLASH LAGOON

Erie - Peach Street (I-90 exit 24, Rte. 19 south) 16509. Phone: (866) 3-SPLASH.
Web: www.splashlagoon.com   Hours: Generally 9:00am-10:00pm. Admission: Waterpark passes are $15.00 each. Miscellaneous: 4 hotels are part of the indoor waterpark resort and are directly connected to Splash Lagoon (range $140-$300, include 4-6 waterpark passes and one or two complimentary meals).

A new indoor waterpark resort with a: Tree House packed with interactive water fun, 48-Ft Tall Tipping Bucket regularly dumps 1,000 gallons of water, 4 twisting & turning 4-story high Body Slides, A Swirling Body Coaster with speeds of over 40 MPH, Swirling Tube Coaster for 1 or 2 riders, Two 25 Person whirlpools, Laaaazy River, Activity Pool featuring 8 water basketball hoops, Dancing

...it looks like a giant "Mouse-Trap" game...what fun!

Water Play Area, Little People Activity Pool with zero depth entry, 6,000 Sq. Ft. Arcade, Lazer Tag Arena, and Food Court. We recommend going online and reserving one of the SPLASH LAGOON overnight stay packages because you get two day waterpark passes and hotel accommodations in large rooms with complimentary continental breakfast (real value for the money). You'll want to break up your day(s) at the waterpark every two hours or so with a rest - all that play makes you tired and hungry…naps and several light meals at local eateries (our favorite, Quaker Steak & Lube) are recommended. And Splash Lagoon is outstanding! Clean, fresh (check out all the filters they use…both air and water) and full of something for every child and adult to ride and lounge in. Compared to other indoor waterparks, we especially liked that every ride had a different "twist" and they even have some of the new rides we affectionately call "toilet bowls"…chute down a tube, then swirl around a bowl and drop out the middle. None of the rides are strenuous and plenty of staff are on hand to gently escort you to another area or help you out of your raft. On busy days (esp. rainy day Saturdays), be prepared for long lines up the dozens of steps to the big rides (watch out for your neighbors raft bumping). Everyone in our party, from 6 to 66, enjoyed the park!

DEBENCE ANTIQUE MUSIC MUSEUM

Franklin - 1261 Liberty Street (Downtown, off I-80 to exit 3) 16323. Phone: (814) 432-5668 or (888) 547-2377. Web: www.debencemusicworld.com Hours: Tuesday-Saturday 11:00am-4:00pm, Sunday 12:30-4:00pm (mid-March - October). Admission: $8.00 adult, $7.00 senior (60+), $3.00 child (3-12).

"To See and Hear Museum". 100+ antique, automated music machines from the gay 90's - roaring 20's. See and hear demonstrations of nickelodeons, Swiss & German music boxes, waltzes and polkas, merry-go-round band organs, calliopes, player pianos, and a variety of antique organs. We were most fascinated by the nickelodeons that had glass panel inserts showing the musical instrument "guts". This was the first time we have ever seen a violin or accordion playing as an accompaniment. Bring the grandparents along for this visit.

GREENVILLE CANAL MUSEUM

Greenville - 60 Alan Avenue (Lock 22 - Alan Avenue, near Riverside Park) 16125. Phone: (724) 588-7540. Web: www.greenvillecanalmuseum.org Hours: Saturday-Sunday 1:00-5:00pm (summer). Weekends only (May, September, October). Admission: Small admission for students+.

History of Erie Extension Canal - artifacts like tools and photographs. The Erie Extension Canal played a vital role as the first efficient transportation into northwestern Pennsylvania for settlers and commerce. Great Lakes iron ore was shipped on the canal, which was combined with coal at iron and steel mills. Small settlements along the canal grew, forming new towns. See a full size replica of an 1840s canal boat - Rufus Reed, and view a working model of a canal lock.

GREENVILLE RAILROAD PARK AND MUSEUM

Greenville - 314 Main Street - Rte. 358   16125. http://members.tripod.com/~greenville/rrpark.html Phone: (724) 588-4009. Hours: Weekends 1:00-5:00pm (Summer).

Climb aboard the largest switch engine - #604 - used in the steel industry. Plenty of railroad cars - hopper cars, cabooses, and a 1914 Empire auto touring car. World's first parachute invented by local Stefan Banie in 1914. Stationmasters quarters, dispatch office and displays of railroad uniforms.

WENDELL AUGUST FORGE

Grove City - *620 North Madison Avenue (I-79, exit 31 or I-80, exit 3A - follow signs) 16127. Phone: (800) WAF-GIFT or (724) 458-8360.* **Web: www.wendellaugust.com** *Hours: Monday-Saturday 9:00am-4:00pm (except several days surrounding holidays). Admission: FREE Miscellaneous: Country's oldest and largest forge producing aluminum, pewter, sterling silver, and bronze items by hand. Old time Nickelodeon, W.A. Parrot (who talks and does impressions), LGB train on a surrounding track up above and a 225 gallon ocean reef tank. These keep the kids amused while adults gift shop.*

A self-guided tour of the production workshop is fascinating to watch as metal is taken through an eleven step process. The gift metal is hammered over a pre-designed template with random hand, or machine-operated hammer motions. At one point, you'll get a chance to pick up a hammer that is used - they weigh up to 3 pounds. You'll understand why a craftsman thought to automate the hammering process - tired, tired hands! Once the impression is set, the item is forged (put in a log fire) to produce smoke marks that bring out the detail of the design.

..."edging" the metalwork

The item is cooled and cleaned and finished by thinning the edges. Each piece is marked with a sign particular to the craftsman. This is a wonderful place to show children the balance between old world craft and new, automated craftsmanship.

PHILADELPHIA CANDIES

Hermitage - *1546 East State Street (off SR18 North) 16148. Phone: (724) 981-6341.* **Web: www.philadelphia-candies.com** *Hours: Daily 9:00am-4:00pm (lunch between 12:00-1:00pm). Admission: FREE Miscellaneous: annual "Chocolate Factory Tour" from 9:00am-4:00pm, Saturday, two weeks before Easter, showing the public where and how all the delicious candy is made for shipment to its own stores as well as other fine stores throughout the country. You will be able to see skilled candy makers creating milk chocolate bunnies, specialty baskets, and delicious chocolates. The 7,000-pound chocolate tank, chocolate enrobers, a chocolate bunny depositor, and a lollipop machine will be labeled and operating for the self-guided tour.*

Chocolate covered potato chips...yummm!

Philadelphia Candies *(cont.)*

Have you ever tried chocolate covered potato chips? We have - and this is where you can see them being made! Here are some "fun" numbers for you: 30,000 square foot facility, 80 year old family business, 7000 pounds of chocolate are melted at one time, sugar comes in 50 pounds bags, and corn syrup is delivered in 55 gallon drums!

PYMATUNING DEER PARK

Jamestown - Route 58, East Jamestown Road (off US 322, 3 Miles South of Pymatuning Dam) 16134. Phone: (724) 932-3200. Web: www.pymatuning.com/ DeerPark.htm Hours: Monday - Friday 10:00am-5:00pm, Saturday, Sunday, Holidays 10:00am-6:00pm (Summer). Weekends only in May, September & October (weather permitting). Admission: Average $4.00 per person. Miscellaneous: Train & pony rides.

Petting zoo plus other animals like lions, tigers, bears, camels, and kangaroos (and farm animals). 200 animals in all.

PYMATUNING STATE PARK

Jamestown - Box 425 (accessible by U.S. Route 6, U.S. Route 322, PA Route 18, PA Route 285, and PA Route 58) 16134. Phone: (724) 932-3141. Web: www.dcnr.state.pa.us/stateparks/parks/pymatuning.aspx

Flood control reservoir along the Ohio border. The spillway is perhaps one of the best known locations because the fish being fed are so plentiful that the "ducks walk on the fishes' backs" to compete for the food fed by the visitors. The largest body of water in the state. More people visit Pymatuning than almost any other PA state park. But the biggest thing about Pymatuning is the fun you can have boating, fishing, swimming, camping and enjoying other recreational opportunities. In addition to the state park facilities, the PA Fish and Boat Commission operates a fish hatchery and the PA Game Commission has wildlife viewing areas. Wildlife Museum - state's largest colony of nesting eagles. Beach, Boat Rentals, Sledding, Campsites, Modern Cabins, Fishing, and Trails.

CORNPLANTER STATE FOREST

North Warren - 323 N. State Street 16365. Phone: (814) 723-0262. Web: www.dcnr.state.pa.us/forestry/stateforests/cornplanteractivities.aspx

1,256 acres named for Chief Cornplanter, a famous Indian Chief of the Seneca tribe. Highlights include Hunter Run Demonstration Area and Lasure Trail. This is a combined interpretive area with about 1-1/2 miles of self guided foot trails. It is heavily used by the surrounding schools for environmental education. There are seven miles of cross-country ski trails for the winter sports enthusiast. The trail is located 4 miles N. of Tionesta off SR 36. ATV Trails.

OIL CREEK STATE PARK

Oil City - RD 1, Box 207 (the main entrance to the park is off of PA Route 8) 16301. Phone: (814) 676-5915. Web: www.dcnr.state.pa.us/stateparks/parks/oilcreek.aspx

The site of the world's first commercial oil well, this park tells the story of the early petroleum industry by interpreting oil boom towns, oil wells and early transportation. Many sites can be seen while traveling the 9.5-mile paved bicycle trail through the scenic Oil Creek Gorge, or on an excursion train. Displays and programs are at Petroleum Centre, the focal point of the early oil boom. "A Contrast in Time" slideshow takes you on a six-minute journey through time. The noise of pumping wells and shouting  men in the 1860s contrasts with the rustling leaves in a gentle breeze in present day Oil Creek. The train station is open noon-4:00pm Saturdays and Sundays. Visit the Train Station Visitor Center for historical displays, an exciting diorama and an interactive computer information center. A train still chugs through the valley and stops at the Train Station in Petroleum Centre, just as it did over 100 years ago! Petroleum Centre - displays and programs on oil history. Wildcat Hollow - outdoor classroom and 4 theme trails. Boat Rentals, Sledding, Fishing, and Cross-Country Skiing.

GODDARD STATE PARK, MAURICE K.

Sandy Lake - 684 Lake Wilhelm Road (I-79 exit 34, west on Rte. 358) 16145. Phone: (724) 253-4833. Web: www.dcnr.state.pa.us/stateparks/parks/mauricekgoddard.aspx

The 1,860-acre Lake Wilhelm is an angler's paradise. The large lake, abundant wetlands, old fields and mature forests provide a diversity of habitats which attract wildlife in all seasons. Boat Rentals, Sledding, Trails, & Winter Sports.

DAFFIN'S CANDIES

Sharon - 496 East State Street (Factory - 7 Spearman Avenue, SR60 in nearby Farrell) 16146. Phone: (724) 342-2892. Web: www.daffins.com Hours: Monday-Saturday 9:00am-9:00pm, Sunday 11:00am-5:00pm. Admission: FREE Miscellaneous: Tours in the fall and winter are best - more activity preparing for Christmas and Easter

Holidays. The Chocolate Kingdom is available to view whenever the store is open.

Start in the Chocolate Kingdom. The display is filled with giant rabbits, elephants, turtles and castles made of chocolate. Snap a picture or pick up

free postcard pictures of these unique creatures. Each giant figurine can require up to 700 lbs. of chocolate! As the tour continues, you'll learn how cocoa beans are removed from pods, mashed into paste, and finally processed into the chocolate forms we all know and love. Daffin's still hosts its annual event known as Swizzle Stick Day on the Sunday before Palm Sunday. The facility holds plant tours

A display made from hundreds of pounds of chocolate...sweet!

that day, drawing nearly 8,000 people during the four-hour session. Regular factory tours are also available year-round. At the Factory, the group will see a short video tape of Daffin's and the History of chocolates. The seven foot Rabbit and other artistic chocolate items are also on display at the factory. Then, the group will take a tour thru the factory and see how some chocolates are made. At the end of the tour, each person will receive a candy sample.

DRAKE WELL MUSEUM

Titusville - East Bloss Street, 205 Museum Lane (I-80 to exit 3, off SR8 North) 16354. Phone: (814) 827-2797. Web: www.drakewell.org Hours: Monday-Saturday 9:00am-5:00pm, Sunday Noon-5:00pm (May-October). Tuesday-Saturday 9:00am-5:00pm, Sunday Noon-5:00pm (November-April). Closed most holidays except summer holidays. Admission: $5.00 adult, $4.00 senior (50+), $2.00 student (7-17). Reduced adult fares, winter hours. Miscellaneous: Head over to Pithole City (off SR227 between Pleasantville and Plummer) Visitor's Center (June-Labor Day). Within

the park is a bike trail and tourist train ride depot. Magic Lantern Shows (old-fashioned movies using glass slides to illustrate stories, songs and comedy) and Blacksmith demos occasional Saturdays each month. Look at Calendar of Events.

The birthplace of the petroleum industry. Edward Drake drilled the first oil well in 1859 through layers

Lots of fun pushin' the buttons and learning...

of sandstone. Start your visit with a video about the challenges Drake and his driller, "Uncle" Billy Smith faced to succeed. The museum's indoor and outdoor exhibits explain the progress of the oil industry. Operating oil field machinery, historic buildings, and scale models demonstrate primitive and modern drilling processes. Many exhibits have "push buttons" and "cutaways" of the machinery in action (the kids will really like pushing the small button to make all the working parts move). And, they can "squeeze and sniff" oil samples from all over the world, make plastic, send telegraph messages, and find unusual items made from oil in the museum lobby. Some will surprise you (ex. Tape, aspirin). Be sure to purchase a souvenir vial of real crude Pennsylvania oil in the Museum Store and eat your ice cream on the patio.

OIL CREEK & TITUSVILLE RAILROAD

Titusville - 409 South Perry Street (I-80 exit Route 8 north to Perry Street Station) 16354. Phone: (814) 676-1733. **Web: http://octrr.clarion.edu** *Hours: Weekend departures at 1:00pm (June-October). Selected weekday runs in July, August and October. Admission: $15.00 adult, $13.00 senior (60+), $9.00 child (3-12). Miscellaneous: Railroad memorabilia displays, souvenir area, and snack shop.*

See the first oil fields in the world tell a story of the oil rush boom days in the valley (similar to the gold rush). Stop by Rynd Farm and Drake Well Park. Ride in restored 1930s passenger cars. One car is the only working railway Post Office car - have

A railcar post office?

your postcard to grandma hand-stamp cancelled while on board.

ALLEGHENY NATIONAL FOREST

Warren - PO Box 847, 222 Liberty Street 16365. **Web: www.fs.fed.us/r9/allegheny/** *Phone: (814) 723-5150.*

Visit Pennsylvania's wilderness land with 400-year-old forests, 120 miles of trout streams, and where deer, elk, and bear roam the hills. 600 miles of trails. Hundreds of Mountain Laurel in June. 1/2 million acres of land. Twin Lakes and Loleta Recreation Areas. Black Cherry and Tracy Ridge trails. Longhouse Byway and Old Powerhouse. Rimrock Overlook, Jake's Rock, Buzzard Swamp and Owl's Nest.

KINZUA DAM/ BIG BEND VISITOR'S CENTER

Warren - *1205 Kinzua Road - Route 59 (I-79 to Route 6 east to Route 59 east) 16365.*
Phone: (814) 726-0661.   ***Web: www.lrp.usace.army.mil/rec/lakes/kinzuala.htm***
Hours: Daily 10:00am-4:00pm (Summer). Weekends (September, October).
Admission: FREE.

A flood control dam has created a vast waterway known as the Allegheny Reservoir (within the Allegheny National Forest). Center features exhibits,

displays, and slide programs which explain the purpose of the dam and power plant. In the summer, there are numerous activities ranging from swimming, boating and water-skiing, to camping, fishing and sightseeing. During the autumn, the Kinzua countryside produces colorful displays of fall foliage with miles of hiking trails and country roads from which to enjoy the brilliant fall scenery. Winter doesn't signal an end to the enjoyment of the outdoors. Hikers turn to cross-country skiing, fishermen continue their sport on the ice and snowmobiles speed along the many trails and forest roads. The blossoming of the woodland wildflowers signals the arrival of spring in Kinzua Country; and with it, the arrival of trout fishermen, canoeists and nature enthusiasts.

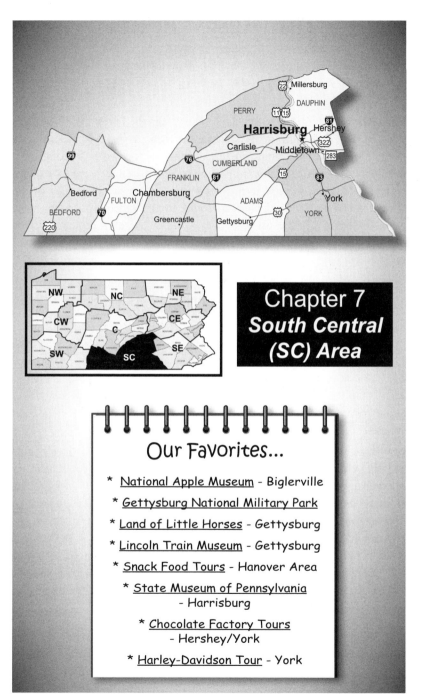

Chapter 7
South Central (SC) Area

Our Favorites...

* __National Apple Museum__ - Biglerville

* __Gettysburg National Military Park__

* __Land of Little Horses__ - Gettysburg

* __Lincoln Train Museum__ - Gettysburg

* __Snack Food Tours__ - Hanover Area

* __State Museum of Pennsylvania__
  - Harrisburg

* __Chocolate Factory Tours__
  - Hershey/York

* __Harley-Davidson Tour__ - York

FORT BEDFORD MUSEUM

Bedford - Fort Bedford Drive (I-76, exit 11, SR320 - Pitt Street - Downtown) 15522. Phone: (814) 623-8891 or (800) 259-4284. Web: www.bedfordcounty.net Hours: Wednesday-Sunday 11:00am-5:00pm (mid-May thru mid-October). Admission: Generally $3.00-$5.00.

The French and Indian War fort site - "The Fort in the Forest". A blockhouse structure that houses the large scale model of the original fort along with Native American household artifacts. From flint rock rifles to hand tools to clothing – each help you explore pioneer and frontier days in western Pennsylvania. In order to secure the water and secure the banks of the stream, a gallery with loopholes extended from the central bastion on its north front down to the water's edge. A ladder-like arrangement of steps led down the river's bluff-like south bank. This enclosed gallery was a real military curiosity. The fort controlled the river gap and served a British stockade against the French for years.

OLD BEDFORD VILLAGE

Bedford - 220 Sawblade Road (1/2 mile south of PA Turnpike (I-70/76), exit 11- Route 220) 15522. Web: www.oldbedfordvillage.org Phone: (814) 623-1156 or (800) 238-4347. Hours: Daily (except Wednesday) 9:00am-5:00pm (Memorial Day-Labor Day). Thursday-Sunday 10:00am-4:00pm (September/October). Admission: $8.00 adult, $4.00 student (age 6+). Ask about senior discount. Miscellaneous: Dress for walking on the natural roadways. Pendergrass Tavern. Many warm weather re-enactment weekends.

Craftsmen are in action as you relive the past walking through 40 log homes and shops (see them making brooms, baskets, bread, pottery). There are seasonal productions such as "Welcome to Early America" - a recreated world of the 1790s Pioneer America or summer theatre musical, comedies or mysteries (814-623-7555 for reservations). In 1794, President George Washington led federal troops with his battle headquarters here in Bedford. After the troops left, the colonial industry flourished with blacksmiths, attorneys, a doctor, distillers, innkeepers, soldiers, millers, and farmers setting up shop in the village. In all, over 14 period skills are represented at the Village, and many of the products made on site can be found at the Village Craft Shop. And don't miss the opportunity to learn one of the many crafts available through Old Bedford Village's educational programs.

GRAVITY HILL

Bedford (Schellsburgh) - Bethel Hollow Road 15522. . Web: www.gravityhill.com

Tucked away in the "less traveled" area of
Bedford County is a marvel. Often talked about,
but seldom found, Gravity Hill is a phenomenon.
Cars roll uphill, water flows the wrong way ...
it's a place where gravity has gone haywire.
Some people like to take water or various other

non-flammable, bio-degradeable liquids and pour them onto the road. The
liquids will flow uphill. There are directions on the website about finding
Gravity Hill with a minimum of wrong turns. Daylight hours suggested.

NATIONAL APPLE MUSEUM

*Biglerville - 154 West Hanover Street (US 30 west to York to SR234 & SR394 - Look
for big red barn) 17307. Web: www.nationalapplemuseum.com Phone: (717) 677-
4556. Hours: Saturday 10:00am-4:00pm, Sunday 1:00-4:00pm (May-October). Call
for special group arrangement during other days and times. Admission: $2.00 adult,
$1.00 child (6-12). Miscellaneous: Picnic area. Gift shop - guess what...everything
in there has apples on it!*

What a treat this place is! America's favorite fruit (red delicious, the most
popular) is highlighted here. Kids can get involved right from the beginning
(they eat a snack of apple juice and cookies). As you sip on your juice, they
show a film about apple varieties, picking, and production (bet you didn't
know the apple is part of the rose family!). This film is very entertaining (not
boring at all) and the kids are thrilled seeing thousands of apples in every
scene. Because many apple production facilities don't give tours, you'll get a
great video look at how they "produce" apples for applesauce. How do they

keep apples unbruised and ripe all year
long? Antique equipment displays and
old town dioramas are upstairs. The bug
displays really appeal to the kids. See the
"apple biz" come to life when you drive
just up the road through apple orchards.
Do you know why orchards love bees,
ladybug beetles, and dwarf trees?

Miles and miles of sweet,
juicy apples...

HOPE ACRES FARM, HOME OF THE BROWN COW

Brogue - *2680 Delta Road (PA Rte. 74 southeast off US 30) 17309. Phone: (800) 293-1054. Web: www.hopeacres.com Admission: $4.00-$6.00 per person. Includes a free ice cream cone at end of tour.*

This 75-minute tour is fun and educational for all ages. See the latest innovations in milking technology. Tour the Brown Cow's processing facilities, then head to Hope Acres farm where you will see 100% automated robotic milking. They call them Astronauts machines. They are currently one of four farms in the country testing these robotics. While touring the fully robotic milking facility, you'll see how cows are "pampered" with waterbeds and back scratchers. The tour includes a trip to the calving barn to see HOPE ACRES newest arrivals. Complete the tour with a visit to The Brown Cow Country Market for a scoop of HOPE ACRES ice cream - free with the price of your tour ticket!

KINGS GAP STATE PARK

Carlisle - *500 Kings Gap Road   17013. Phone: (717) 486-5031. Web: www.dcnr.state.pa.us/stateparks/parks/kingsgap.aspx*

Kings Gap offers a panoramic view of the Cumberland Valley. Sixteen miles of hiking trails interconnect three main areas and are open year-round. Kings Gap offers environmental education programs from the pre-school environmental awareness program to environmental problem solving programs.

SKI LIBERTY

Carroll Valley - *78 Country Club Trail (Rte. 30 to Rte. 116, Liberty Mountain Resort is 8 miles on the left) 17320. Phone: (717) 642-8282.. Web: www.skiliberty.com*

Skiing, Snowboarding and Snow Tubing. Longest Run: 5300 ft.; 16 Slopes & Trails. Snow Monsters Kids club.

CALEDONIA STATE PARK

Fayetteville - *40 Rocky Mountain Rd (US Route 30) 17222. Phone: (717) 352-2161. Web: www.dcnr.state.pa.us/stateparks/parks/caledonia.aspx*

Known locally as South Mountain, Caledonia located on the northern-most section of the Blue Ridge Mountains fifteen miles west of Gettysburg via Route 30. The Appalachian Trail passes through the central portion of the park. It is a great place for family outings: Pool, Visitor Center, Campsites,

Modern Cabins, Fishing, Trails, and Cross-Country Skiing. Mr. Ed's Elephant Museum (a collection of 6000 elephants) is open daily just 2 miles east of the park on Rte. 30 (717-352-3792).

MICHAUX STATE FOREST

Fayetteville - 10099 Lincoln Way East 17222. Phone: (717) 352-2211. **Web:** *www.dcnr.state.pa.us/forestry/stateforests/forests/michaux/michaux.htm*

The Michaux State Forest spans Adams, Cumberland and Franklin counties. In 1785, a French botanist, Andre Michaux, sent by France to gather plants for the Royal Gardens, identified numerous flowers, shrubs and trees. From the mid-eighteenth century to the early twentieth century, large iron companies owned much of the forest. Iron furnaces processed iron ore, which was forged into iron implements, cannonballs, and stoves. The iron companies needed large tracts of woodland to cut and burn for the charcoal-fueled furnaces. There are miles of trout streams and many lakes and reservoirs for fishing. Camping, hiking, horseback riding, bicycling, cross-country skiing and snowmobiling are some recreational activities.

TOTEM POLE PLAYHOUSE

Fayetteville - 9555 Golf Road, Caledonia State Park (Junction of US 30 & PA233) 17222. Phone: (717) 352-2164. **Web:** *www.totempoleplayhouse.org* *Season: June-August Admission: Varies by performance, $27.00+ (Children under 5 not admitted). Junior Tickets (Ages 5 to 25) - $12 for all shows.*

Professional theatre featuring comedies and musicals plus Summer Theatre Camps.

COWAN'S GAP STATE PARK

Fort Loudon - (PA 75 North to Richmond Furnace, follow signs) 17224. Phone: (717) 485-3948. **Web:** *www.dcnr.state.pa.us/stateparks/parks/cowansgap.aspx*

Logging Road Trail: 1.7-mile, easy hiking. This old logging road can be walked from one end of the park to the other and is a good trail to use to make loop hikes with other trails on the side of Cove Mountain. Lakeside Trail: 1.5-mile, easy hiking. This very pleasant, nearly level, scenic trail encompasses Cowans Gap Lake. This is the most popular trail in the park. Beach, Visitor Center, Boat Rentals, Campsites, Rustic Cabins, and Winter Activities. Buchanan's Birthplace State Historical Park nearby. Environmental Education and Interpretation (April-November).

PINE GROVE FURNACE STATE PARK

Gardners - 1100 Pine Grove Road (PA Route 233 & 34) 17324. Phone: (717) 486-7174. Web: www.dcnr.state.pa.us/stateparks/parks/pinegrovefurnace.aspx

This park was once the site of the Pine Grove Furnace Iron Works that dates from 1764. Historical buildings include the ironmaster's mansion, a gristmill, an inn and several residences. The self-guiding historical trail leads you through the remains of the iron works. The Appalachian Trail passes through the park. Beach, Visitor Center, Boat Rentals, Campsites, Kite-flying Area. Fishing, Trails, and Cross-Country Skiing.

AMERICAN CIVIL WAR MUSEUM

Gettysburg - 297 Steinwehr Avenue (US15 - Business Route) 17325. Phone: (717) 334-6245. Web: www.e-gettysburg.cc Hours: Daily 9:00am-9:00pm (Summer), Daily 9:00am-7:00pm (mid-April - mid-June), Daily 9:00am-5:00pm (September - December, March - Mid-April), Weekends Only (Winter). Admission: $5.50 adult, $3.50 student (13-17), $2.50 child (6-12).

More than 200 life-size wax figures in 30 different scenes re-create crucial moments but also describe the cause and effects of the conflict. Besides strategic planning and battle scenes, voices from history blend with scenes and words to recreate the past. Jennie Wade bakes bread before being fatally shot in her sister's kitchen. John Brown, bound in ropes, walks to the gallows. Slaves using the Underground Railroad try to escape to freedom. And Abraham Lincoln sits in the theatre on that fateful day. The last scene is of an animated wax figure of Lincoln making his speech the night before his famous address. At the end of the tour, you'll enter the Battleroom Auditorium where the battle is re-enacted (with wax figures and lighting). It's an easy explanation of the three days of battle (not too technical for kids). Lincoln arrives and gives his address at the end.

BATTLEFIELD BUS TOURS

Gettysburg - 778 Baltimore Street 17325. Web: www.gettysburgbattlefieldtours.com Phone: (717) 334-6296. Hours: Daily 9:00am-9:00pm (Summer), 9:00am-7:00pm (Spring & Fall), 9:00am-5:00pm (rest of year). Weather permitting. Admission: $21.95 adult, $12.35 child (4-11).

A Hollywood cast of actors, technicians, and special effects recreate the Battle of Gettysburg as you tour the Battlefield from the famous Double Decker buses (seasonal, warm months) that have become a landmark in Gettysburg. Enclosed bus for other cold, rainy season tours.

BOYD'S BEAR COUNTRY

Gettysburg - 75 Cunningham Road (off Bus. Rte. 15, near Emmitsburg Rd.) 17325. Phone: (717) 630-2600. **Web: www.boydsbearcountry.com** *Hours: Daily 10:00am–6:00pm except New Years, Easter, Thanksgiving and Christmas. Admission: FREE. Miscellaneous: Restaurants on premises. Dress-your-own bears & seasonal crafts area.*

The World's Most Humongous Teddy Bear Store and museum. Get a history of the Boyd's Collection…its product and the life story of the founder. Your tour is led by Bennie B., an overstuffed (and overfed!) Boyd's Bear who serves as the resident historian. The museum includes a replica of Gary's father's butcher shop in New York City (where Gary learned business tricks and tips!); neat photos and memorabilia of Gary's growin' up years and experiences as a Peace Corps volunteer; displays of early Boyd's duck decoys, Gnomes Homes, early plush and resin, and other stuff that made Boyd's famous; and sections dedicated to QVC shows, collectors' club, and charitable activities. They've built a display of virtually every Boyd's plush critter ever made.

The Nursery is open…where baby bears are born every day. Nurse Carin welcomes perspective parents of all ages to adopt their beary own cuddly bear. Look at the bears in their cradles, pick one, fill out the adoption papers and get your photo taken. Also, they have occasional Breakfasts with Molly & Sebastian, a Mother's Day Tea or Father's Day Breakfast, hayrides in October, or Breakfast with Santa in December. Entertainment on the porch most summer weekends, too.

EXPLORE & MORE CHILDREN'S MUSEUM

Gettysburg - 20 East High Street (near the circle) 17325. Phone: (717) 337-9151. **Web: www.exploreandmore.com** *Hours: Monday-Saturday 10:00am-5:00pm (May– August). Closed Wednesdays but open Sunday afternoons (rest of year). Admission: $4.00 adult (age 15+), $6.00 child (2-14). Miscellaneous: Toy store.*

Located in an historic home, they have seven rooms where children can create a work of art, play house the way people lived around the time of the Civil War, make a bubble large enough to stand inside of, or experiment with mixing colors (make color explosions in milk!) and waterworks. Children can make puppets and then perform a show with them. More pretend play in the Hard Hat area (receiving, conveyor, shipping, recycling – clean up) or the Black Light Dress Up Room (wild!). At this place, you can even play with an overhead projector, just like teacher. Give your children a break from the battlefield nearby!

GETTYSBURG BATTLE THEATRE

Gettysburg - 571 Steinwehr Avenue 17325. www.gettysburgbattlefieldtours.com/Battle.html Phone: (717) 334-6296. Hours: Daily 9:00am-5:00pm (March-December). Admission: $3.50-$6.00 (age 6+). Miscellaneous: Try General Pickett's Buffet located downstairs in the Battle Cafeteria.

Begin with a viewing of a movie featuring a multi-media battle re-enactment. To further visualize the battlement during the Civil War, take a close look at the electronic map and a complete Battlefield Diorama of 25,000 hand-painted miniature soldiers. Learn what role your home state played in the Battle. See the armies' arrival, battle lines forming, and the advances and retreats of the struggling armies. Jim Getty, who portrayed Abraham Lincoln in the first person, occasionally can be still be seen at the Gettysburg Battle Theatre.

GETTYSBURG NATIONAL MILITARY PARK

*Gettysburg - 97 Taneytown Road (SR134 or Steinwehr Ave. -Bus. 15) 17325. **Web:** www.nps.gov/gett Phone: (717) 334-1124 Park or (717) 338-9114 Eisenhower Site. Hours: Daily 8:00am-5:00pm. Closed Thanksgiving, Christmas and New Years. Admission: VISITOR CENTER/BATTLEFIELD - FREE. CYCLORAMA/ELECTRIC MAP - $3.00-$4.00 (age 6+) for each exhibit. EISENHOWER SITE - $7.00 adult, $4.00 child (13-16) and $2.50 child (6-12).*

Here is the site of the major Civil War battle and Abraham Lincoln's Gettysburg Address:

BATTLEFIELD - The most important major blow to the Confederate Army and the most casualties (51,000) on the first few days of early July 1863. See key places: Cemetery Hill and Ridge, Culp's Hill, Little Round Top, and Observation Tower. (We suggest the audio tape tour for kids).

NOVEMBER 19, 1863, CEMETERY - President Lincoln dedicated the National Cemetery on the battlefield and delivered his famous speech "The Gettysburg Address".

CYCLORAMA - A 30 minute description while standing in the middle of a 360 degree circular wall painting of the battlefield and Pickett's Charge, the climactic moment of the battle (a sight & sound experience). 9:00 am - 4:30pm (every 1/2 hour).

ELECTRIC MAP - A 30 minute show with highlights of strategic moves of battle. (every 45 minutes)

MUSEUM OF THE CIVIL WAR - A large collection of Civil War artifacts, especially weapons and uniforms.

EISENHOWER HISTORIC SITE SUMMER HOME - Visit the web site at **www.nps.gov/eise**. During his Presidency, President and Mrs. Eisenhower used the farm as a weekend retreat, a refuge in time of illness, and a comfortable meeting place for world leaders. From 1961 to 1969, it was the Eisenhower's home during a vigorous and active retirement.

GETTYSBURG SCENIC RAIL TOURS

Gettysburg - 106 North Washington Street (Near Lincoln Square - Downtown) 17325. Phone: (717) 334-6932. Web: www.gettysburgrail.com Admission: $9.00-$17.00 per customer. Miscellaneous: The "Famous" Civil War Train Raid: An exciting special drama unfolds as Civil War Re-enactors from the Union Army guard the train before departure and then board for the 22-mile trip to protect our train from possible attack by the Confederates.

Relax aboard one of the vintage rail coaches or the unique double-decker open car, pulled by classic railroad locomotives. Enjoy a nostalgic train ride, first passing the famous "railroad cut", through the countryside and then passing through the First Day Battlefield of the Gettysburg National Military Park.

HALL OF PRESIDENTS

Gettysburg - 789 Baltimore Street 17325. Phone: (717) 334-5717. Hours: Daily 9:00am-5:00pm (later hours in summer season). (March-Thanksgiving Weekend). Admission: $7.25 adult. $3.50 child (4-11). Web: www.gettysburgbattlefieldtours.com/

Watch life-sized reproductions tell the "Story of America" through taped messages. First ladies appear in the type of gown they wore at the inauguration of their husbands. They've also added a heartwarming "Eisenhower at Gettysburg" exhibit. If your children are studying Presidential history, this is an easy way to learn or re-learn important facts about each man.

JENNIE WADE HOUSE & OLDE TOWN

Gettysburg - 547 Baltimore Street (Adjacent to Olde Town) 17325. Phone: (717) 334-4100. Hours: Daily 9:00am-9:00pm (Summer), Daily 9:00am-5:00pm (March-Thanksgiving Weekend). Admission: $4.00-$6.00 (age 6+). Miscellaneous: Caution: Due to the dramatic nature and story of this tour - parents with children younger than 1st or 2nd grade should probably arrange to be part of a school tour. They only give brief descriptions of the events and not explicit details.

Jennie Wade was the only civilian killed during the battle of Gettysburg and the situations that led to her death were quite dramatic. While baking bread for the soldiers in her kitchen, a stray bullet hit and killed young 20 year old Jennie. (a realistic hologram of Jennie is seen in the kitchen - and you see the actual bullet hole). A soldier tells you all the details including the fact that her fiancé was killed just days later in battle, but never knew of Jennie's fate!

LAND OF LITTLE HORSES

Gettysburg - 125 Glenwood Drive (3 miles West on US30, then follow signs) 17325. Phone: (717) 334-7259. **Web:** *www.landoflittlehorses.com Hours: Monday-Saturday 10:00am-5:00pm, Sunday Noon-5:00pm (April-Labor Day). Weekends only (September, October). Admission: $12.00 (age 2+). Miscellaneous: Air-conditioned arena. The Gift Horse Shop. Carousel, train tram, petting farm. Put on a "feed bag" at the Hobby Horse Café.*

As you enter, you'll be greeted by those adorable small horses (most only a few feet tall) that seem to be just the right size for kids to enjoy. Many are in separate pens throughout the park, some are in the barn, others are getting ready for the show in the arena. We took in the Barn Show first and loved the chance to see the horses prance around and be gently petted. Especially cute are the mothers with their young. The highlight of this farm is the Performing

...just the right size for kids!

Animals Show. They get the kids involved by "kissing a pig" (there's a trick involved - 2 kids volunteered and did it!), or helping with the animal tricks. "Something Special" is a daily event at the Land of Little Horses. The event changes every day, and can be anything from Miniature Horse costume parades (where you dress up horses and show them off to the entire park), fun games with prizes for the winners, goat milking & sheep sheering, photo opportunities with the stars of our daily Arena Performances, and much more! They also have cart races, saddle kids, and host weekend chicken races - so cute, pick your favorite animal and cheer it on! A great attraction for children of all ages.

LINCOLN TRAIN MUSEUM

Gettysburg - 425 Steinwehr Avenue 17325. Phone: (717) 334-5678. Hours: Daily 9:00am-9:00pm (Summer), Daily 9:00am-5:00pm (March-Thanksgiving). Admission: $4.00-$6.00 (age 6+). Miscellaneous: Events (in the diorama display) that led up to this historic train ride. Large train collection layout that reproduces the Civil War Era.

A simulated 1836 train ride with Lincoln and statesmen on a 12 minute trip. See Civil War grounds and overhear conversations that might have occurred on that trip. They project actual footage of a steam train ride as your seat and floorboards move to the straights, curves, and rumbles of the track. Statesmen speak of this time, in the still present war, Mr. President's ill son, and thoughts of re-election. We suggest this stop for young kids (all ages for that matter) because it easily and uniquely illustrates the emotion/history behind the Gettysburg Address.

SOLDIER'S NATIONAL MUSEUM

Gettysburg - 777 Baltimore Street 17325. Phone: (717) 334-4890. Hours: Daily 9:00am-9:00pm (Summer) 9:00am-5:00pm (March-Thanksgiving Weekend). Admission: $4.00-$6.00 (age 6+).

10 dioramas depict battles of the Civil War. There's also a life- sized, narrated confederate encampment. The building was once General Howard's headquarters and later the Soldier's National Orphanage.

LAKE TOBIAS WILDLIFE PARK

Halifax - 760 Tobias Drive (Rt. 322/22 West to Dauphin. Rt. 225 North to Halifax. Four miles on Rt. 225 North to Fisherville) 17032. Web: www.laketobias.com Phone: (717) 362-9126. Hours: Monday-Friday 10:00am-6:00pm, Saturday & Sunday 11:00am-7:00pm (Summer), Weekends only (May, September, October). Admission: $3.00-5.00 per activity- adult, $2.00-4.00 per activity, child (2-12).

Hundreds of wild and exotic animals - alligators, buffalo, llamas, monkeys and reptile animal shows. Specially designed cruisers take you across 150 acres of rolling land where you see herds of wild and exotic animals from around the world. Tour guides travel with you giving expert information on the various species and their habitats. You will be surprised at how close you come to these animals. Also a petting zoo and fishing ponds for "tamer" activity.

CODORUS STATE PARK

Hanover - 1066 Blooming Grove Road (PA Route 216) 17331. Phone: (717) 637-2816. Web: www.dcnr.state.pa.us/stateparks/parks/codorus.aspx

The 1,275-acre Lake Marburg is popular with fishermen, boaters and swimmers. Codorus is also an excellent place to observe spring and fall migrations of waterfowl and warblers. The park offers interpretive programs and hikes. Boat rentals are available and a restaurant is convenient to the park. Pool, Visitor Center, Horseback Riding, Sledding, Campsites, Fishing, Trails, Winter Sports.

UTZ POTATO CHIPS

Hanover - 900 High Street (SR94 North and Clearview Streets) 17331. Phone: (717) 637-6644. Web: www.utzsnacks.com Hours: Monday-Thursday 8:00am-4:00pm. Occasional Fridays, by appointment. Admission: FREE Miscellaneous: Outlet store just down the road. Lots of sampling and buying goes on there.

Walk along an elevated, glass enclosed observation gallery to observe potato chips in production. View close up TV monitors and listen to the descriptions of each step of the process. This is a modern and very clean facility. We probably got the closest to large conveyors of fried chips here (behind glass of course!).  A new experience was watching home-cooked kettle chips being made. As you study family history photographs, enjoy a free bag of chips! We especially liked the "platform bridges" that they had throughout the tour so the "little ones" could see too!

SNYDERS OF HANOVER

Hanover - 1350 York Street 17731. Web: www.snyders-han.com Phone: (800) 233-7125 ext. 8592. Admission: FREE

Meet at the factory storefront (where you'll no doubt be nibbling on samples before touring). It's no wonder that Pennsylvania is the "snack food" capital of the US. Watch a  short video covering the company history starting with potato chips made at home in the early 1920s to the 1970s when they established sourdough hard pretzels. The differences you'll notice on this snack food tour are the numerous and extra large baking ovens and highly automated packaging systems. Machines build boxes while another machine fills the bags and yet another machine boxes the bags and then seals the cases shut. Kids love all the automation!

STATE CAPITOL BUILDING

Harrisburg - Third & State Streets   17101. Phone: (800) TOUR-N-PA. **Web:** *www.legis.state.pa.us/cfdocs/legis/home/toursWelcome.cfm Hours: Monday-Friday 8:30am-4:00pm, Saturday, Sunday, & Holiday 9:00am, 11:00am, 1:00pm, & 3:00pm. Closed major holidays. Admission: FREE Miscellaneous: Stop at the Information Center first for a brochure on the self-guided tour. Welcome Center is open weekdays only.*

The 272-foot dome will stun everyone as you stand underneath it and look up. Your neck could get sore because you'll be staring a good while. As you pass though bronze and ornately carved wooden doors, you can climb the stairs to the second and fourth floors to view the elegant and handsome Senate and House chambers. The favorite (and most educational) area is the Welcome Center. From the Ben Franklin video in miniature, to Hello History (take a telephone call from famous Pennsylvania leaders and

...inside the rotunda!

athletes) to the glass window case full of colored balls (representing the number of bills that a state legislator considers in a year - there's a lot!). Other exhibits that encourage learning about laws (for kids and adults) are interactive displays of a "Day in the Life of a Legislator" (try to get your birthday as a holiday), voting (actually sit in a voting desk) and the making of a law (presented through a colorful display - like the game "Mousetrap" full of tracks, pulleys, and chains that follow a funny course). What a wonderful way to teach government!

WHITAKER CENTER FOR SCIENCE AND THE ARTS

Harrisburg - 222 Market Street (Downtown - Diagonal to the State Capitol) 17101. Phone: (717) 214-ARTS. **Web: www.whitakercenter.org** *Hours: Monday-Saturday 9:30am-5:00pm. Sunday 11:30am-5:00pm. Admission: $6.75 adult, $5.25 senior (55+), $5.25 child (3-12). IMAX additional charge. Combo discounts offered.*

Miscellaneous: IMAX Theatre - call (717) 214-IMAX for showtimes. Center closed Thanksgiving and Christmas Day. Food court attached by walkway. In addition to hands-on interactive exhibits, the Harsco Science Center also features Stage Two, a "black box" theater; and Big Science Theatre productions.

Their motto is "Question Everything". Nine different themed exhibit areas use performing arts to teach science concepts. How is dancing linked to science and physics? What are backstage secrets of how lighting and special effects contribute to the theater experience? Have you ever "walked through" a kaleidoscope? (you can here!). The younger kids will spend most of their time in the "kids hall" (ages 8 and below) where they too, get to experiment with light and sound! Other exhibits: Health and Wellness which includes The Gallery of Anatomy, The Five Senses, Medical Technology, and Wellness; The Gallery of Mathematics in Nature and Art; People and Diversity which includes Genetics, and Culture and Communication; Environment and Ecology which includes Global Environment, Watersheds, and Pennsylvania Environments; Physics which includes Forces and Motion, Simple Machines, Bodies In Motion: The Physics of Human Movement, and Backstage Science. Kids Hall which includes Sound and Music, Light and Color, Gizmos, the Theater, ArtWorks, and Kids Garden.

NATIONAL CIVIL WAR MUSEUM

Harrisburg - 1 Lincoln Circle at Reservoir Park (Interstate 83, Take Exit 50 West (Progress Exit & US Route 22 / Walnut Street) 17103. Phone: (717) 260-1861 or (866) BLU-GRAY. Web: www.nationalcivilwarmuseum.com Hours: Monday-Saturday 10:00am-5:00pm, Sunday Noon-5:00pm. (Closed Thanksgiving, Christmas & New Year's Day). Closed Mondays and Tuesdays in the winter. Admission: $8.00 adult, $7.00 senior, $6.00 student, $30.00 family.

Mission Statement: The only museum in the United States that attempts to portray the story of the Nation's Civil War - Equally balanced presentations are humanistic in nature without bias to Union or Confederate causes. Dioramas, digital videos and simply displayed showcases ease you through the facts. A House Divided features comparisons of the Northern and

Southern economies, the John Brown raid on Harpers Ferry, the election of Abraham Lincoln, and a map showing the division of the country. The "We the People" video introduces you to ten Americans – Northerners and Southerners, men and women, white and black, military and civilian – who endured typical hardships and heartache in the four-year conflict. Tours are educational, entertaining, sometimes emotional and look at the issues of slavery, war strategies, motivations and music.

CITY ISLAND

*Harrisburg - Walnut & Market Street Bridges (Susquehanna River) 17104. . **Web:** www.harrisburgpa.gov/parksRec/cityIsland/ Hours: Dawn-Dusk.*

Enjoy 63 acres of parkland developed as a recreational center. Once ashore, a miniature train provides a leisurely round-the Island tour of all the sights and attractions. Some of the Island's most popular activities are located on its north end, where the unique Water Golf miniature golf course awaits. Nearby, the distinctive Harbourtown Children's Play area beckons visitors with a scaled-down re-creation of an 1840s canal town. Playhouse-type structures include a pirate ship, lighthouse and stores. Within feet are large sandboxes and volleyball courts, and the city's historic Beachhouse and Beach (one of the cleanest rivers in the nation). Skyline Sports Complex & Riverside Village Park eateries (east shore) include crab cakes, burgers, fries, ice cream and more. This mid-19th Century-themed retail village contains a variety of picnic facilities, gazebos, scenic decks and plenty of places to feed the Island's ever-hungry ducks and geese. Nestled against the Walnut Street Bridge is the City Island Arcade. Elegant horse-drawn carriage rides are offered in-season along the waterfront. What a treat for locals and a nice appeal to visitors!

PRIDE OF THE SUSQUEHANNA RIVERBOAT TOUR

*Harrisburg - (Docked at City Island) 17104. **Web:** www.harrisburgriverboat.com Phone: (717) 234-6500. Hours: Tuesday-Sunday Noon-3:00pm (June-August) Admission: $6.50 adult, $6.00 senior, $3.50 child (3-12). Wednesday has reduced fares. Miscellaneous: Dinner cruises are $35.00 per person from May-October with reservation.*

Pass under 6 bridges and by the grave of the city's founder, John Harris on an authentic paddlewheel boat. Take your children and their special friends back to yesteryear, and experience a unique method of transportation that was used over 150 years ago. The boat is docked on the wonderful city park, City

Island, which is situated in the middle of the Susquehanna River. History tells us that the Susquehannock Indians lived on the islands in the river and fished the waters of the Susquehanna River in the 17th Century.

HARRISBURG SENATORS BASEBALL

Harrisburg - PO Box 15757 Commerce Bank Park (City Island) 17105. Phone: (717) 231-4444. Web: www.senatorsbaseball.com   Admission: $3.00-$9.00

AA Class affiliate of the Washington Nationals. Meet Rascal, the mascot on Sunday afternoons.

STATE MUSEUM OF PENNSYLVANIA

Harrisburg - 3rd & North Streets - PO Box 1026 (Downtown) 17108. Phone: (717) 787-4978. Web: www.statemuseumpa.org   Hours: Tuesday-Saturday, 9:00am -5:00pm., Sunday 12:00-5:00pm. (Closed holidays except Memorial Day and Labor Day) Admission: FREE. Curiosity Connection requires small fee. Miscellaneous: Planetarium (additional charge) shows. Gift shop - we bought some neat Dinosaur DNA dust (cherry or grape flavor) to commemorate our Dino Lab experience.

The Official Museum of the Commonwealth features 4 floors of historical exhibits: Geology, Archeology (pretend to dig like the professionals - what types of things are found at a typical site?), Military (Gettysburg, etc.), Industry, The Arts, Technology. Do you know what animal has the most highly developed brain? Do you know the difference between a paleontologist and an archaeologist? Do you know what important document served as an instrument of peace during a time of great turmoil? Do you know what camp near Harrisburg had more soldiers trained and organized into regiments than any other camp during the Civil War? Do you know what kind of wagon early Pennsylvania farmers used to haul their products to market?

Our favorite was the Dino Lab - a real paleontology lab tech at work carving a skeleton from a fossil rock. It is a fascinating experience - and you can even ask questions while they work! The original charter granted to William Penn by King Charles II in 1861 is also on display. CURIOSITY CONNECTION -

Interactive Computer and dress up for kids age 7 and below. The adventure begins in a Child's Magical Bedroom and continues through secret portals leading to an entire miniature world of Curiosity. Other areas such as The Living Forest, Industry and Transportation Zone, Farm Land, Construction Zone and

...be a bee!

Art Wall allow children to discover the world around them and express their creativity through interactive play. Infants and toddlers will find activities, puzzles, puppets and more in their own special place. Kids will want to check out activities that correspond to the displays in the museum.

WILDWOOD LAKE SANCTUARY

Harrisburg - 100 Wildwood Way (Lucknow Industrial Park, north of Harrisburg Area Comm. College) 17110. Phone: (717) 221-0292. ***Web: www.wildwoodlake.org*** *Hours: Dawn to dusk. Nature Center Tuesday-Sunday 10:00am-4:00pm. Admission: FREE general admission , small fee for special programs.*

It's a 212 acre lake with wonderful walkways through marshes, meadows and woodlands. The nature center has great interactive displays for children... they take a card through the exhibit and get stamps at various stations which teach them about the wetlands while creating a picture. There's also a Discovery Room with quick, easy arts and crafts. The pathways outside are well marked, paved or mulched, and lend themselves to a lot of discovery... turtles on logs, butterflies, etc. Gift shop with exploration toys. Our relatives from Pennsylvania love this place!

SHOE HOUSE

Hellam - 195 Shoe House Road (Just south of Rt. 30, west of Hellam, north off Hwy 462) 17315. Phone: (717) 840-8339. ***Web: www.shoehouse.us*** *Hours: Wednesday-Sunday 11:00am-5:00pm (summer). Weekends 1:30-5:00pm (September, October). Admission: $2.00-$3.00 (age 4+).*

The odd shaped building seen from the Lincoln Highway was built by a shoe store chain owner as a promotional gimmick. Colonel Haines was a flamboyant millionaire aptly named the "Shoe Wizard." The house measures 48 ft. in length, 17 ft. in width at the widest part and 25 ft. in height. The interior consists of three bedrooms, two baths, a kitchen and living room. Take a personal tour of the Shoe House and view the interesting rooms on the five different levels. See the curved eating booth in the kitchen located in the heel of the shoe

...and there it is...a shoe house!

house. Count the number of stained-glass windows with pictures of shoes. Relax in the soul of the shoe with a snack and some homemade ice cream, or picnic on the grounds. Look for the shoe dog house and the shoe mailbox.

ANTIQUE AUTOMOBILE CLUB OF AMERICA MUSEUM

Hershey - 161 Museum Drive (322 East into Hershey and exit onto HERSHEYPARK Drive). Turn left onto Hershey Road (Rte. 39 West) at GIANT Center) 17033. Phone: (717) 566-7100. **Web: www.aacamuseum.org** *Hours: Daily 9:00am-5:00pm (except major winter holidays). Admission: $7.00-$9.00 (age 4+).*

What was your first car? Do you have a Dream Car? You may find them at the Museum. Museum collections currently number over 150 vehicles, at any given time, you can see 85-100 classic cars and trucks on display. The Museum's highly detailed dioramas present carefully restored vintage vehicles in elaborate scenes that bring the history of the automobile to life. From a tiny machine shop in turn-of-the-century New York to the asphalt apron of San Francisco's Golden Gate Bridge. Be sure to see the Lakeland Bus used in the Academy Award winning movie Forrest Gump. For children, the Lower Level is a place to get up close and personal with automotive stuff. In the activity room, younger visitors can ride a pedal car, do a crayon rubbing of an antique license plate and engage in a variety of hands-on projects and activities. At the Photo Stop, kids of ages can dress up in period clothing and have their picture taken sitting in a car from the Museum's sit-in fleet.

HERSHEY BEARS HOCKEY

Hershey - 100 West Hershey Park Drive (Giant Arena) 17033. Phone: (717) 534-3911. **Web: www.hersheybears.com** *Admission: $14.00-$20.00. Family Four Packs with food offered at a discount.*

AHL, Washington Capitals affiliate. Join CoCo the Bears Kids Club.

HERSHEY GARDENS

Hershey - 170 Hotel Road (on the grounds of the Hotel Hershey) 17033. Phone: (717) 534-3492. **Web: www.hersheygardens.org** *Hours: Daily 9:00am-5:00pm (April-October). Extended summer evening hours. Admission: $6.00-$10.00 (age 3+).*

This 23-acre botanical gem has over 7,000 roses and seasonal flower displays, 25,000 tulips in the spring, a Japanese garden and an outdoor Butterfly House with 400 butterflies. The Butterfly House Opens first weekend in June and will remain open through the third Saturday in September, weather permitting. The Children's Garden provides opportunities for hands-on learning, self-discovery, and fun with water features, hideaways, creatures, surprises, whimsical characters, and more all within nearly 30 themed areas.

HERSHEY MUSEUM

Hershey - 170 West Hersheypark Drive (next to arena) 17033. Phone: (717) 534-3439 or (800) HERSHEY. **Web: www.hersheymuseum.org** *Hours: Daily 10:00am-6:00pm (Summer). 10:00am-5:00pm (Winter). Admission: $7.00 adult, $6.00 senior (62+), $3.50 child (3-15).*

KISSTORY - The Story of An American Icon. From their introduction in 1907, HERSHEY'S KISSES chocolates have enjoyed a phenomenal popularity that remains to this day. Explore this fun-filled, interactive exhibit that takes a nostalgic look at one of America's most treasured treats. Learn how Mr. Hershey failed as a candy maker in Philadelphia and New York - but

became a millionaire manufacturing caramels in Lancaster, Pennsylvania. He sold that business to start a chocolate factory in his birthplace farmland. See how it developed as Hershey, Pennsylvania. (Also exhibits on Pennsylvania German and Native American clothing, tools, art). We also fell in love with the Apostolic Clock Procession which performs at 20 minutes before each hour. Notice which Apostle doesn't greet Christ. Look for the "Marys" or try to find the Devil. They've enhanced the Discovery Room - now there are more "rooms" to play 1830s Victorian Home,

the 13' clock ...built over 11 years

Kitchen, and General Store. Elsewhere in the museum, kids can "punch a real time clock" or sit in an original HersheyPark roller coaster car (kind of virtual reality).

HERSHEY TROLLEY WORKS

Hershey - (Departs at entrance to Hershey's Chocolate World) 17033. Phone: (717) 533-3000. **Web: www.hersheypa.com** *Hours: Rain or Shine. Same hours as the park. Last tour is 1 hour before closing Admission: $12.95 adult, $11.95 senior (62+), $5.95 child (3-12).*

Family adventure through America's sweetest town. Old time songs and visits throughout from famous "characters" plus lots of little-known facts about the town as you pass historic sites.

HERSHEYPARK

Hershey - 100 W. Hersheypark Drive (Off SR 743 & US 422) 17033. Phone: (800)
HERSHEY. Web: www.hersheypa.com Hours: Daily - opens at 10:30am (summer).
Weekends only (May, September). Admission: Range $25.00-$45.00 (Ages 3+).

Begin by "measuring up" for size. From "Kisses" on up, the rides are rated by candy type. 110 acre theme park with 60 rides and attractions. You'll also find: German Area, English Area, Penn Dutch Area (and food to match), a SeaLion & Dolphin Show, Night Lights Musical Laser Spectacular. 21 kiddie rides and live entertainment at Music Box Theater or the Amphitheatres. Rollercoasters you'll find include: GREAT BEAR - inverted looping roller coaster; SUPER DOOPER LOOPER - is a milder form of Great Bear; and ROLLER SOAKER - an awesome interactive water coaster. As a grand tribute to the boardwalks of the East Coast beaches, The Boardwalk At HERSHEYPARK will captivate you with over 100 fun-in-the-sun experiences--from the flavors, sounds, and activities of an old-fashioned boardwalk, to the exhilarating refreshment of five distinctive water attractions, including the largest water-play structure in the world! The entire park is very clean and the staff, friendly.

Fun with our cousins
& their good friend
"KitKat"

HERSHEY'S CHOCOLATE WORLD VISITOR'S CENTER

Hershey - 800 Park Blvd 17033. Web: www.hersheyschocolateworld.com Phone:
(800) HERSHEY. Hours: Daily 9:00am-5:00pm (everyday but Christmas). - Extended
hours for special events. Admission: FREE. Miscellaneous: 8 unique gift shops.
Food court. Chocolate Town Café. HERSHEY'S Really Big 3-D Show, an immersive
three-dimensional musical featuring the HERSHEY'S Product Characters as they
come to life for the first time on the big screen (movie charges fee).

A factory tour on an automated tram into the simulated world of chocolate production! Start at the cocoa bean plantation (rainforests and tropic) to dairy farms to making chocolate through the years at Hershey. Actual video footage of a real factory and the wonderful scent of chocolate pervades. It even gets warmer as you pass through the "roaster oven" part of the ride. Souvenir photographs are taken of the passengers in each car. You can purchase them for around $10.00 at the end of the tour. Learn why different chocolate manufacturers have different flavors (the secret is where the cocoa beans came from). The updated Chocolate Making Tour Ride is an exciting and informative immersive experience…and it ends with a free sample!

…a bunch of Hershey bar wrappers - a treat at the end of the tour…

ZOO AMERICA NORTH AMERICAN WILDLIFE PARK

Hershey - Park Avenue (opposite Hershey Park) 17033. Phone: (717) 534-3860. Web: www.hersheypa.com Hours: 10:00am-5:00pm. (Open until 8:00pm in the summer). ZOOAMERICA is open year-round except Thanksgiving, Christmas and New Year's Day. Admission: $7.50-$8.50 (age 3+)

An eleven acre North American attraction that hosts wildlife from 5 regions (200+ species). "Desert of Night" area is unique and wonderful. "Visit" with creatures of the night like owls, snakes and bats. The American crocodile exhibit and interactive Maze learning stations are newer to the zoo.

INDIAN ECHO CAVERNS

Hummelstown - 368 Middletown Road (Off I-283 and US 322 at Hummelstown / Middletown Exits) 17036. Web: www.indianechocaverns.com Phone: (717) 566-8131. Hours: Daily 9:00am-6:00pm (Summer). 10:00am-4:00pm (Spring/Fall). Call for times (Winter). Admission: $12.00 adult, $9.00 senior (62+), $6.00 child (3-11). Miscellaneous: Gift shop - Southwestern, Rocks. Pan for gems at Gem Mill Junction (open seasonally). Wagon ride to the Petting Barnyard. Playground with Indian Tepee and Conestoga Wagon.

You'll walk the same paths that the Susquehannock Indians did hundreds of years ago and be entertained with many stories and legends surrounding Indian Echo. Check out the Wilson Room and the Story of William Wilson who lived in the caverns for 19 years - "the Pennsylvania Hermit". The Indian

Ballroom is the largest room. There are 3 lakes and a variety of stalactites, stalagmites, and flowstone.

BLUE KNOB STATE PARK

*Imler - RR 1, Box 449 16655. Phone: (814) 276-3576. **Web:** www.dcnr.state.pa.us/ stateparks/parks/blueknob.aspx*

Bob's Creek is great for trout fishing and Blue Knob boasts the second highest peak in the state, which gives great views of up to 42 miles. Off-peak season, ride the ski resort's chairlift for great views. All park trails are open to mountain biking. Pool, Horse-back Riding, Down-hill Skiing, Campsites, Fishing, Winter Sports.

GIFFORD PINCHOT STATE PARK

*Lewisberry - 2200 Rosstown Road (Route 177) 17339. Phone: (717) 432-5011. **Web:** www.dcnr.state.pa.us/stateparks/parks/giffordpinchot.aspx*

Pinchot Lake is a great warm water fishery and is popular for sailing. The trails between the campground and the Conewago Day Use Area are for joint-use by hikers, cross-country skiers and bikers. Beach, Visitor Center, Boat Rentals, Horseback Riding, Sledding, Campsites, Modern Cabins, Fishing, Trails, and Cross-Country Skiing.

SKI ROUNDTOP

*Lewisberry - 925 Roundtop Road 17339. Phone: (717) 432-9631. Snow Report: (717) 432-7000. **Web:** www.skiroundtop.com*

Magic Mountain area is set aside just for kids. With its own Magic Carpet lift, your children can learn in a secure area physically separated from the other slopes. Longest Run: 4100 ft.; 15 Slopes & Trails - Skiing and Snowtubing.

BUCHANAN STATE FOREST

*McConnellsburg - 440 Buchanan Trail 17233. Phone: (717) 485-3148. **Web:** www.dcnr.state.pa.us/forestry/stateforests/forests/buchanan/buchanan.htm*

The Buchanan State Forest was named in honor of James Buchanan, 15th President of the United States. The area consists of five principle tracts that cover seventy-five thousand acres of Commonwealth owned forest lands. In Bedford County, there is a saltpeter cave within the Sweet Root Natural Area where saltpeter had been produced for gunpowder before and during the American Revolution. ATV Trails (26 miles), Fishing, Camping, Trails, and Winter Sports.

WHITETAIL SKI RESORT AND MOUNTAIN BIKING CENTER

Mercersburg - 13805 Blairs Valley Road 17236. Web: www.skiwhitetail.com Phone: (717) 328-9400.

Longest Run: 4900 ft.; 17 Slopes & Trails. Terrain Park: 1 rail, 8 snow features, and a fun box for snow tubing and snow boarding. SnowMonsters kids program.

MIDDLETOWN AND HUMMELSTOWN RAILROAD

Middletown - 136 Brown Street (SR283 to Middletown exit - Race Street Station) 17057. Phone: (717) 944-4435. Web: www.mhrailroad.com Hours: Memorial Day Weekends - October. July & August - Tuesday and Thursday also. Admission: $5.00-$10.00 (age 3+). Miscellaneous: Special event trains (see seasonal chapter). Reservations suggested.

The yard has several rail cars on display. During the ride, the train follows the towpath of the historic Union Canal and alongside the peaceful Swatara. The narrator relates the history of the Canal (completed in 1827) and the location of Canal Lock #33, as well as a century old limekiln and Horse Thief Cave. Passengers will want to have their cameras out while crossing a 35-foot bridge above the Swatara Creek. On the return trip from Indian Echo Cave Platform, you will enjoy a "sing-a-long" of tunes from the railroading days, as well as fun songs for young and old alike. Can you still "Chicken Dance"?

LITTLE BUFFALO STATE PARK

Newport - RD 2, Box 256A (PA Route 34) 17074. Phone: (717) 567-9255. Web: www.dcnr.state.pa.us/stateparks/parks/littlebuffalo.aspx

Explore historical features including a covered bridge, restored grist mill, an old farm house built on the site of a colonial tavern, and a narrow gauge railroad. Programs are offered year-round. Many programs feature Shoaff's Mill. Over 12,000 people visit the mill annually. Today, the Perry County Historical Society operates and maintains a museum and library in the farmhouse. Members volunteer to open the museum every Sunday during the summer months. For more detailed information on programs, contact the park office. Pool, Visitor Center, Year-round Education & Interpretation Center, Boat Rentals, Sledding, Fishing, and Trails.

COLONEL DENNING STATE PARK

Newville - 1599 Doubling Gap Road (Doubling Gap, North Cumberland County, along PA Route 233) 17241. Phone: (717) 776-5272. **Web: www.dcnr.state.pa.us/ stateparks/parks/coloneldenning.aspx**

The wooded park area nestles at the side of a mountain and has a scenic lake and excellent hiking trails. A hike on a 2.5 mile trail rises to Flat Rock for a beautiful vista of the Cumberland Valley. Beach, Visitor Center, Campsites, Fishing, and Cross-Country Skiing.

SHAWNEE STATE PARK

Schellsburg - Box 67 (Ten miles west of historic Bedford along Route 30) 15559. Phone: (814) 733-4218. **Web: www.dcnr.state.pa.us/stateparks/parks/shawnee.htm**

Of particular interest is Shawnee's long sand and turf beach that receives ample use between Memorial Day and Labor Day. The lake is popular for boating and fishing. Boat Rentals, Mountain Biking, Sledding, Campsites, Modern Cabins, Trails, and Winter Sports.

MARTIN'S POTATO CHIPS

Thomasville - 5847 Lincoln Highway (US Route 30) 17364. Phone: (717) 792-3565 or (800) 272-4477. **Web: www.martinschips.com** *Admission: FREE*

Enjoying the benefit of the rich loamy soil, farmers had to find ways to use their excess crops. From the farm kitchen of Harry and Fairy Martin in 1941, a unique potato chip found its way into homes. All potato chips and popcorn are made in their 40,000 sq. ft. Thomasville facility which produces over one million bags each month.

WRIGHTSVILLE CIVIL WAR DIORAMA

Wrightsville - 124 Hellam Street 17368. Phone: (717) 252-1169.   Hours: Sundays 1:00-4:00pm (March thru November, except holidays).

The diorama is a show with a sight and sound program in a restored old post office and store. The story told by the diorama is one of adventure and history. It tells how the Confederacy under General John B. Gordon reached Wrightsville in June 1863, looking for a way across the Susquehanna, the last major obstacle between them and the riches of Pennsylvania, including Harrisburg and Philadelphia. It tells of half-trained local militia, using makeshift fortifications and their efforts to stop the Confederates. Finally, it tells of the burning of the Wrightsville-Columbia Bridge, one of the longest covered bridges in the world, to stop the eastern advance of Lee's army, and the cooperation of the residents and the invaders to save the town from fire. Had the Confederates been able to cross the river at Wrightsville, it is entirely possible that the Battle of Gettysburg would not have been fought, and perhaps the Civil War would have had a different ending.

HARLEY-DAVIDSON MOTORCYCLE MUSEUM TOUR

York - 1425 Eden Road (on US30 or Exit 21 East of I-83) 17402. Phone: (877) 883-1450. Web: www.harleydavidson.com Admission: FREE Miscellaneous: Tours are wheelchair accessible. Souvenir Shop.

What little traveler hasn't seen (or better yet - heard) a Harley-Davidson motorcycle pass by? Founded in 1903, Harley-Davidson has become a passion of the American dream. See over 20 vintage and famous Harleys (Malcolm Forbes' custom bike) on the museum tour that is available for all ages (even a Kids Rally area for the little tykes). You will see photographs and videos of the 24 step manufacturing process that produces a  completed motorcycle every 6 minutes! They are so confident in their quality and reliability that the first time an engine is started (it contains over 400 parts!) is when the bike is completely finished. An associate takes a few spins around the 1 mile long test track (what a great job!) to be sure that it meets all the standards and expectations of the waiting customer. More than 3,000 employees work around the clock assembling Touring and Softail® models, as well as limited production, factory-custom motorcycles. They perform a variety of manufacturing operations - from machining, polishing and chrome plating, to forming, welding and painting. What does a doctor, a lawyer, machine operator, actor, business owner, and pastor all have in common… a Harley-Davidson motorcycle!

AGRICULTURAL & INDUSTRIAL MUSEUMS

York - 480 East Market Street / 217 West Princess Street (US30 to George Street exit, Rte. 462 into downtown) 17403. Phone: (717) 852-7007. Web: www.yorkheritage.org Hours: Tuesday-Saturday 10:00am-4:00pm. Admission: $6.00 adult, $5.00 senior (65+) & student (age 12+). One ticket for Ag & Industrial, Fire & Historical Museums. We recommend the Industrial Museum (Princess Street) for sure.

A lot of products produced here have clothed, sheltered, transported, fed, and entertained the nation. Learn how the modern day farm evolved from

York industry has reached
around the world!

the time of Native Americans. Then, go a few streets away to explore the numerous products made in York. Begin in an old gristmill (still working - you'll see), pull a factory whistle (time to go home!) or use an old rotary phone to dial up a friend next door (watch the mechanics of the operation station tapping out the numbers). The Pfaltzgraff pottery exhibit is well done with several stages of pottery being made (sometimes a potter comes in for live demonstrations). Since the Pfaltzgraff tour has age restrictions and is rather long, you may vote this exhibit more family-friendly than an actual tour. Don't forget about CAT trucks (get in the cab) and York Peppermint Patties!

YORK COUNTY HERITAGE MUSEUMS

*York - 250 East Market Street (US 30 to George Street exit, follow signs to downtown) 17403. Phone: (717) 848-1587. **Web: www.yorkheritage.org** Hours: Tuesday-Saturday 10:00am-4:00pm, Sunday Noon-4:00pm. Winter hours only weekends. Admission: $6.00 adult, $5.00 senior (65+) & student (age 12+). One ticket for Ag & Industrial, Fire & Historical Museums.*

When you venture downtown, be sure to visit the campus of historical buildings on West Market Street. These buildings include a replica of the courthouse where the Second Continental Congress met, as well as an authentic tavern dating back to 1741. A reproduction of original York village square with Bonham House (beautiful home), General Gates House, and Bobb Log House. The Golden Plough Tavern (c. 1741), the city's oldest structure, gives a taste of life during the years when the Tavern housed travelers and served local residents. The General Horatio Gates House (c. 1751): this English-style house was the General's home while he attended the Continental Congress, and is said to have been the site of LaFayette's famous toast to Washington that sent a signal to conspirators that the French would not support a plot to replace Washington with Gates. The Bobb Log House (c. 1812) is an example of the simple structures popular along the Pennsylvania frontier at the turn of the 19th century. The Horace Bonham House, with original furnishings of the artist, reveals the social and cultural changes that took place between the Civil War and the turn of the century.

YORK LITTLE THEATRE

*York - 27 South Belmont Street 17403. Phone: (717) 854-3894. **Web: www.ylt.org***

Family hits like Sound of Music and Seuss....Many productions include youth performers.

YORK COUNTY FIRE MUSEUM

*York - 757 West Market Street 17404. **Web: www.yorkheritage.org** Phone: (717) 843-0464. Hours: Saturday 10:00am-4:00pm. Closed winter. Admission: $6.00 adult, $5.00 senior (65+) & student (age 12+). One ticket for Ag & Industrial, Fire & Historical Museums.*

The Fire Museum of York County displays more than 200 years of firefighting. All seventy-two fire companies of York County are represented here, with some of them dating back to before the American Revolution. The beautiful turn-of-the-century fire house contains a series of displays of how firefighters progressed from the early Leather Bucket Brigades to Hand Drawn Carts and Pumps, to Horse Drawn Apparatus, and finally to Motorized Equipment. All  of the equipment is original and full-size. Pull a Fire Alarm Box or visit an old fashioned Fire Chief's Sleeping Quarters, complete with brass slide pole.

WOLFGANG CANDY COMPANY

*York - 50 East 4th Avenue (SR30 to North George Street - south to Fourth Avenue) 17405. Phone: (717) 843-5536 or (800) 248-4273. **Web: www.wolfgangcandy.com** Hours: Monday-Friday 8:00am-5:00pm, Saturday 9:00am-4:00pm. Admission: FREE Miscellaneous: Candy shoppe and soda fountain (Das Sweeten Haus Center). Relax on an antique stool (and watch the girls make hand dipped raisin clusters) as you enjoy a dish of Wolfgang's ice cream and sip a coffee or hot chocolate.*

When you enter the Bavarian style shop to wait for your tour, you undoubtedly first glance at the antique truck parked in the middle of the main floor. This was the original delivery truck used to sell chocolate candies door to door back in the 1920s. It is also the truck that helps "Candy Dan" in his flying video tour of the factory. If you choose not to go on the tour at all, this video is a great "birdseye view" of a tour but with a children's twist. The actual facility started in the back of the Wolfgang house and grew and grew.

I really was excited about the tour... just didn't like the hair net...

You'll pass retired family members' homes as you adorn a white hair net and walk up to the factory. Their corn starch machine is still used and original to the factory. Smell and taste samples as you go. The guide kept the kids' attention by pointing out lessons they learn in school. The girls and guys on the line must pick partners and pay attention (sound like school?). We recommend Fall through Easter as the best time to see candy and fillings actually made on the line (it's easier to understand the tour during full production). Summertime has minimal production.

SUGGESTED LODGING AND DINING

HERSHEY LODGE, **Hershey**. West Chocolate Avenue. (717) 533-3311 or **www.hersheypa.com**. A very family-friendly way to stay in the area comfortably. With lodging rates in the $100-$150 range, it includes a free shuttle to HersheyPark and other attractions, plus, free admission to Hershey Gardens (Butterfly House) and Hershey Museum (Discovery Room). You have the opportunity to make reservations for Breakfast in the Park with Hershey Characters, too. On site, at the lodge, are tennis courts, basketball courts, miniature golf, gameroom, bocce ball, bike rentals, and their fabulous pools – indoor and outdoor. Kids will like to eat at Lebbie Lebkichers casual buffet or the Bears' Den hockey-themed sports café. Watch the game on a 9'x12' video wall, check out the game room, and order from the Kids Menu (we recommend the Bear Puck Dessert). Great way to enjoy Hershey, PA without a lot of hassle.

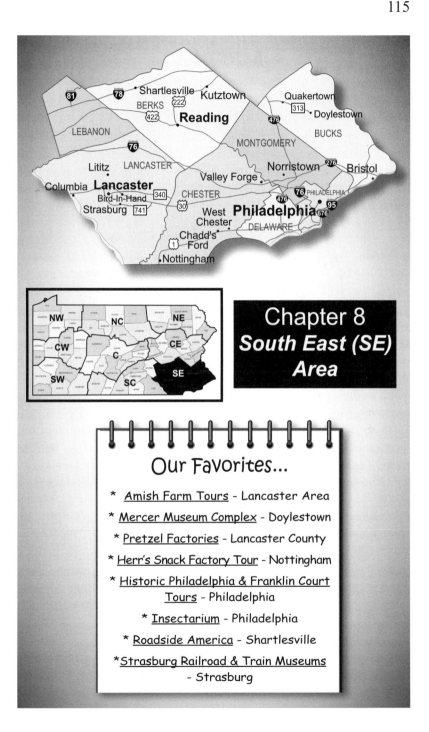

Chapter 8
South East (SE) Area

Our Favorites...

* <u>Amish Farm Tours</u> - Lancaster Area

* <u>Mercer Museum Complex</u> - Doylestown

* <u>Pretzel Factories</u> - Lancaster County

* <u>Herr's Snack Factory Tour</u> - Nottingham

* <u>Historic Philadelphia & Franklin Court Tours</u> - Philadelphia

* <u>Insectarium</u> - Philadelphia

* <u>Roadside America</u> - Shartlesville

*<u>Strasburg Railroad & Train Museums</u> - Strasburg

MILL GROVE, THE AUDUBON WILDLIFE SANCTUARY

Audubon - Audubon & Pawlings Roads 19407. Web: http://pa.audubon.org Phone: (610) 666-5593. Hours: Tuesday-Saturday 10:00am-4:00pm, Sunday 1:00-4:00pm. Admission: $2.00-$4.00 (age 4+).

Early 1800s home of noted artist, author and nature lover, John James Audubon. The house displays Audubon's paintings of birds and a complete set of his greatest work, "The Birds of America". Kids seem to admire the stuffed bird collection and birds' eggs. Grounds with nature trails and bird sanctuary are open dawn to dusk.

NESHAMINY STATE PARK

Bensalem - 3401 State Road (State Road and Dunks Ferry Road) 19020. Phone: (215) 639-4538. Web: www.dcnr.state.pa.us/stateparks/parks/neshaminy.aspx

Neshaminy State Park provides boating access to the Delaware River. The picnic areas and swimming pool are the most popular park attractions. River Walk Trail: The trailheads for both River Walk trails begin and end on Logan Walk. The River Walk Trail follows the shoreline and gives views of the river with its boating traffic, and also explores the tidal marsh. The River Trail Inner Loop explores the interior of the park and is a great way to discover animals and plants. The River Walk Brochure compares the past to the present, and describes some of the river inhabitants like sturgeon, shad and eel. Puzzles help children explore the estuary, river and tidal marsh. This self-guiding brochure is available at the park office. Fishing, Boating, Hiking, Cross-Country Skiing.

AMERICANA MUSEUM

Bird-in-Hand - 2709 Old Philadelphia Pike, Rte. 340 17505. Phone: (717) 391-9780. Web: www.bird-in-hand.com/americanamuseum/ Hours: Tuesday thru Saturday 10:00am-5:00pm (April thru November). Admission: $2.00-$4.00 (age 6+).

Step back to a time when cigars were two for a nickel, a can of soup cost a dime, and a shave was only fifteen cents. Take a nostalgic walk through small town America at the dawn of the 20th century. Museum exhibits include a barber shop, woodworking shop, tea parlor, print shop, millinery, toy store, blacksmith shop, tobacco shop, apothecary, wheelwright shop, and a country general store, where neighbors often gathered to share news and play a friendly game of checkers beside the potbelly stove. Self-guided tours are offered throughout the day.

PLAIN & FANCY FARM

Bird-In-Hand - *3121 Old Philadelphia Pike (7 miles east on SR340) 17505. Phone: (717) 768-4400 or (800) 441-3505.* **Web:** *www.plainandfancyfarm.com Hours: Monday-Saturday 8:30am-5:00pm, Sunday 10:30am-6:00pm (April-October). Extended summer hours. Monday-Sunday 10:00am-5:00pm (November-March). Admission: $5.00-$10.00 per person/ per activity (Depending on Activity). Combo pricing packages and coupons online. Miscellaneous: Plain & Fancy Restaurant - all you can eat home style meals.*

Here's what you can do (choose one or a combo):

The Amish Experience Theater ♥ Bird-in-Hand ♥ Pennsylvania

"THE AMISH EXPERIENCE" - Only one of three "experimental" F/X theatres in North America - they use actual props, 5 projectors, 3D imagery, dramatic stage lighting and "surround sound" to tell a story. The story is of an Amish family and their teenage son who is in a "runabout time" - trying to decide which world he wants to embrace. (85% of Amish teens stay within the church even after experiencing the outside world). It tells a great Amish story (past and present) and is very dramatic - probably best for ages 8 and older. **www.amishexperience.com**.

AMISH COUNTRY HOMESTEAD - see how Amish live today through a 9-room house. Learn about Amish living, furniture, chores and clothing.

AARON & JESSICA'S BUGGY RIDES - 3.5 mile buggy ride tour of Amish farmlands. Sleigh rides too (winter)! **www.amishbuggyrides.com** (717) 768-8828.

DANIEL BOONE HOMESTEAD

Birdsboro - *400 Daniel Boone Road (off US422 - 1 mile north) 19508. Phone: (610) 582-4900.* **Web:** *www.danielboonehomestead.org Hours: Tuesday - Saturday 9:00am-5:00pm, Sunday Noon-5:00pm. Closed non-Summer holidays. Reduced schedule January & February Admission: $2.00-$4.00 (age 6+). Miscellaneous: The Daniel Boone Homestead offers a variety of walking/hiking possibilities throughout the site. The gravel path winds around the historic area and is about ¾ of a mile in distance. A short trail takes you around the Lake and there are hiking/bridle trails. Daniel Boone Lake, created by damming the Owatin Creek, runs through the Homestead property. Fishing is permitted with a valid fishing license during regular visiting hours.*

Daniel Boone Homestead *(cont.)*

Born here in 1734, the birthplace interprets the colonial Pennsylvania rural life of Daniel Boone. Daniel spent his first 16 years here before his family migrated to North Carolina. Today, the site tells the story of Daniel's youth and the saga of the region's 18th century settlers by contrasting their lives and cultures. A  restored 10 room Boone homestead (originally a log cabin), a similar cabin, sawmill, smokehouse, spring kitchen, blacksmith, and barn are on site. Be sure to watch the video presentation (re-enacted) to get a sense of the Boone family's life here and out-of-state.

BOYERTOWN MUSEUM OF HISTORIC VEHICLES

Boyertown - 28 Warwick Street (SR73 and 562 - South to Warwick) 19512. Phone: (610) 367-2090. Web: www.boyertownmuseum.org/ Hours: Tuesday-Sunday 9:30am-4:00pm. Admission: $4.00-$6.00 (age 6+).

See Pennsylvania's transportation heritage - carriages, wagons, trucks, bicycles, and cars. Also on display are 18th and 19th century vehicles built by Pennsylvania Dutch craftsmen and the tools that were used to assemble them. See rare vehicles, learn about some of America's earliest auto manufacturers. See custom bodied cars by Fleetwood, steam and electric vehicle technology, high wheel bicycles, children's vehicles and tools of the craftsman.

TERRY HILL WATERPARK

Breinigsville - 10000 Hamilton Road (SR222) 18031. Web: www.terryhill.com Phone: (610) 395-0222. Hours: Daily Noon-6:00pm (June), Monday-Friday Noon-7:00pm, Weekends until 8:00pm (July & August). Admission: $10.00 -$16.00.

A family waterpark with nine different water slides (tunnel, pirate, wild river), three pools, and kiddie waterplay area. Lazy River Ride; Tarzan Rope; Hand Over Hand Rope; Lilly Pads to Run On; & 18-Hole Miniature Golf. Snack bars.

BRANDYWINE BATTLEFIELD PARK

Chadds Ford - Box 202 (US1, 1 mile east of SR100) 19317. Phone: (610) 459-3342. Web: www.ushistory.org/brandywine Hours: Tuesday - Saturday 9:00am-4:30pm, Sunday Noon-4:30pm. Admission: Grounds FREE (building tours $1.50-$3.50 per person) Miscellaneous: Museum shop. Plenty of picnic areas. Battle re-enactment every September.

Giant park and museum focused on actual Revolutionary War events. Watch the audiovisual introduction to the park first, then drive along a tour that includes 28 historic points taking you back to 1777. Remember, this defeat of American forces (led by George Washington) left the Philadelphia area open to attack and conquest by the British.

BRANDYWINE RIVER MUSEUM

*Chadds Ford - US 1 & PA Rte. 100 19317. **Web: www.brandywinemuseum.org** Phone: (610) 388-2700. Hours: Daily 9:30am-4:30pm. Closed Christmas. Admission: $8.00 adult, $5.00 student/child (age 6+).*

American art in a 19th century gristmill. Known for collections by three generations of Wyeths. The house where N.C. Wyeth raised his extraordinarily creative children and the studio in which he painted many of his memorable works of art have been restored to reflect their character in 1945, the year of the artist's death (House & Studio Tour $5.00 extra, April-November).

BYERS' CHOICE LTD

*Chalfont - 4335 County Line Road (Just north of Rt.309 & Rt. 202) 18914. Phone: (215) 822-0150. **Web: www.byerschoice.com** Hours: Monday-Saturday 10:00am-5:00pm, Sunday Noon-5:00pm (Closed major holidays).*

Family and friends (employees) hand sculpt precious Caroler figurines. By a walk-through observation deck, you can watch them mold delicate faces and then apply makeup (paint) to add dimension and features. See all the costumes and background landscapes available to make each singing doll unique. What you don't see in production that day, you can watch by pre-taped video.

FREEDOM CHAPEL DINNER THEATRE

*Christiana - 15 North Bridge Street, P.O. Box 63 (Rt. 30 East into Gap. Turn right Rt. 41 South (Newport Pike) 2 1/2 miles toward Christiana) 17509. Phone: (610) 593-7013. **Web: www.800padutch.com/z/freedomchapel.htm***

Newest theatre in Lancaster County. Intimate, up close and personal, seating only 100 with a meal served at your table. "Amish Vows in Paradise" - true, original, Amish show. Local Amish have attended, saying, "You're right on", "We love it". Broadway and original shows. (season: mid-February thru just before Christmas)

EVANSBURG STATE PARK

Collegeville - 851 May Hall Road (off US Route 422) 19426. Phone: (610) 409-1150. Web: www.dcnr.state.pa.us/stateparks/parks/evansburg.aspx

This park is a haven for hikers, equestrians and folks who want to picnic and relax. You can take a walk along Skippack Creek or visit the Friedt Visitor Center that provides insight into German Mennonite living in the 18th and 19th centuries. This farmhouse was built in the early 1700s. This historic building interprets the lifestyles of the German Mennonite families who owned the home for 190 years. Outside, the root cellar, well, and herb and sensory gardens add to the eighteenth century atmosphere. An exhibit room in the house is devoted to the natural history of the area, and the house also provides an area for visitors to watch songbirds and other animals. Fishing, Hiking, Cross-Country Skiing.

NATIONAL WATCH & CLOCK MUSEUM

Columbia - 514 Popular Street (off US30 west - follow signs) 17512. Phone: (717) 684-8261. Web: www.nawcc.org/museum/museum.htm Hours: Tuesday-Saturday 10:00am-4:00pm (year round). Sunday Noon-4:00pm (April-December). Open Tuesday-Saturday until 5:00pm (April-December). Admission: $4.00-$7.00 (age 6+). Miscellaneous: "Yours, Mine and Hours" Museum Shop. Library.

You've got the time, they've got the place! The National Association of Watch and Clock Collectors have a school (of horology), offices, and this fabulously renovated museum. One staff member described it as the "Disneyland of Clocks and Time". Start at the beginning, Stonehenge, then travel through time as you browse past displays of time-keeping history. You'll see thousands of watches (many still working), unique water and candle clocks, sundials and even an alarm clock that pinches you when it rings! Bells, chimes, music boxes, and organs sound on the hour.

WRIGHT'S FERRY MANSION

Columbia - 38 South 2nd Street (US30 - Columbia/Marietta Exit SR 441 South) 17512. Phone: (717) 684-4325. Hours: Tuesday & Wednesday, Friday & Saturday 10:00am-3:00pm, Closed July 4 (May- October). Open hours vary from year to year. PLEASE VERIFY OPEN HOURS BEFORE VISITING. Admission: $5.00 adult, $2.50 child (6-18). Group tours (Call for reservations - 30 days in advance).

Discover the fascinating and visionary life of Susanna Wright, a bright, creative Quaker woman whose diverse talents have benefited many. She ran a ferry here, was an unofficial doctor and lawyer, launched the silk industry in this region, and shared ideas with people like Ben Franklin with whom she corresponded regularly. The 1738 house reflects Quaker lifestyles prior to 1750 and its collections are one of the most complete and representative in the country. Because this is an "open" museum (no velvet ropes separating you from the displays) you certainly get the feeling that the occupants have just left for a little while…and may be returning shortly! We recommend close supervision for younger children, or better yet only bring them if your children are age 8 or older.

CORNWALL IRON FURNACE

*Cornwall - Rexmont Road - PO Box 251 (4 miles North of US76 off SR 72 on SR419) 17016. Phone: (717) 272-9711. **Web:** www.cornwallironfurnace.org Hours: Tuesday-Saturday 9:00am-5:00pm, Sunday Noon-5:00pm. Closed most holidays, except Summer holidays. Admission: $2.00-$4.00 per person (age 6+).*

A 1742 - 1833 iron making complex. The preserved facility once produced farm tools, kitchenware, stoves, cannons and ammunition. You can see the original furnace stack, blast machinery, blowing tubs, and a Great Wheel (76 feet around). Remember this site was water-powered. An ironmaster's mansion and the Charcoal House Visitor's Center are on the premises.

MARSH CREEK STATE PARK

Downingtown - 675 Park Road (two miles west of the village of Eagle on PA 100) 19335. Web: www.dcnr.state.pa.us/stateparks/parks/marshcreek.aspx Phone: (610) 458-5119.

Marsh Creek Lake is especially popular with sailboaters and windsurfers who take advantage of the prevailing wind to enjoy their sport. Nature lovers will enjoy a pleasant walk on hiking trails or the Larkins covered Bridge located in the northeast section of the park. Pool, Boat Rentals, Sledding, and Fishing.

MERCER MUSEUM

Doylestown - 84 South Pine Street (off SR202, rear SR313 and SR611) 18901. Phone: (215) 345-0210. Web: www.mercermuseum.org/mercermuseum/index.html Hours: Monday-Saturday 10:00am-5:00pm, Sunday Noon-5:00pm (open until 9:00pm on Tuesdays). Admission: $8.00 adult, $7.00 senior (62+), $4.00 youth (5-17).

The receptionist promised us that the best part of the self-guided tour was the walk into the Center Court. It's amazing! Artifacts are hanging everywhere!

While searching through junk in a barn, Henry Chapman Mercer found a jumble of objects made obsolete by the Industrial Revolution. His collection,

housed in a "cement castle", represents more than 60 crafts and trades - pre 1850. Called "The Tools of the Nation Maker", play a game to try to find one tool from at least 50 trades (every year, they produce a different themed scavenger hunt worksheet - ask for one). Some are easy to see, but over 40,000 pieces of "junk" are in every nook and cranny. In the museum's

Cool old stuff housed in a big stone castle...

Imagination Gallery, located nearby, young children can explore other hands-on activities related to the museum's collection, including puppet play, tile rubbings, puzzles, and storybooks. This is the most eccentric, yet curiously fun, museum you'll ever find! By the way, the cement and leaded glass windows truly give that medieval feeling inside and out.

MORAVIAN POTTERY AND TILE WORKS & FONTHILL

Doylestown - 130 Swamp Road/East Court Street (Court St. and Swamp Rd., off of Rte. 313, which runs north/south of Doylestown) 18901. Phone: (215) 345-6722. Web: www.cr.nps.gov/NR/travel/delaware/mor.htm Hours: Daily 10:00am-5:00pm, except Sunday Noon-5:00pm. Admission: Averages $2.00-$3.50 per person for Tile Works or $4.00-$9.00 per person for Fonthill. Discount combo pricing with Mercer Museum. Miscellaneous: Tile Shop.

This facility, beginning in 1912, produced tiles and mosaics for floors, walls and ceilings. Mercer's artistic floor tiles adorn the rotunda and halls of the Pennsylvania State Capitol, depicting 400 scenes in the Commonwealth's history. Today, the facility makes reproductions of Mercer's original line of tiles. Mercer was a visionary architect who was one of the first designers to work with reinforced concrete as a building material.

Watch the clay being prepared, then stamped with designs, then fired, glazed and fired again.

Kids will appreciate FONTHILL (Mercer's mansion/castle that is next door) or the Mercer Museum a little more if they understand what made him rich and famous. His mosaics are probably the prettiest to look at. **www.mercermuseum.org/fonthill/**

44 rooms, 18 fireplaces and more than 200 windows...

RALPH STOVER STATE PARK

Doylestown (Pipersville) - 6011 State Park Road (State Park Road and Stump Road) 18947. Web: www.dcnr.state.pa.us/stateparks/parks/ralphstover.aspx Phone: (610) 982-5560.

45 acres along the Tohickon Creek. Warm-water fish species found in Tohickon Creek include smallmouth bass, sunfish, carp and catfish. They stock trout, a cold-water fish. There is one mile of easy walking trails that pass through many habitats and near the millrace. The 'High Rocks' section of the park features an outstanding view of a horseshoe bend in Tohickon Creek and the surrounding forest.

FRENCH CREEK STATE PARK

*Elverson - 843 Park Road (off Route 345) 19520. Phone: (610) 582-9680. **Web:** www.dcnr.state.pa.us/stateparks/parks/frenchcreek.aspx*

French Creek offers two lakes - Hopewell and Scotts Run, extensive forests and almost 40 miles of hiking trails. Adjacent to the park lies Hopewell Furnace. Pool, Boat Rentals, Horseback Riding, Mountain Biking, Campsites, Modern Cabins, Fishing, and Cross-Country Skiing.

HOPEWELL FURNACE NATIONAL HISTORIC SITE

*Elverson - 2 Mark Bird Lane (PA Rt. 724 East, turn right onto PA Rt. 345 South) 19520. Phone: (610) 582-8773. **Web:** www.nps.gov/archive/hofu/index.html Hours: Daily 9:00am-5:00pm. Closed most holidays. Admission: $4.00 adult (over 17). Children FREE. Miscellaneous: Younger children would prefer summers when living history actors are in costume throughout the village. Older kids really get into the stories told on the tour.*

The Visitor's Center features an audio visual program and exhibits of the original iron castings and tools used in Colonial cold blast charcoal furnaces. See a restored cast house, water wheel cooling shed, tenant houses and ironmaster's mansion (The Big House). Learn about "pig iron" (formed in troughs), and stoves and weapons produced here - recreated by actual blacksmiths shaping the hot slabs of iron alongside molders. This is mostly a living history village (summers and special events) and the "villagers" are well educated on iron casting. Call ahead to be sure you get to see live demonstrations during your visit.

FORT WASHINGTON STATE PARK

Fort Washington - *500 Bethlehem Pike (2 miles from PA Turnpike exit 26) 19034. Web: www.dcnr.state.pa.us/stateparks/parks/fortwashington.aspx Phone: (215) 646-2942.*

This beautiful park interests historians of the American Revolution. The park takes its name from the fort built by George Washington's troops in the fall of 1777, before heading to Valley Forge. The park is popular with hikers and bikers. Birders enjoy the seasonal migration of raptors from the Observation Deck. Hawks, Washington Encampment, Fishing, Trails, Winter Sports.

MEMORIAL LAKE STATE PARK

Grantville - *RD 1, Box 7045 (I- 81 at exit 29 /Fort Indiantown Gap, take PA Route 934 North) 17028. Web: www.dcnr.state.pa.us/stateparks/parks/memoriallake.aspx Phone: (717) 865-6470.*

This quaint park has a lake for canoeing, wind surfing and fishing, and hiking trails and lots of beautiful scenery. A short woodland trail winds along the northern shoreline. The open nature of the park allows the visitor to take casual walks through most of the park. Scenic views of the lake provide a tranquil setting, especially during the spring and autumn days. Boat Rentals, Fishing, Cross-Country Skiing.

INTERCOURSE PRETZEL FACTORY

Intercourse - *3614 Old Philadelphia Pike (at Cross Keys) (at the intersection of Route 340 and Route 772 East) 17534. Phone: (717) 768-3432. Web: www.amishnews.com/ Attractions/intercoursepretzelfactory.htm Admission: FREE Miscellaneous: Snack Bar.*

How do you like your pretzels? Soft, stuffed, or hard? Plan on visiting this factory for a lunch/dessert treat. As you watch all the pretzels being made by hand and learn to twist your own pretzel...try to decide which flavors you're going to try now and which you'll take home. Their stuffed pretzels are wrapped around cheeses, meats, relishes, and jams. Soft and hard pretzels come in a variety of seasonings (doesn't brown butter topping sound warm and cozy?) and their chocolate covered varieties are smothered in Wilbur's *(our favorite in Pennsylvania)* chocolate. Do you see why we suggest to save "tummy room" for snacking?

HAWK MOUNTAIN

Kempton - 1700 Hawk Mountain Road (I-78, exit 9B north to Route 895 east) 19529. Phone: (610) 756-6961. Web: www.hawkmountain.org Hours: Daily 9:00am-5:00pm (most of year), 8:00am-5:00pm (September-November). Admission: Trail Fees (to get to lookouts): $5.00-$7.00 adult, $4.00-$7.00 senior, $3.00 child (6-12).

Between mid-August and mid-December an average 18,000 hawks, eagles, and falcons fly past this site. Bookstore. Wildlife viewing windows. Exhibits. Trails. FREE Live-raptor programs on weekends (April-November).

W.K. & S. STEAM RAILROAD

Kempton - PO Box 24 (SR143 or SR737 into Kempton. - follow signs) 19529. Phone: (610) 756-6469. Web: www.kemptontrain.com/pages/741740/index.htm Hours: Sundays (May-October), Saturdays also (July, August, October). Departures from 1:00pm-4:00pm leave every hour on the hour. Admission: $3.50-$7.00 (age 2+).

Scenic train ride on the Hawk Mountain Line. Passengers enjoy a three-mile ride to Wanamaker through Pennsylvania's picturesque countryside, passing several historic sites and structures. Nice short ride (40 minutes) where you can get off at picnic groves throughout the countryside and get back on later. Gift shop. Snack bar.

LONGWOOD GARDENS

Kennett Square - US Route 1, PO Box 501 (northeast of town) 19348. Phone: (610) 388-1000. Web: www.longwoodgardens.com Hours: Daily 9:00am-5:00pm (open later during peak Spring / Summer & Holiday seasons) Admission: $14.00 adult ($10.00 on Tuesdays), $6.00 youth (ages 16-20), $2.00 child (ages 6-15), Under age 6 FREE. Miscellaneous: Stop by the Terrace Restaurant for Kids Value Meals (offered daily). Breakfasts with the Easter Bunny and Santa, and Family Fireworks BBQs are featured seasonally by reservation.

See exotic plants from around the world, examine insect-catching plants up close, enjoy dancing fountains that shoot water 130 feet in the air, and be dazzled by 40 colorful indoor and outdoor displays every day of the year. Daily activities feature fun and educational adventures and activities for kids and families. Conservatory and rainbow fountains. Special too, are the water platters, Topiary garden and Idea Garden. Special children's programs like Peter Rabbit and Friends, Christmas and Mazes.

CRYSTAL CAVE

Kutztown - Crystal Cave Road (Off US 222. Follow signs) 19530. Phone: (610) 683-6765. Web: www.crystalcavepa.com Hours: Daily 9:00am-5:00pm (March-November) Summer to 6:00 or 7:00pm. Holidays & Weekends to 6:00pm. Admission: $6.50-$10.50 (age 4+). Miscellaneous: Food. Gift shop. Rock shop. Mini-golf. Gem Panning. Museum and nature trails.

The 45 minute tour begins with an eight minute video presentation in the theatre. Trained guides take you past milky white formations enhanced by indirect lighting. Look for the Giant's Tooth, Prairie dogs, Indian Head, Totem Pole, Natural Bridge and the Ear of Corn formations.

RODALE INSTITUTE FARM

Kutztown - 611 Siegfriedale Road (off US222, just northeast of town) 19530. Phone: (610) 683-1400. Web: www.rodaleinstitute.org Hours: Monday-Saturday 9:00am-5:00pm, Sunday 10:00am-3:00pm (early May - mid-October). Admission: Average $3.00 per person (age 5+) Miscellaneous: International Café features organic light fare and beverages. Gift shop - suggest you try homemade organic apple sauce or butter.

Regenerative Organic Farming and Gardening - Do you know what that means? If you've eaten one too many frozen or fast food meals this week - start feeling healthier here. Learn the connection between healthy soil, healthy food, and healthy people, all through demonstrations and children's gardens. A tour highlight for children is watching how earthworms help aerate and fertilize the soil. Initial shrieks turn to keen interest as the children handle the subterranean workers, feed them kitchen scraps and watch them burrow. They can then take a trip through a child-size "Earthworm Tunnel™" for a first-hand experience.

DUTCH APPLE DINNER THEATRE

Lancaster - 510 Centerville Road (off US 30 west) 17601. Web: www.dutchapple.com Phone: (717) 898-1900.

Children's matinee and Sunday twilight. Dine while watching children's musicals like Sleeping Beauty, Willy Wonka or Cinderella. Tickets range $18.00-$33.00.

HANDS-ON HOUSE CHILDREN'S MUSEUM

*Lancaster - 721 Landis Valley Road (US 30 to Oregon Pike N exit) 17601. Phone: (717) 569-KIDS. **Web: www.handsonhouse.org** Hours: Tuesday-Friday 11:00am-4:00pm, Saturday 10:00am-5:00pm, Sunday Noon-5:00pm. Open Mondays and extended hours in the summer. Closed major winter holiday times. Admission: $6.00 general. Miscellaneous: Recommended for ages 2-10. Everything is simply explained to allow parents and kids' imagination to explore possibilities.*

All of the exhibits at Hands-on House are custom-designed and unique. There exhibits include a variety of activities appropriate for children ages 2-10 years. Each exhibit has a theme with a variety of activities to do that relate to the theme. Favorite "spaces" include: a Lancaster Farming Area, Grocery Store and Art Smart Fun. In Marty's Machine Shop, you'll wear safety goggles to work on an assembly line or sort and deliver mail at a kid-friendly factory. The Space Voyage Checkpoint takes kids on a spaceship ride to learn about health and wellness as earthlings get a checkup before their journey into space. At Feelings, talk to a giant stuffed bear.

LANDIS VALLEY MUSEUM

*Lancaster - 2451 Kissel Hill Road (3 miles north on Oregon Pike - SR272) 17601. Phone: (717) 569-0401. **Web: www.landisvalleymuseum.org** Hours: Monday-Saturday 9:00am-5:00pm, Sunday Noon-5:00pm. Admission: $9.00 adult, $7.00 senior (60+), $6.00 child (6-17). Miscellaneous: Weathervane gift shop.*

The largest Pennsylvania German museum in the U.S. (100 acres). See 20 buildings including the craft shop, schoolhouse, country store, leather crafts, farmstead, blacksmith, transportation building, hotel, pottery shop plus others. Exhibits interpret rural life prior to 1900 through artisans and demonstrations of traditional skills. Special performances, craft demonstrations and living history programs change monthly. Don't  forget about the traditional walkways of dirt, pebble or brick.

AMISH FARM AND HOUSE

Lancaster - 2395 Route 30 East 17602. Web: www.amishfarmandhouse.com Phone: (717) 394-6185. Hours: Daily 8:30am-6:00pm (Summer). 8:30am-5:00pm (Spring & Fall), 8:30am-4:00pm (November-March). Admission: $7.25 adult, $6.50 senior (60+), $4.75 child (5-11) Miscellaneous: Dutch Food Pavilion (April - October). Weekend craft demonstrations (branch carvings for example). Nighttime lamp tours (late September -late October). Buggy rides.

Guided tours of an Amish home (10 rooms) - learn the history, religious customs and a simple way of life. Self-guided tour of a working farm with local crops, barns, and farm animals. Most interesting is a unique Lancaster County device - a water wheel powered pump (smaller pump in meadow) operates a larger pump via wire. In the Spring House, a large water wheel powers a pump which forces cold spring water into a kitchen refrigerator. A limestone quarry on the property supplied stone to build this barn and house. New to the property is a tour of the Amish One Room Schoolhouse.

BIBLICAL TABERNACLE REPRODUCTION / MENNONITE INFORMATION CENTER

Lancaster - 2209 Millstream Road - Off US30 17602. Web: www.mennoniteinfoctr.com Phone: (717) 299-0954. Hours: Monday-Saturday 8:00am-5:00pm (April-October). 8:30am-4:30pm (November-March). Admission: FREE for info center. Film is $2.50-$4.50 (age 7+). Tabernacle is $3.50-$6.00 (ages 7+). Miscellaneous: Gift shop featuring crafts (reproduction) from biblical times & craft kits to recreate tabernacle.

Film and displays explaining the faith and culture of Amish and Mennonites called "Postcards From a Heritage of Faith" or the 3-screen documentary from Peoples' Place, "Who are the Amish?" Shown every hour. Included is a reproduction of a Hebrew Tabernacle with lecture tours given on the history, construction, function, and significance on the hour (every 2 hours in the Winter). Most kids leave with an understanding of the Arc of the Covenant and can answer as to why the 66 lumps in the candleholder were prophecy of the future.

DISCOVER LANCASTER COUNTY HISTORY MUSEUM

Lancaster - 2249 Route 30 East 17602. **Web: www.discoverlancaster.com** *Phone: (717) 393-3679. Hours: Daily 9:00am-4:00pm. Open later in the summer and many weekends. Only closed major winter holidays. Admission: $8.50 adult, $7.25 senior (60+), $5.25 child (5-11). Miscellaneous: Gift shop.*

After you've exhausted yourself outside at Dutch ___, head next door, and inside for a little history. See 34 life ___ (diovisuals) scenes of historic events in Pennsylvani ___ the 1600s to the present. Exam ___ Treaty, Ephrata Cloister, "Pe ___ early settlers. Some of t ___ wax museum are d ___ young ones, but, aft ___ niel Boone area, the ___ look at. Press buttons f ___ ions. They even have an area wh ___ can dress as a settler like young Daniel Boone and walk in a magic booth as young Daniel turns into a man before your eyes. Next, use a large bellow to help heat the

Last minute press update: This museum closed December 30, 2006.

Settler Dressup...

blacksmith's fire or learn to twist a pretzel. Watch a 10 minute animatronics of an Amish Barn Raising - actually it takes one day in real life - a major accomplishment until you learn about their consistent, organized teamwork. There's a computer quiz at the end relating to presidents and politics (best for the tweens to adult to play).

DUTCH WONDERLAND FAMILY AMUSEMENT PARK

Lancaster - 2249 Route 30 East 17602. **Web: www.dutchwonderland.com** *Phone: (717) 291-1888. Hours: Daily 10:00am-7:00pm (Memorial Day-Labor Day), Weekends only 10:00am-6:00pm (Spring & Fall). Admission: Range $23.00-$30.00 (ages 3+). Discount packages available adding nearby attractions.*

It's a Kingdom for Kids. Come and meet "Duke The Dragon" and the "Princess of Dutch Wonderland". It's cute...with many clean, safe rides for kids (probably best age range is 4-12, with their adults). Water splash and ride areas with new features every year. Cute little interactive shows and a wonderful "High Dive" show. It's hard to believe those guys really dive from 30 to 80 feet...until you see it! Rides include: Roller Coaster, Giant Slide, Double Splash Flume, Flying Trapeze, Space Shuttle, Lady Riverboat rides, Mini-Train rides, Sky ride, and Voyager motion simulator.

Monster Truck fun...

HERITAGE CENTER MUSEUM OF LANCASTER COUNTY

Lancaster - 13 West King Street (Penn Square-Downtown) 17603. Phone: (717) 299-6440. Web: www.lancasterheritage.com Hours: Tuesday-Saturday 10:00am-5:00pm, Sunday Noon-5:00pm (mid-April-December). Admission: FREE.

You'll find out why Amish dolls have no faces, why there's an ever-watchful eye peering down from the ceiling and why the face in the tall-case clock changes from sun to moon. Focuses on local furniture, folk art and toys. Children's activity area (summertime) and self-guided Children's Guide available.

LANCASTER BARNSTORMERS PROFESSIONAL BASEBALL

Lancaster - Clipper Magazine Stadium, 650 North Prince Street 17603. Phone: (717) 509-HITS. Web: www.lancasterbarnstormers.com.

Family entertainment and exciting Atlantic League Baseball come together at state of the art Clipper Magazine Stadium in downtown Lancaster, May-September.

NORTH MUSEUM OF NATURAL HISTORY AND SCIENCE

Lancaster - 400 College Avenue (Franklin Marshall College) 17603. Phone: (717) 291-3941. Web: www.northmuseum.org Hours: Tuesday-Saturday 10:00am-5:00pm, Sunday Noon-5:00pm. Admission: $6.00-$7.00 (ages 3+). Small additional fee for planetarium.

From the foundations of our earth to the wonders of space, dinosaurs to Native Americans, hands-on discovery for children to live snakes and turtles, the

North Museum offers fun learning experiences about science and the natural world. Child's Discovery Room. Planetarium shows weekend afternoons.

WHEATLAND

Lancaster - *1120 Marietta Avenue (PA 23 off US30 west) 17603. Phone: (717) 392-8721.* **Web: www.wheatland.org** *Hours: Daily 10:00am-4:00pm, except Sunday opens at Noon (April-October) plus long weekends in November (Friday-Monday). Admission: $7.00 adult, $6.00 senior, $5.00 student, $2.00 child (6-11). Miscellaneous: Gift shop. Snack bar.*

The Federal Style mansion was home to the nation's 15th President (and the only President from Pennsylvania), James Buchanan. Tours begin in the

carriage house where you view a film about Mr. Buchanan and see the actual carriage his family used to travel around town. Also, see the library that served as a headquarters for his Presidential campaign. Kids are invited to dress in top hats

or hoop skirts and may be asked questions like, "How often did people take baths in the mid-1800s?" Guess? (Answer - An average of 2 times per year!) His response to inquiries about "Wheatland" was…"I am now residing at this place, which is an agreeable country residence…I hope you may not fail to come this way…I should be delighted with a visit…"

AMERICAN MUSIC THEATRE

Lancaster - *2425 Lincoln Highway East (US 30) 17605. Phone: (717) 397-7700 or (800) 648-4102.* **Web: www.amtshows.com**

American Sights. American sounds. American Songs. American spirit. Musicals plus 30+ celebrity concerts year round. Morning, matinee and evening shows. Spring thru the Holidays. $19.00-$37.00 avg. Friday Family Night Rates (discounted early shows).

NATIONAL CHRISTMAS CENTER

Lancaster (Paradise) - 3427 US 30 (Lincoln Highway) 17562. Phone: (717) 442-7950. Web: www.padutch.com/z/nationalchristmasctr.htm Hours: Daily 10:00am -6:00pm (May - first week of January). Open weekends in March & April. Admission: $9.50 adult, $5.00 child (3-12). Miscellaneous: Santa visits November 20th - December 23rd. Gift shop.

As you enter, you're greeted by a cute 1950s Christmas morning scene as a little boy opens and tries on his new cowboy outfit. Another scene depicts "Yes Virginia, There is a Santa Claus". Can you find Santa patiently waiting

for a little girl to go to bed? This scene depicts a Christmas 100 years ago. Life cast artists create theme walk-thru displays with story lines. "Tudor Towne" is of Jolly Old England, a Once-Upon-A-Time World. "Return to Christmas Past" features antiques dating back to the early 1800s . "The First Christmas" probably has the most impact as you walk down a life-size recreation of the journey of Mary and Joseph to Bethlehem. It's very touching.

HANS HERR HOUSE

Lancaster (Willow Street) - 1849 Hans Herr Drive (between Pennsylvania route 741 / U.S. route 222 (Beaver Valley Pike) and Penn Grant Road) 17584. Phone: (717) 464-4438. Web: www.hansherr.org Hours: Monday-Saturday 9:00am-4:00pm (April-November). Admission: $5.00 adult, $2.00 child (7-12).

The 1719 Hans Herr House, built in that year by Hans' son Christian, is the oldest surviving dwelling place of European settlers in what is now Lancaster County, Pennsylvania. It is the oldest still-standing Mennonite meeting house in the Western Hemisphere. The 1719 House, or "Hans Herr House" as it is known locally, was a home to several generations of Hans Herr's family until the 1860s, after which it was used as a barn and storage shed. It was restored to colonial-era appearance in the early 1970s. It is now part of a Museum complex which includes three Pennsylvania German farmhouses, several barns and other outbuildings, and an extensive collection of farm equipment spanning three centuries.

TYLER STATE PARK

Langhorne (Newtown) - 101 Swamp Road (Follow I-95 north to the Newtown-Yardley exit 30) 18940. **Web: www.dcnr.state.pa.us/stateparks/parks/tyler.aspx** *Phone: (215) 968-2021.*

The meandering waters of Neshaminy Creek flow through the park along with 10 miles of paved bicycling trails, a playhouse - -Spring Garden Mill, and several children's play areas. Boat Rentals, Horseback Riding, Fishing, Trails, Winter Sports.

STURGIS PRETZEL

Lititz - 219 East Main Street (Route 772 - off Route 501) 17543. Phone: (717) 626-4354. **Web: www.sturgispretzel.com** *Hours: Monday-Saturday, 9:00am-5:00pm generally. Closed Sundays and winter Mondays. Admission: General $2.00-$4.00 (A pretzel is given as your admission ticket. Be careful not to eat it all before the tour starts!) Miscellaneous: Gift shop with all sorts of fresh baked pretzels (flavorings, galore!) to purchase.* **(early 2007 update - temporarily closed for renovations. Check website for updates)**.

Boy, did the memories flow at this place! Over 20 years ago, my family (Michele's) took the same tour, in the same building and I still have my "Official Pretzel Twister" *(see right)* certificate. (By the way, they still do that - our daughter now has one too!). This is the first pretzel bakery in America (1861) and they still make their original soft pretzel by hand in the original 200 year old ovens. Julius Sturgis started the pretzel industry with a recipe he learned from a hobo. Learn the history of the "pretiola" derived from monk's gifts to nearby children if they said their prayers. As you learn to fold your own pretzel, you'll learn how each step is related to prayer or marriage or the trinity. Definite "must see" while in Amish country.

Michele & her brother & sister (left) and Jenny (right) earning their official Pretzel Twister Certificate...

WILBUR CHOCOLATE AMERICANA MUSEUM

Lititz - *48 North Broad Street* - *(Route 501)   17543. Web: www.wilburbuds.com* Phone: *(717) 626-3249. Hours: Monday-Saturday 10:00am-5:00pm. Admission: FREE Miscellaneous: Gift shop - suggest chocolate pretzels or Wilbur Buds (free sample).*

Candy Americana Museum - antique metal molds, tin boxes, advertisements. View Video – "The World Of Wilbur Chocolate" - see smooth chocolate made from the start. Pass by the Candy Kitchen where specialty candy is hand-made right before your eyes. Pick up a 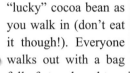 "lucky" cocoa bean as you walk in (don't eat it though!). Everyone walks out with a bag full of store bought variety chocolates. P.S. - For a walk back in time, try their hot cocoa mix that you prepare over a stove - it's worth shoveling snow just to enjoy entering a warm house full of an aroma of the rich liquid chocolate.

Famous, yummy
Wilbur Buds

RIDLEY CREEK STATE PARK

Media - *Sycamore Mills Road (entrances on PA3, PA 252 or PA352) 19063. Phone: (610) 892-3900. Web: www.dcnr.state.pa.us/stateparks/parks/ridleycreek.aspx*

Shaded equestrian, hiking and bicycling trails lace the woodlands and old meadow. Within the park is the Colonial Pennsylvania Plantation that depicts a Delaware County Quaker farm prior to the American Revolution. On weekends from April to November, visitors can observe the farm family cooking over the open hearth, preserving foods, processing textiles, tending field crops and performing other chores necessary for survival in the 18th century world (small fee, 610-566-1725). Fishing and Winter Sports.

PENNSBURY MANOR

Morrisville - *400 Pennsbury Memorial Lane (on the Delaware River) 19067. Phone: (215) 946-0400. Web: www.pennsburymanor.org Hours: Tuesday-Saturday 9:00am -5:00pm, Sunday Noon-5:00pm (open Summer holidays). Admission: $5.00 adult, $4.50 senior, $3.00 child (6-17) . Miscellaneous: Best for kids to visit (April - October) Sundays for living history days. Picnic areas.*

A quaint, Quaker, simple homestead of William Penn, the founder of Pennsylvania. See a replica of the boat Penn used to "commute" to Philly. They may be baking bread (up to 30 loaves at one time!) in the bake house or checkout the farm where sheep and geese roam. Inside the Visitor's Center, try writing with the original "pen" - a quill pen. You can also learn about Colonial James writing style here.

NEW HOPE AND IVYLAND RAILROAD

New Hope - PO Box 634 (Depot at West Bridge and Stockton Street) 18938. Phone: (215) 862-2332. **Web: www.newhoperailroad.com** *Hours: Daily (April-Holidays). Admission: Anywhere from $5.00 to $30.00 per ticket.*

This ride is famous for the trestle called "Pauline" upon which actress Pearl White was bound to in the 1914 silent film "The Perils of Pauline". It might be the best way to expose young kids to the silent movies era (pictures available at the depot, too).

NEW HOPE BOAT RIDES

New Hope - 18938.

CORYELL'S FERRY HISTORIC BOAT RIDES. 22 South Main Street at Gerenser's Ice Cream. (215) 862-2050 or **www.spiritof76.com** - 1/2 hour tours on path once used to commute passengers by canoe (now they use paddleboats). (April - October)

WELLS FERRY - Ferry Street and River Road. (215) 862-5965 OR **www.wellsferry.com**. Guided tour on a 36 passenger boat highlighting history of river and canal plus famous homes and wildlife. Admission. (May - October)

ELMWOOD PARK ZOO

Norristown - 1661 Harding Blvd (I76 to Rte. 202 to Johnson Hwy.) 19401. Phone: (610) 277-BUCK. **Web: www.elmwoodparkzoo.org** *Hours: Daily 10:00am-5:00pm. Closed major winter holidays. Admission: $6.50-$9.00 (ages 2+). Miscellaneous: Pony rides add $2.00 (seasonally). Snack shop. Gift shop. Picnic area.*

Highlights of the zoo include: Petting Barn (goats & sheep), Duck Lake, Prairie Dog exhibits, and Aviary Wetland (waterfowl, beaver, otters), The Bayou (murky home to lovely alligators, turtles, and snakes - everything that hisses or snaps!). There's also your basic natural Grasslands (bison, elk, and new "bears" area). Animal shows on Summer weekends.

HERR'S SNACK FACTORY TOUR

Nottingham - PO Box 300 (US 1 and SR272 to Herr Drive) 19362. Phone: (800) 63-SNACK. **Web: www.herrs.com** *Admission: FREE. Miscellaneous: Gift shop. Chippers Café with crunch and munch lunchroom. Very reasonable snack bar prices.*

There's no fake machinery or actors - it's the REAL factory, the REAL workers, and the REAL process. "Watch a groovy-chip movie" starring "Chipper" your tour guide and mascot. The whimsical (combination guide

and TV monitor) tour takes you through the simple process of snack food production. Lots of hot oil and hot air drying, moisturizing and "spritzing" going on - a salon for snacks! Try samples warm off the "beltway" - those were a favorite point of the tour. Yes, you can have more than one! Also see other snacks made like cheesepuffs (corn meal dollops filled with air), tortilla chips, popcorn (huge poppers!) and pretzels. Your kids

Jenny ♦ Daniel and their good friend "Chipper"

will be amused at the sideway mixers churning out 10 pound mounds of pretzel dough. The dough takes a long trip on a conveyor and then a "dough-bot" (robot) removes them to be shaped & baked. An excellent, organized tour - voted our best pick of snack food tours.

PHILADELPHIA SPORTS

Philadelphia - . .

KIXX SOCCER - MISL - Major Indoor Soccer League. May-September. Wachovia Complex. **www.kixxonline.com**. Look for their mascot, SocceRoo.

PHILADELPHIA 76ers BASKETBALL - www.nba.com/sixers. Wachovia Complex. National Basketball Association. Family Pack Nights.

PHILADELPHIA EAGLES FOOTBALL -www.philadelphiaeagles.com. Lincoln Field. NFL Professional football team (August-December). Meet and greet players at the annual Eagles Carnival in August.

PHILADELPHIA FLYERS HOCKEY - www.philadelphiaflyers.com. Wachovia Complex. National Hockey League (October-March).

PHILADELPHIA PHILLIES BASEBALL - www.phillies.com. Citizens Bank Park. National League East. Take a romp in the Phanatic Phun Zone, the largest Softplay area for kids in Major League Baseball. Take a stroll through Ashburn Alley, an outdoor entertainment area. Features include the All-Star Walk, Citizens Bank Games of Baseball, Memory Lane, Rooftop Bleacher Seats, Wall of Fame, Alley Store, and more! Opens 2 1/2 hours prior to game time so fans can watch batting practice.

PHILLY TRANSPORTATION TOURS

Philadelphia - (Downtown). Admission: Call for rates. Pay as you board.

PHILADELPHIA TROLLEY WORKS ('76 Carriage Company): www.phillytour.com. This longtime Philadelphia company offers several exciting options for touring town, including Victorian Trolley Tours, Horse Drawn Carriage Tours, LandShark Tours and Double Decker Bus Tours. Entertaining staff will treat you to a fun and informative trip around the city. Both day and evening tours available, and take advantage of free daytime shuttle service.

PHILLY PHLASH - (215) 4-PHLASH. Purple and teal buses run in a loop around downtown.

RIVERLINK FERRY - (215) 925-LINK. Passenger ferry across the Delaware River between Penn's Landing and the Camden waterfront sites.

BIG BUS TOURS - www.bigbustours.com. Now you can experience the unique history and beauty of Philadelphia from an authentic London-style double-decker bus. An open-top tour of the city offers you spectacular views and make sure your ears are tuned in to the entertaining live commentaries from fully-trained and friendly guides.

PHILADELPHIA ORCHESTRA

*Philadelphia - 260 South Broad Street, 16th Floor (most performances at Kimmel Center) 19102. Phone: (215) 893-1900. **Web: www.philorch.org***

Sound All Around Series (ages 3-5), learn about the different families of instruments. Family Concert Series (ages 6-12) - music featuring puppets, magicians, storytellers, and young soloists. (Saturday mornings).

ACADEMY OF NATURAL SCIENCES

Philadelphia - 1900 Benjamin Franklin Parkway (off I-76 and corner of 19th Street) 19103. Phone: (215) 299-1000. Web: www.acnatsci.org Hours: Monday-Friday 10:00am-4:30pm, Saturday, Sunday & Holidays 10:00am-5:00pm. Closed Thanksgiving, Christmas, and New Year's Day. Admission: $10.00 adult, $8.00 senior (65+), $8.00 child (3-12). Part of CityPass discount card. Miscellaneous: Ask for Scavenger Hunts sheets (age appropriate) when you enter. The kids stay focused this way. Films show daily. Ecology Café and gift shop.

The oldest dinosaur and natural science exhibit in the world is here. Actually peer into, or walk under, dinosaurs. You're greeted by a roaring robotic

dinosaur at one entrance. A giant dinosaur skeleton hangs over the information desk at the main entrance. Most families' favorite area is the Dinosaur Hall. This is hands-on paleontology including a fossil dig (child equipped with goggles and tools), fossil prep lab, and Time Machine (get your picture image appearing with dinosaurs!). You'll also meet T-Rex, plus 11 friends, and even get to climb into a dinosaur skull. The North American Hall has some

"Friendly" dinosaurs everywhere...

stuffed large animals that are almost 200 years old. Butterflies!, a completely redesigned permanent exhibit, features a lush, tropical garden filled with colorful plants and a multitude of exotic butterflies from around the globe. Educational demos and computer interactives add to this Metamorphysis space ($2.00 extra admission). There are live animals shows and "Outside In"... hands-on, touching mice, snakes, frogs, and huge bugs. Touch a real meteorite, view a stream from underneath, crawl through a fallen log, look for fossil footprints, pan for shark teeth, watch a working beehive, build a sandcastle or read a book on Lucy's Back Porch. There's also a crystals and gems exhibit that features a 57 pound amethyst and "Living Downstream" - a showcase of life in a watershed or Egyptian Mummies.

FRANKLIN INSTITUTE SCIENCE MUSEUM

Philadelphia - 222 North 20th Street (intersection of 20th Street and the Benjamin Franklin Parkway, downtown) 19103. Phone: (215) 448-1200. Web: www.fi.edu Hours: Daily 9:30am-5:00pm. Admission: $13.75 adult, $11.00 child (4-11) and senior (62+). Sci-Pass includes museum, science demos, and planetarium. IMAX and *special exhibits extra. Miscellaneous: Ben's Bistro - Lunch, Café, Museum Stores. Special exhibits change in the Mandell Center. IMAX Theatre (additional charge). Science Park out back (open May-October).*

What began as a national memorial to Ben Franklin is now a hands-on exhibit and demonstration complex. At the entrance are displays of some of Franklin's personal effects and a famous statue by James Earle Fraser. Some exhibits have been there forever. Walk through a "Human Heart" - hear a heart beating as "blood" races through the arteries. Also, see a full-size train or airplane cockpit! Learn how Sports and Physics mix or how Art & Physics collide. Here's a look at other areas:

SPACE COMMAND - Visit a research station right here on Earth! Locate your house using a satellite home-tracking device! Travel through time to

uncover what our ancestry thought about space! Embark on a mission to discover a lost, unmanned space probe! Check out equipment used by real astronauts to explore space!

KIDSCIENCE CENTER - Flight and optical illusions. Planetarium. Interactive Franklin… he's electric! Liquid air show - weather.

OMNIVERSE THEATER - 180 degree field of view motion picture made for all age groups. Titles vary seasonally.

PLEASE TOUCH MUSEUM

Philadelphia - 210 North 21st Street (21st and Race Streets) 19103. Phone: (215) 963-0667. Web: www.pleasetouchmuseum.org Hours: Daily 9:00am-4:30pm. Open until 5:00pm during the summer. Admission: General $9.95 (over age 1). Miscellaneous: Strollers are NOT permitted on the gallery floor, but may be parked on the first level at the start of your visit; Snuglies® are available for use, free of charge. Education Store - take ideas from the museum home as souvenirs or projects. Barnyard Babies for kids 3 and under.

A hands-on museum for kids 8 and under with activities that are educational, fun, and safe. Here are the highlights to look forward to:

SENDAK - You probably recognize the name - does "Where the Wild Things Are" book ring a bell? Maurice Sendak's (Philadelphia native) popular books come to life as Max's giant bedroom is filled with jungle life. Children use fantasy play and daydreams to respond to feelings like anger and joy.

Please Touch Museum *(cont.)*

MOVE IT! - Hop in a real full-sized bus or monorail. Learn to sail a boat or fill up your tank at the service station.

SUPER MARKET SCIENCE - Shop and cook in a child sized, fully stocked grocery store, kitchen, and food science lab. Use a microscope or magnifying glass to examine those foodstuffs more closely.   **Move it!**

ALICE IN WONDERLAND - The tale is explained in miniature (little doors to peek through) and then full size. Try on cover ups and pretend you're the Queen of Hearts ready for a tea party with Mad Hatter & rabbit (a great photo opportunity!).

Although the setups are classic in here, the fresh aspects of creativity through role playing are really different. It's pricier than most kid's museums we've been to in our travels, but its uniqueness is worth it - be sure to take advantage of science park (free with admission) across the street.

SCIENCE PARK

Philadelphia - (21st Street between Winter & Race Streets) 19103. . Hours: Daily 10:00am-3:00pm, weather permitting - (May-October) Admission: Included with either "Please Touch Museum" or "Franklin Institute Museum" admission.

A 38,000 square foot learning playground. Climb on and over high tech learning structures like mazes and optical illusions. Sky bike, miniature golf, radar detector and echo chambers. Its bright colors and unusual shapes entice kids.

PHILADELPHIA ZOO

Philadelphia - 3400 West Girard Avenue (I-76, exit 36) 19104. Phone: (215) 243-1100. Web: www.phillyzoo.org Hours: Daily 9:30am-4:30pm (March-November). Daily 9:30am-4:00pm (December-February). Closed Thanksgiving, December 24, 25 and 31 plus New Years Day. Admission: $16.95 adult, $13.95 child (2-11) Zoo. $5.00-$10.00 Zooballoon Ride. Parking $10.00. Miscellaneous: Zoo shop. McDonald's restaurants. Victorian picnic groves. Stroller and wheelchair rentals.

Camel, elephant and pony rides and "Treehouse" interactive areas have additional fees. Behind-the-Scenes tours available occasionally. Dodge Wild Earth. Kids and grown-ups can climb inside one of the award-winning Dodge Wild Earth Durango adventure simulators for a thrilling 3-D ride through the plains of Africa.

The first zoo in the country - now has 1600 animals on 42 acres of beautiful landscape. Favorites include the famous white lions, Jezebel and Vinkel, the first white lions ever to be exhibited in North America. Presently, there are no white lions in the wild. Big Cat Falls! - home to endangered big cats from around the world, including three new playful snow leopard cubs, three adorable new puma kittens and a beautiful new black jaguar cub. Carnivore Kingdom has the country's only giant otters. Bear Country allows you to interact (viewing , that is) with playful bears that love to show off. The Children's Zoo has your typically petted animals plus cow-milking and other live demonstrations in the pavilion. The first passenger carrying balloon in the world to be located at a zoo is available for rides (Zooballoon).

UNIVERSITY OF PENNSYLVANIA MUSEUM OF ARCHAEOLOGY & ANTHROPOLOGY

*Philadelphia - 3260 South Street (I-76 to South Street exit to 33rd and Spruce Streets) 19104. Phone: (215) 898-4001. **Web:** www.upenn.edu/museum Hours: Tuesday-Saturday 10:00am-4:30pm, Sunday 1:00-5:00pm (Closed Mondays, Holidays, and summer Sundays from Memorial Day to Labor Day) Admission: $8.00 adult, $5.00 senior (62+) and student (age 6+). Miscellaneous: Snack café. Pyramid Gift Shop. Most fun to come during a Family Fun Day Event (215) 898-4890.*

Exhibits outstanding findings from Ancient Egypt, Asia, Central America, North America, Mesopotamia, Greece, and Africa, uncovered by University staff and student expeditions. See a giant Sphinx and real mummies. The stories of the archeologists' thoughts and accompanying pictures of "digs" might inspire a budding career.

ATWATER KENT, MUSEUM OF PHILADELPHIA

*Philadelphia - 15 South 7th Street 19106. **Web:** www.philadelphiahistory.org Phone: (215) 922-3031. Hours: Wednesday-Sunday 1:00pm-5:00pm. First Friday, 5:00-8:00pm, free and open to the public. Admission: $5.00 adult, $3.00 senior and youth (13-17).*

Whatever history you don't catch visiting buildings in the area, you'll get a touch of here. Included are: the wampum belt received by William Penn from the Lenni Lenape at Shakamaxon in 1682, the first German Bible in North

America printed by Christopher Saur in 1743, personal items from Benjamin Franklin, and Phillies' Mike Schmidt's game-worn jersey. You'll also see Norman Rockwell's America showcasing all 322 magazine covers created by the country's most admired 20th-century illustrator for The Saturday Evening Post. Family Programs - toys of the past, hat making, children of the past.

BETSY ROSS HOUSE

Philadelphia - 239 Arch Street, Historic area (Between 2nd & 3rd Streets) 19106. Phone: (215) 686-1252. **Web: www.ushistory.org/betsy/** *Hours: Tuesday-Sunday & Monday Holidays 10:00am-5:00pm. Also open summer Mondays. Closed Thanksgiving, Christmas and New Years. Admission: Donations. Miscellaneous: Ask for the "house hunt" sheet for kids.*

In 1777, the first American flag made by Colonial Mrs. Ross was sewn here. You can tour her modest, working class home. Did she design the flag? Each

room has a description, in Betsy's words (in old English), of what led up to her sewing the flag. She and the fellas that made the Liberty Bell were just ordinary folks who had a skill needed to enhance the cause of Independence. What was considered a routine job lead to national recognition many years later!

CARPENTER'S HALL

Philadelphia - 320 Chestnut Street, Historic area 19106. Phone: (215) 925-0167. **Web: www.ushistory.org/carpentershall/** *Hours: Tuesday-Sunday 10:00am-4:00pm (Closed January & February Tuesdays). Admission: FREE*

Displays of early carpenter's chairs and tools used by the First Continental Congress in 1774. A 10 minute video chronicles the history of the carpenter's company (they still own and operate the hall).

CHRIST CHURCH

Philadelphia - 20 North American Street 2nd Street (between Arch & Market Streets) 19106. Phone: (215) 922-1695. **Web: www.christchurchphila.org** *Hours: Monday-Saturday 9:00am-5:00pm, Sunday 1:00-5:00pm (March-December). Wednesday-Sunday (Rest of year). Admission: Donation. Miscellaneous: Services (Episcopal) held on Sunday mornings and Wednesday at 12:00pm.*

Fifteen signers of the Declaration of Independence worshiped here including George Washington and Benjamin Franklin. A brass plaque marks each pew of famous Colonists including Betsy Ross. The church was built in 1727 and originally had dirt or wood floors. Ask a guide what those marble rectangles are in the floor. Careful - though they won't mind…you may be stepping on the memory of a notable patron of the church!

DECLARATION (GRAFF) HOUSE

Philadelphia - 7th & Market Streets 19106. Phone: (215) 597-8974. **Web:** *www.nps.gov/inde/declaration-house.html Hours: Generally 9:00am-Noon. Vary by season. (Call ahead) Admission: FREE*

Catch the short video and then see the rooms that Continental Congress delegate, Thomas Jefferson rented in this building where he penned the actual Declaration of Independence. Like the other buildings in this national park, our history studies come alive in these authentic places where great men once walked, worked, and lived.

FIREMAN'S HALL

Philadelphia - 147 North 2nd Street (Historic district near Elfreth's Alley) 19106. Phone: (215) 923-1438. **Web:** *www.firemanshall.org Hours: Tuesday-Saturday 10:00am-4:00pm. Admission: FREE*

An 1876 firehouse depicts the history of firefighting. See memorabilia, films, and early equipment. Did your kids know Benjamin Franklin founded the first Philadelphia Fire Department in 1736? See old-fashioned leather buckets, fire wagons and an "around the world" display of firefighter helmets. Play pretend in the re-created living quarters or steer a fireboat. Taped firemen's stories recall high level exciting moments on the job. The Spider Hose Reel (1804) has a chariot look with brass bells and shiny mirrors. Also be on the lookout for the fire pole and injured firemen's hats (charred & broken).

FRANKLIN COURT

Philadelphia - 3rd, 4th, Chestnut & Market Streets (Chestnut or Market Street entrance) 19106. Phone: (215) 597-8974. **Web:** *www.nps.gov/inde Hours: Usually daily 10:00am-5:00pm but can vary. Call for details. Admission: FREE*

Today the site contains a steel "ghost structure" outlining the spot where Franklin's house stood and features an underground museum with a film and displays about his personal life. Check out Franklin's numerous inventions, then walk and talk in the Phone Room where dozens of phones can call famous friends of Franklin. Hear "voices" of historic men such as Thomas Jefferson and Mark Twain talk about Franklin and how they felt about his character. In the courtyard, peek in the pits below to see actual excavations of rooms of Franklin's home. "Bump into" Mr. Franklin as you roam his court and he'll invite you to gather around to hear stories of his life. What a wonderful way to study this amazing historic man!

Once owned by Ben Franklin who lived in Philadelphia from 1722-1790, the complex of buildings also includes:

NEWSPAPER OFFICE - Working reproduction of 1785 printing press and bindery.

POST OFFICE - In 1775, Ben Franklin was appointed as the first Postmaster General. The name "Free Franklin" was used as the hand cancellation signature because Mr. Franklin was referring to America's struggle for freedom. See actual hand-canceled letters, then, purchase a post card & send it from this working post office!

INDEPENDENCE HALL

*Philadelphia - 5th & 6th Streets on Chestnut 19106. Phone: (215) 965-7676. **Web:** www.independencehall.org   Hours: Daily 9:00am-6:00pm.   Admission: FREE*
Miscellaneous: Congress Hall (where the first US Congress met and inaugurations of Presidents occurred) and Old City Hall (Supreme Court original house) are across the street. Hours vary but it is a must see for kids studying the setup of the United States Government.

Hey…this is the place that we see in countless movies and pictures. You will get a patriotic chill as you enter the hall where the Declaration of Independence was adopted and the U.S. Constitution was written. The Assembly Room looks just as it did in 1776 (you'll feel like you're in a movie) and you can see the original inkwell the Declaration signers dipped quills in to sign the famous freedom document.

INDEPENDENCE SEAPORT MUSEUM

*Philadelphia - 211 South Columbus Blvd, Penns Landing (I-95 exit 20) 19106. Phone: (215) 925-5439. **Web: www.phillyseaport.org** Hours: Daily 10:00am-5:00pm. Closed major winter holidays. Admission: $9.00 adult, $8.00 senior (65+), $6.00 child (5-12). Miscellaneous: The Museum Store. Ask about the Philadelphia Citypass - it's a great value if you're seeing more than just historic area. Family Saturdays at the Seaport is a program where kids craft while pretending to be a pirate or ship captain.*

"Climb in, Pull this, Please"…are common signs here (hands on area). For example, ride a waterbed boat, blow a fog horn, play the Crane Game or Climb aboard bunks on a ship. In clever dioramas, hear and see immigrant and crew stories. Take a few moments to watch and talk to boat builders as they build skiffs, then head

"Everyone remain calm!" screams Capt. William…

outdoors to the walk-on battleship Olympia and submarine Becuna. This is what the kids really come for! Self-guided tour lets kids "feel" like sailors, captains, or pirates. The kids will move quickly following the self-guided arrows so try to keep up! Be prepared, they may want to tour again, and again.

History lessons are woven between these additional exhibits:

WHAT FLOATS YOUR BOAT? - Put weights in different places on a model boat to study its center of gravity, or pull different shapes through a ten-foot tank of water to examine how drag affects speed. Assemble a four-foot wooden boat puzzle. And further on, the curious can walk or crawl through a full size replica of a 22-foot 19th century Delaware River Shad Skiff.

DIVERS OF THE DEEP - Diving gear and underwater archeology.

INDEPENDENCE VISITOR CENTER (FOR THE NATIONAL HISTORICAL PARK)

Philadelphia - *One North Independence Mall West (northeast corner of 6th & Market Sts - across from the Liberty Bell) 19106.* ***Web: www.nps.gov/inde*** *Phone: (215) 597-8974. Hours: Daily 9:00am-7:00pm. Extended summer hours. Admission: FREE Miscellaneous: This is where to park (below center) and purchase tickets or schedule times for tours. Plan to spend 5-8 hours in the Independence Historical Park. Audio Walk & Tour Historic Philadelphia. CDs and players are available to rent.*

Start here before you explore the well-known sites. See award winning historical and tourism films shown throughout the day. Ben Franklin, George Washington, John Adams and others come back to life to tell the Independence story. Older children will want to sign up for the walking tour here (little ones up to grades 1 or 2 will want to wander at their own pace and usually aren't interested enough to stay with the group). To keep attention spans high, we noticed they create a theme (seasonally) of historical significance. Actors called "Town Criers" present impromptu conversations and "street stage" presentations along with that theme. They admired our "carriage" (known to you and me as a wagon) and our "horse" that was pulling it (Daddy!) Most events are daily in the summer and weekends the rest of the year.

LIBERTY BELL

*Philadelphia - 6th Street, between Market and Chestnut Streets (across from Independence Hall, entrance on Market Street) 19106. **Web: www.nps.gov/inde** Phone: (215) 597-8974. Hours: Daily 9:00am-6:00pm. Admission: FREE Miscellaneous: Glass encased bell is viewable 24 hours a day. Interpretive kiosk displays explain details of the Bell.*

Made a few blocks away by two crafters who only made pots and pans (usually), its famous "crack" has many folklore stories associated with it.

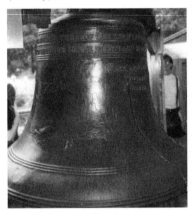

It would be nice to believe that each crack was the result of zealous ringing; however, it just wasn't cast properly to withstand its large size and temperature variances. Initially, it was just a bell ordered to be placed in the tower of the meeting hall (now called Independence Hall). Later, abolitionists used it as a symbol of freedom for slaves and proclaimed it the Liberty Bell (not until 1840 though!) - and the name stuck! It'll give you goosebumps to stand inches from it. Be sure to take advantage of the photo opportunity time provided by park rangers.

So close to history...

LIGHTS OF LIBERTY

*Philadelphia - Public Ledger Building (6th and Chestnut Streets) 19106. Phone: (215) LIBERTY or (877) GO-2-1776. **Web: www.lightsofliberty.org** Hours: At Dark (April-September). See website additional scheduled dates. Admission: $19.50 adult, $16.50 senior (65+) and student (w/ID), $13.00 child (6-12). Discount promotions on their website.*

History comes alive at night...

For updates & travel games visit: **www.KidsLoveTravel.com**

One evening during a visit, be sure you reserve a spot for the LIGHTS OF LIBERTY. Using headsets with 3D sound, visitors follow the drama of the American Revolution as it happened, where it happened. The sound system and enormous five-story images projected on buildings immerse visitors into events leading up to the Colonists' fight for freedom from the British. Start in Franklin Court, end at Independence Hall where the battle rages with swirling 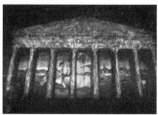 smoke and flashes from imaginary musket blasts. Hear the hurried sound of horses' hoofs on cobblestone streets. You'll find yourself cheering for the Patriots and clapping on several occasions. The ending "God Bless America" is very moving. Our six year old really got engaged! Although anyone can see the giant projected images, only those wearing the high tech headsets hear the stories. Ask for the youth show (a fictional family, the Warren children, serve as headset hosts). Recommended ages: 6+. So unique and what an adventure!

NATIONAL CONSTITUTION CENTER

Philadelphia - (Independence National Park, between Arch & Race, 5th & 6th Streets) 19106. Phone: (215) 923-0004. Web: www.constitutioncenter.org Hours: Daily 9:30am-5:00pm (except Thanksgiving Day, Christmas Day, and New Years Day) Admission: $7.00-$9.00 (age 4+).

The first-ever national museum honoring and explaining the U.S. Constitution...designed to increase awareness and understanding of the US Constitution, the Constitution's history, and the Constitution's relevance to our daily lives so that all of us -- "We the People" -- will better understand and exercise our rights and our responsibilities. It begins with an introduction to the extraordinary beginnings of our nation and Constitution. Wandering a "street scene" in 1787 Philadelphia, you can eavesdrop on fellow citizens and discover the forces that inspired the creation of the document. "Signers Hall," is where visitors are invited to play the role of Signer amidst life-size statues of the Founding Fathers. You then enter a theater-in-the-round, where you view The Founding Story, a multi-media production which orients you to the major themes of the Center and the basic historical context of the Constitution. The "National Tree" will interpret the theme by using video stories of Americans throughout history. The exhibit will illustrate how the diversity of American citizens has changed with the changes in the Constitution.

RIDE THE DUCKS TOURS

*Philadelphia - 6th & Chestnut Depot 19106. **Web: www.phillyducks.com** Phone: (215) 227- DUCK (3825). Hours: Daily (mid-March - December). Admisson: $25.00 adult (13+), $24.00 seniot (62+), $15.00 child (3-12).*

This fun tour provides passengers with an 80 minute entertaining, historically accurate, land and water sightseeing adventure aboard amphibious WWII Duck vessels. Each tour features a scenic "bus" tour past Philly's historical and cultural sites, then splashes down into the Delaware River for a floating tour along Penn's Landing (the kids, and kids-at-heart, get to try driving the boat on the water, too). You'll find yourself quacking (with provided official quackers) at interesting people as the

This tour vehicle is at "home" on land and water - QUACK!

captain commentates with theme music – party music – that really gets you in the mood! Learn about different ethnic eateries or some history "with a twist" – just little funny tidbits that never bore the kids (i.e. What happened if you didn't have fire insurance? Who is famous for cake and ice cream?). Don't worry, the Duck Trucks look silly but you feel great as you travel this fun way…the new, hip way to see historic old Philadelphia!

THADDEUS KOSCIUSZKO NATIONAL MEMORIAL

*Philadelphia - 301 Pine Street (I-676 or I-95 Independence Hall exit) 19106. Phone: (215) 597-9618. **Web: www.nps.gov/thko** Hours: Wednesday-Sunday Noon-4:00pm (rest of year). Admission: FREE*

Exhibits & audiovisual displays (English & Polish language) describing the help Thaddeus gave to the American Revolution. Learn why he was loved and then kicked out of his native Poland, why he carried a crutch and how his skills helped Americans strategically beat the British. He was a genius engineer!

TODD HOUSE

Philadelphia - *4th & Walnut Streets 19106.* **Web: *www.ushistory.org/tour/tour_todd.htm***
Phone: (215) 597-8974. Hours: Open house daily from 4:00pm-5:00pm. Admission: $2.00 adult.

This was the home of Dolly Todd before her marriage to James Madison (Dolly Madison pastries will get the kids on the same page). Representing a middle-class Quaker home, she became quite a First Lady when she moved from this house and married James Madison, fourth President of the United States.

U.S. MINT

Philadelphia - *5th & Arch Streets 19106.* **Web: *www.usmint.gov/mint_tours/*** *Phone: (215) 408-0112. Admission: FREE*

While in the historic district of Philadelphia, be sure to take your family to the world's largest coinage operation (seen through a glass enclosed gallery). They make a million dollars worth of coins per day! (29 million coins!). See them start with blanks that are cleaned and then stamped, sorted, and bagged. To see coins in large bins or spilling out of machines is mesmerizing! Even little kids eyes sparkle. A "Stamp Your Own Medal" machine (press a big red button to operate) is located in the Gift shop. Great souvenir idea!

So many types of coins are minted here...

PHILADELPHIA CITY HALL OBSERVATION DECK

Philadelphia - *Broad & Market Streets 19107. Phone: (215) 686-2840.   Hours: Daily 9:30am-4:15pm. Admission: Donation.*

Every city has one building that stands as one of the tallest in town and usually it has a lot of history behind it. Most noted is the courtroom (available to view on the tour only) where a motion picture film was made and the 548 foot tall tower that has a statue of William Penn on top. At the base of the statue is the observation deck. This building is so breathtakingly beautiful and stands in the center of downtown…believe us, you can't miss it!

EASTERN STATE PENITENTIARY

Philadelphia - *2124 Fairmount Avenue (I-95 exit 22, follow I-676 west. Get off at "Art Museum/Benjamin Franklin Parkway" Exit. Turn right and go five blocks past the Museum of Art) 19130. Phone: 215-236-3300.* **Web: www.easternstate.org** *Hours: Daily 10:00am-5:00pm (April-November). Admission: $9.00 adult, $7.00 senior and student, $4.00 child (7-12). Children under the age of 7 cannot be admitted to the site.*

Let's go to jail. Kids are fascinated by the massive cellblocks, dark cells, and stories of punishment and escape at Eastern State Penitentiary. Tours include: The central rotunda, restored cells, the solitary confinement yards, the baseball diamond, death row and Al Capone's Cell.

The "Keys to the Past" Family Tour is recommended for families with kids age seven to twelve. In this hands-on, interactive program, families unlock boxes, examine artifacts, and piece together the story of the world's first true penitentiary. Families record their findings in "travel journals" and also take home a special memento of their visit to Eastern State Penitentiary. (available during all hours).

A "voices of Eastern State" audio tour is available during all hours. Although the subject matter is family friendly, it's recommended for kids 12 and up.

PHILADELPHIA MUSEUM OF ART

Philadelphia - *26th Street and Ben Franklin Parkway   19130. Phone: (215) 763-8100.* **Web: www.philamuseum.org** *Hours: Tuesday-Sunday, 10:00am-5:00pm. Friday evening until 8:45pm Admission: $12.00 adult, $9.00 senior (62+), $8.00 child & students (age 13+). Sundays - pay what you wish.*

The 3rd largest museum in the country. 2000 years of fine and applied arts (crafts, interiors, architecture) with 200 galleries. Many rooms have themes that transport you back to when the works were created. Museum restaurant.

Your kids (or parents!) will love running up the numerous steps to the top like Rocky *(from the movie by the same name).* Pretend you  hear the crowd cheer as you step onto the brass glazed imprints of Rocky's shoes! Family Art Activities.

The famous steps from famous movies...

FAIRMOUNT PARK

Philadelphia - *Benjamin Franklin Parkway (info at Visitor's Center at Memorial Hall) 19131. Phone: (215) 685-0000. Web: www.fairmountpark.org*

Along both sides of Schuylkill River, one of the world's largest city park's features include:

ANDORRA NATURAL AREA - (215) 685-9285. Bartram's Historic Garden - (215) 729-5281. 18th Century home of colonial botanist, John Bartram.

SMITH PLAYGROUND & PLAYHOUSE - (215) 765-4325. Emphasis on playhouse (3 story) for preschoolers with trains, foam blocks and comfortable reading rooms. Pick up a Cozy Car and drive along the play roads with stop signs and traffic lights. This 100 year old playground has a Giant Slide that on which four generations have slid down.

JAPANESE HOUSE & GARDEN - Horticultural Center. (215) 878-5097. Small admission for tours.

FOX CHASE FARM - tours.

WISSAHICKON CREEK GORGE - hiking trails.

INSECTARIUM

Philadelphia - *8046 Frankford Avenue (1-95 Cottman Avenue exit thru, right on Frankford for several blocks) 19136. Web: www.insectarium.com Phone: (215) 338-3000. Hours: Monday-Saturday 10:00am-4:00pm. Admission: $6.00 (ages 2+).*

While in Philly, maybe add a creepy trip over to the INSECTARIUM, north of downtown. Did you know we eat  bugs every day? They're ground up in plants as they are harvested. See a glow in the dark scorpion or bugs with noses. There's giant bugs and little

George, "calmly" holding a scorpion...yikes!

bees (do you know what honey really is?). Pet live bugs like Martin the cockroach or Harry the millipede (yes, Mommy actually pet them!). Interact as you climb thru a spider web, eat fried worms, or push buttons. The highlight has to be the Cockroach Kitchen & Bathroom! How do they keep them inside the room? They live here and are welcome! Great photo ops and their gift shop has inexpensive craft kits and bug food and toys. You will learn so much here and the guides really add the "magic". Outside, there's a learning garden where you go on bug hunts.

MUMMERS MUSEUM

Philadelphia - 1100 South 2nd Street & Washington Avenue 19147. Phone: (215) 336-3050. Web: www.mummersmuseum.com Hours: Tuesday-Saturday 9:30am-4:30pm, Sunday Noon-4:30pm. Closed Sundays in July and August and all Holidays. Open evenings in summer. Admission: $2.50-$3.50.

What is a mummer? Audio and interactive displays, musical instruments, costumes, and artifacts from the traditional New Year's Day parade. See videos of past parades or watch how those colorful sparkly costumes are made.

WACHOVIA CENTER / SPECTACOR TOURS

Philadelphia - 3601 South Broad Street (South Broad Street & Patterson Avenue) 19148. Web: www.comcast-spectacor.com/arenaInfo/tours.asp Phone: (215) 389-9543.

Guided tours of the home of the Philadelphia 76ers, Flyers, and Wings. In your personal guided tour through the Wachovia Center, you will be given an exclusive chance to visit and explore the private luxury seating levels, the press box, Arena Vision studio control room, Comcast SportsNet, and the official NBA and NHL locker rooms. See playing floors and learn great inside scoops on the history of favorite players and teams.

FORT MIFFLIN

Philadelphia - Fort Mifflin Road (I-95 to Island Avenue Exit - follow signs) 19153. Phone: (215) 685-4167. Web: www.fortmifflin.com Hours: Wednesday-Sunday 10:00am-4:00pm. (March-November) Admission: $6.00 adult, $5.00 senior (65+), $3.00 child (5-12). Military FREE. Miscellaneous: Sundays suggested as there are military drills and craftspeople demonstrating their skills. Check out their educational Treasure Hunts for group tours.

"What Really Happened at Fort Mifflin?"... you'll find out that a lot happened here. Starting in 1772, it was built by the British to protect the colonies. Ironically, in 1777, it was used by Americans trying to protect the Philadelphia and Delaware River from the British (7 long, grueling weeks of siege). It also protected the city of Philadelphia during the War of 1812 and was active as a Confederate and Union prison camp during the Civil War. Until 1954, it was still used to store ammunition for the United States military. A great place to check out and study several wars all in one spot.

HEINZ NATIONAL WILDLIFE REFUGE

Philadelphia - Lindbergh Blvd. & 86th Street 19153. Phone: (215) 365-3118. Web: http://heinz.fws.gov/

Visitor contact station. Hiking trails to explore butterflies, muskrats, frogs, flying geese, and loads of wildflowers is open dawn to dusk. Observation tower. The Cusano Environmental Education Center is open daily from 8:30 AM to 4:00 PM, free of charge.

MORRIS ARBORETUM

Philadelphia (Chestnut Hill) - 100 Northwestern Avenue (University of Pennsylvania) 19118. Phone: (215) 247-5777. Web: www.business-services.upenn.edu/arboretum/ Hours: Daily 10:00am-4:00pm (year round). Open until 5:00pm on Saturday and Sunday (April - October) Admission: $10.00 adult, $8.00 senior (65+) and student, $5.00 child (3-12).

Romantic 92 acre Victorian garden with many of Philly's rarest and largest trees, a sculpture garden, a rose garden and the Fernery. A canopy into the limbs of the Metasequoias is the latest addition to the Morris Arboretum experience. A stairway brings visitors front and center into one of the Arboretum's most spectacular groves of trees via an installation called meta Metasequoia. Garden Railway Display changes each season.

SESAME PLACE

Philadelphia (Langhorne) - 100 Sesame Road (I-95 to US 1 north to Oxford Valley exit. Next to Oxford Valley Mall) 19047. Web: www.sesameplace.com Phone: (215) 752-7070. Hours: Daily 9:00am-8:00pm (mid May - Labor Day Weekend), Weekends (September & October) - Call for current schedule. Admission: ~$45.00+ general admission. Parking $10.00. Miscellaneous: Late afternoon and family discounts. Bathing suits required for water attractions. We'd recommend staying all day to get your money's worth.

While your kids continue to peek over their shoulders for a glimpse of a Sesame Street character like Big Bird (great photograph opportunities), they'll be pulling your hand in every direction so they won't miss anything. Catch a show like "Rock Around the Block", then jump on Ernie's Bed Bounce (that even sounds like fun to adults, doesn't it?) or scale "Cookie Mountain". Mechanical rides include: A roller coaster called "Vapor Trail", or, a 40-foot high balloon tower ride carries you up in one of eight balloon baskets - providing a bird's eye view of the park, and, also a character themed tea cup ride turns you "round and round" - as fast or as slow as you want to go.

Everybody's favorite character hosts the new Elmo's World ride area. There's also 14 refreshing water attractions. As you float, zoom or chute through Big

Bird, Ernie's and Slimey's Rides, you'll be splashed or trickled by a giant rubber ducky. Toddlers can be water trickled in Teany Tiny Tidal Waves. Bet your kids just can't wait to walk down a full-sized replica of Sesame Street and take pictures to show their friends back home!

NOCKAMIXON STATE PARK

Quakertown - 1542 Mountain View Drive (PA Route 563, Northeast Extension of the PA Turnpike, Exit 32) 18951. www.dcnr.state.pa.us/stateparks/parks/nockamixon.aspx Phone: (215) 529-7300 or -7308 (marina).

The name Nockamixon is synonymous with boating. Four public launching areas are provided on the lake and boats may be rented from a park concession. Visitors enjoy watching sailboats from a bench at the marina, and the equestrian, bicycle and hiking trails. Pool, Visitors Center, Horseback Riding, Modern Cabins, Fishing, and Winter Sports.

FULTON (ROBERT) BIRTHPLACE

Quarryville - Box 33 (Rte. 30 west to Rte. 372 west to US222 South of Quarryville) 17566. Phone: (717) 548-2679.   Hours: Saturday 11:00am-4:00pm, Sunday 1:00-5:00pm (Summer). Admission: $1.00 adult, children FREE (12 and under).

Robert Fulton, the inventor, the artist, and the engineer was born here in 1765. On display are many of his drawings, miniature portraits, and models (located throughout the living room). Being most famous for his steamboat, "Claremont" (the first steamboat), you'll see a strong connection between his artistic ability and his engineering ideas. Because his drawings were so well done, supporters could easily visualize his inventive ideas.

MID ATLANTIC AIR MUSEUM

Reading - *11 Museum Drive* - *SR183 (Reading Regional Airport) 19605. Phone: (610) 372-7333.* **Web:** *www.maam.org Hours: Daily 9:30am-4:00pm. Closed major holidays. Admission: $6.00 adult, $3.00 child (6-12). Miscellaneous: Aviation gift shop. Airplane rides weekends in summer for additional fee.*

Restored, ready to fly, classic civilian and military aircraft. Of special interest are the classic commercial airliners, and the first night fighter ever built, history of aircraft manufacturers, and aviation movies and toys.

READING PHILLIES BASEBALL

Reading - *1900 S. Centre Avenue (FirstEnergy Stadium) 19605. Phone: (610) 370-BALL or 375-8469.* **Web:** *www.readingphillies.com Admission: $3.00-$7.00.*

Minor League AA Class affiliate of the Philadelphia Phillies. The Mascot Band members are Quack the Rubber Ducky on lead vocals and guitar, Bucky the Beaver on bass, Change-Up the Turtle on the bongos, and Screwball bringing it all together on the drums – you really have to see it to believe it.

NOLDE FOREST ENVIRONMENTAL EDUCATION CENTER

Reading - *2910 New Holland Road 19608. Phone: (610) 775-1411.* **Web:** *www.dcnr.state.pa.us/stateparks/parks/noldeforest.aspx*

Year-Round Education & Interpretation Center. Nolde Forest encompasses more than 665 acres of deciduous woodlands and coniferous plantations. A network of trails makes the center's streams, ponds and diverse habitats accessible to both students and casual visitors. Teaching stations offer places for students to work and benches for those who wish to sit. There is a short, accessible trail by the mansion.

READING PUBLIC MUSEUM

Reading - *500 Museum Road (follow 222 South/422 East to West Reading/Penn Avenue exit) 19611. Phone: (610) 371-5850.* **Web:** *www.readingpublicmuseum.org Hours: Tuesday - Saturday 11:00am-5:00pm, Sunday Noon-5:00pm. Also Wednesday eve. Closed Christmas. Admission: $7.00 adult, $5.00 child (4-17).*

While the art of many nations and people is represented in the permanent collection, special emphasis has been placed on painting. The fine art collection includes more than seven hundred oil paintings by American and foreign artists such as: Benjamin West, Milton Avery, John Singer Sargent, N.C. Wyeth, George Bellows, Raphaelle Peale, Henry Raeburn, Frederic

Church, Joshua Reynolds, Julien Dupre, and Edgar Degas - names students are familiar with in art history class. In addition, the Reading Public Museum possesses over one hundred sculptures, thousands of graphics, and more than two hundred water colors. Mounted Specimens are prepared to resemble the organism as it would normally appear in the wild. Public Star Shows on Sundays, Public Laser Shows on Saturdays (separate fee).

ROADSIDE AMERICA

Shartlesville - Roadside Drive (I-78 / US22, exit 23) 19554. Phone: (610) 488-6241. Web: www.roadsideamericainc.com Hours: Weekdays 9:00am-6:30pm, Weekends until 7:00pm (July-Labor Day). Monday-Friday 10:00am-5:00pm, Saturday & Sunday 10:00am-6:00pm (September-June). Admission: $6.00 adult, $5.50 senior, $3.00 child (6-11).

Our kids lost their breath as they entered the enormous and wonderful train village! It's the largest known indoor miniature train village! As a young boy, Lawrence Gieringer saw buildings far away and felt they appeared tiny and toy-sized. As his carpentry skills grew, he began whittling blocks of wood

Something for every age here...all in miniature detail...wow!

into different scaled-down models of industries and buildings he saw all around him - all of them important to the development of the area. You'll see scenes of a coal breaker, a Pennsylvania Dutch farm, downtown small town USA, gristmills, and churches. Kids are enchanted by the moving trains (over bridges, through tunnels), trolleys, bubbling fountains, or aircraft swooping and diving through the air (there's even a hot air balloon). Parents relive childhood dreams playing with toy animals, people, machinery, etc. as they examine all the details. Kids' favorites are the 50+ pushbuttons that make trains or figures move - it gives them the chance to feel like they're helping to operate the huge display. Don't leave until you've seen the Night Pageant! Every half hour they turn day into night and back!

ED'S BUGGY RIDES

Strasburg - SR 896 (across from Sight & Sound Theatre) 17572. Phone: (717) 687-0360. Web: www.edsbuggyrides.com Admission: $9.00 adult, $4.00 child.

3 mile tour through Amish farmlands in an Amish buggy. Experience the beautiful Pennsylvania Dutch Country landscape, while watching the everyday routine of the Amish through hilly back roads in an authentic Amish buggy. Daily, year-round.

AMISH VILLAGE

Strasburg - Route 896 - PO Box 115 (1 mile south of US30 & 2 miles north of Strasburg) 17579. Phone: (717) 687-8511. Web: www.800padutch.com/avillage.html Hours: Daily 9:00am-5:00pm (Spring/Summer/Fall) Admission: $6.75 adult, $2.75 child (6-12). Miscellaneous: Amish Village store.

Educational tour of an 1840 Old Order Amish home, authentically furnished. The site includes a blacksmith, one room schoolhouse, operating smokehouse, water wheel, farm animals, spring house and windmill.

CHOO CHOO BARN, TRAINTOWN USA

Strasburg - Route 741 East, Box 130 17579. Web: www.choochoobarn.com Phone: (717) 687-7911. Hours: Daily 10:00am-5:00pm (April - December). Closed major winter holidays and Easter. Admission: $5.50 adult, $3.50 child (5-12).

A 1700 square foot mini display of Pennsylvania Dutch County with area landmarks, 20 operating trains plus over 150 animated and automated vehicles and figurines. The kids shriek with delight at everything there is to see - esp. when it changes from daylight to nighttime. Look for the skiers zooming down the slopes and the dump truck that really moves. The working fire display shows a house burning and then the fire truck comes to put it out, complete with a fireman who climbs the ladder and makes a hole in the roof to put out the fire. Most displays can be seen from "kids-eye" level with only occasional "lifts" to get the "big picture". You have to pass the well-stocked gift shop in and out of the exhibit so plan some extra time for shopping.

RAILROAD MUSEUM OF PENNSYLVANIA

Strasburg - P. O. BOX 15 (300 Gap Road - SR741 East) 17579. Phone: (717) 687-8628. Web: www.rrmuseumpa.org Hours: Monday-Saturday 9:00am-5:00pm, Sunday Noon-5:00pm. Closed Monday & Winter Holidays (November-early April) Admission: $7.00 adult, $6.00 senior (60+), $5.00 child (6-17). Miscellaneous:

Whistle Stop Shop. Outdoor yard restoration available in good weather. Hands-On-Center. Orientation video. 2nd floor observation deck.

This huge indoor/outdoor museum traces the development of railroads and rail transportation in Pennsylvania from restored locomotives to modern streamliners. Inside, you look down on the hall. Aside from viewing the locomotives and rail cars from various vantage points, you can climb into a caboose or a steam locomotive. Docents are often on hand to explain special locomotives and show you how they worked, and other cars are opened during special events. Meet "Diesel", GG 1 Electric, Logging, Freight and Passenger (actually get to look in or

The trains are bigger than life and each has a story...

walk in) trains! More access than most train museums. In the center of the museum is the railroad workshop where you can actually walk under a train! Great place to bring grandmas and grandpas to pass along stories to younger generations.

SIGHT & SOUND THEATRES / LIVING WATERS THEATRE

*Strasburg - Route 896 (off Rte. 30) 17579. **Web: www.sight-sound.com** Phone: (717) 687-7800.*

Their show props are so realistic...

Special effects theatre with live Easter and Christmas performances. Shows the rest of the year focus on familiar bible characters like Ruth or Daniel. Through inspirational productions, they seek to encourage others to be dedicated and wise stewards of our God-given talents and resources. Amazing side stage and live isle-way entrances/exits help bring Bible stories fantastically to life! Most major story scenes are mouth-droppers! Don't be afraid of the price, it's worth it. Tickets range from $15.00-$49.00. Seasonal shows each Christmas and Easter, too.

STRASBURG RAILROAD

*Strasburg - SR741 East - P. O. Box 96 17579. Web: www.strasburgrailroad.com
Phone: (717) 687-7522. Hours: Daily 10:00am-7:00pm (July & August), 11:00am-
3:00pm (April, June, September). Mostly long weekends (weather permitting) Noon-3:00pm
(Rest of the year). Admission: Train Rides: $11.00-$13.00 adult, $6.00-$8.00 child
(3-11).. Activities: $1.00-$5.00 per activity. Additional fees for special events.
Miscellaneous: Several gift shops with train souvenirs, books and loads of Thomas
stuff! Restaurants with casual dining, picnic lunches and sweet treats on premises.*

Offering the most authentic train ride experience of the period, the Strasburg
Railroad takes visitors back to a simpler time. This is the oldest short-line

railroad. The restored Victorian open-air
and coach cars offer wide views of the
landscape (some cars even offer snacks
and the "Lee Brenner" dining car offers
meals). Visitors travel through farm
fields still plowed by horses and mules.
Amish buggies wait patiently at railroad
crossings. Train travelers can even stop at
an old-fashioned picnic grove and enjoy

All aboard !

a snack while the trains rumble by. Each train has a narrator who tells the
railroad's history spiced with a few tall tales.

Other activities on the premises: Hand-propelled cars, which date back to the
1930s, allow little ones to take control as they crank their way around a track;
Cagney Train - built around 1920, this miniature steam train was originally
used at an amusement park; President's Car Tour - Take a self-guided tour
aboard the stationary "mansion on rails." This
restored rail car was used for railroad tycoons and
dignitaries. Also, tour the freight equipment display;
Switch Tower Tour - Built in 1885, this is a classic
example of Pennsylvania Railroad signal tower
design. Get a bird's-eye view of our magnificent
countryside and approaching trains; and Pump Cars
- you provide the power when you operate vintage
Pump Cars - with attendant - along a short track.

Be sure to check on seasonal events that your "little
engineers" will love like "A Day Out With Thomas
the Train!" (One ride on a life-size Thomas plus
storytelling, Sir Topham Hat, Play Tables, Thomas

A Day Out with
Thomas ®!

Coloring and Videos, and Live Musical Entertainment for the wristband price of $14.00 per person/ages 2+ - June, mid-September, early December). This is the place where Thomas spends the most time visiting.

NATIONAL TOY TRAIN MUSEUM

Strasburg (Paradise) - 300 Paradise Lane (off SR 741 East & US 30) 17579. Phone: (717) 687-8976. Web: www.nttmuseum.org Hours: Daily, 10:00am-5:00pm (May-October), Weekends in April, November, and mid-December Admission: $5.00 adult, $4.00 senior (65+), $2.50 child (5-12), $12.00 family.

Five operating push button layouts in panoramic viewing. Meet toy trains from the 1800s to the present in use as part of the layout. One of the displays features large-gauge trains used for outdoors. The Train Collectors Association operates it (they are often featured on national TV). A continuously running video show in the Museum's Theater area features cartoons and comedy films about toy trains.

DELAWARE CANAL STATE PARK

Upper Black Eddy - 11 Lodi Hill Road (Rte. 611 and Rte. 32 18972. Phone: (610) 982-5560. Web: www.dcnr.state.pa.us/stateparks/parks/delawarecanal.aspx

A walk along the 60-mile towpath of the Delaware Canal is a stroll into American History. The Delaware Canal is the only remaining continuously intact canal of the great towpath canal building era of the early and mid-19th century. Mule drawn canal boat rides and the Lock Tender's House Visitor Center are at New Hope. Also, Horseback Riding, Mountain Biking, Fishing, Trails, Cross-Country Skiing.

The Delaware River Canal Boat Co. offers a unique, one hour journey aboard a replica canal boat drawn by a team of mules on the Delaware Canal through historic New Hope and into the scenic Bucks County countryside. Experience life along the Delaware Canal as it was in the 1800s and hear interesting tales of canal days related by an interpreter in period costume. Boats depart starting at noon on Saturdays and Sundays in April, (weather permitting), and daily May through October 31st.

VALLEY FORGE NATIONAL HISTORICAL PARK

Valley Forge - SR23 & N. Gulph Road - PO Box 953 (I-76 to exit 24 - SR202 south to SR422 west to SR23 west) 19482. Phone: (610) 783-1077. Web: www.nps.gov/vafo Hours: Daily 9:00am-5:00pm. Closed Thanksgiving, Christmas and New Year's Day. Admission: $3.00 per person - only if your tour buildings. Often, there is no charge due to ongoing construction around the park site. Miscellaneous: Expanse of outdoor *park areas available. Hiking and bike trails. Stop at the Visitor's Center first. Valley Forge Canteen open 10:00am to 2:00pm Saturday and Sunday.*

Explore the site of the Winter of 1777-78 encampment that was a difficult time for battling elements and disease. Some of the sites that you won't want to miss are:

ARTILLERY PARK - long rows of cannons and forts.

WASHINGTON'S HEADQUARTERS - Isaac Potts' House - looks exactly as it did when General George Washington and his wife, Martha were in residence. (Initially he shared the rough conditions with the soldiers in the field tents). Interpreters are excellent here (weekends and summers).

VISITOR'S CENTER - An eighteen-minute film, "Valley Forge: A Winter Encampment," is shown every 30 minutes on the hour and half-hour, starting at 9:30am, ending at 4:30pm. Be sure to take that in first and look over the dioramas. See a tent headquarters actually used by General Washington.

GRAND PARADE - learn about the other hero (Von Steuben) who turned tattered, confused young men into soldiers.

WORLD OF SCOUTING MUSEUM - A log cabin full of uniforms, handbooks, and badges. Daily, 11:00am - 4:00pm (Summer), Weekends (rest of the year).

 Summer weekends are the best time to visit because the Muhlenberg Brigade is recreated in living history encampments - bringing the drudges of winter camp to life. Remember, these "huts" replaced tents but only offered a little more warmth. Brave a visit Winter weekends to see scout troops living under similar conditions as the soldiers did or inside Washington's Headquarters.

WASHINGTON CROSSING HISTORIC PARK

Washington's Crossing - SR32 and SR532 (off I-95, exit 31) 18977. Phone: (215) 493-4076. Web: www.ushistory.org/washingtoncrossing Hours: Tuesday-Saturday 9:00am-5:00pm, Sunday Noon-5:00pm. Admission: $2.00-$5.00 (age 6+) for walking tour. Park charges $1.00 per vehicle at entrance. Miscellaneous: Every Christmas (at

1:00pm) the park re-enacts Washington's crossing and special events also occur on his birthday. Also on grounds is the Bowman's Hill and Wildflower Preserve.

It's December 25, 1776. Washington planned his attack on the British, first crossing the Delaware River by boat. In the Durham Boat House, you can see the boats that were actually used. A larger than life copy (20 ft. X 12 ft.) of the painting "Washington's Crossing" creates the best image of this historic Christmas Day for freedom. A total of 13 historic buildings are on site and your tour ticket includes Bowman's Hill Tower observation point, Thompson-Neely House (where Washington ate and slept), The Ferry Inn (where Washington dined before crossing the icy Delaware) and the Memorial Building where the giant painting stands. All of this, plus a short historical film is shown of the event. It'll give you goosebumps!

AMERICAN HELICOPTER MUSEUM

West Chester - 1220 American Blvd. (Brandywine Airport - Next to QVC Studios) 19380. Phone: (610) 436-9600. Web: www.helicoptermuseum.org Hours: Wednesday-Saturday 10:00am-5:00pm, Sunday Noon-5:00pm. Admission: $6.00 adult, $5.00 senior (65+), $4.00 child (3-18) or student. Miscellaneous: Older kids will want more information about the engineering of the rotorcraft. Films and mechanics are available to fill in all of the details. Helicopter Rides (every 4th Saturday) - ask for adventure here! Fly-bys...wow!

This very kid-friendly museum exhibits the adventure and history of "rotary wing flight" at the country's only helicopter museum. Visitors come back

here frequently because the kids can actually go on many units and work the rotors and play pretend. Helicopters from the earliest to the most modern are here, inside and outside (Coast Guard, Navy, Army, M.A.S.H.), plus interactive exhibits. Climb aboard and play with the controls inside the giant helicopters being restored. It's lots of fun!

QVC STUDIO TOUR

West Chester - Studio Park (I-76 or I-95, exit US202 to Boot Road - East to Wilson Drive) 19380. Phone: (800) 600-9900. **Web: www.qvctours.com** *Admission: $7.50 adult, $5.00 child (age 6+). Miscellaneous: Must be at least 6 years old.*

Imagine a shopping medium that reaches over 16 million homes instantly and can process more than 30 calls per second! Founded in 1986, this cable shopping service stands for "Quality, Value, Convenience" and has become the largest of its kind. Your tour begins as you are greeted by photographs of famous celebrities that have visited QVC to merchandise their products. You will see 34 sets and 8 studios (there is even an 8000 square foot 2-story house in the studio complete with a garage). All of the cameras are remotely controlled from one central source during taping and the complete facility uses over 1,000,000 watts of power (or enough to power 3000 average households!) You might even have a chance to see "Murphy the Dog" the QVC mascot - he is a golden retriever that is featured on the show and we are told he gets as much e-mail as any of the other hosts! See live broadcasts being done (without cue cards - everything is ad lib!). See the prop production and design facilities - the texture display is awesome! You can even be a part of a live studio audience with advance notice.

PETER WENTZ FARMSTEAD

Worcester - Shearer Road (SR73 and SR363) 19490. Phone: (610) 584-5104. **Web: www.peterwentzfarmsteadsociety.org** *Hours: Tuesday - Saturday 10:00am-4:00pm, Sunday 1:00-4:00pm. Admission: FREE*

A restored, colorfully decorated, 18th century Pennsylvania German working farm and mansion. Did you know that George Washington used this home as his headquarters (from time to time) during the Revolutionary War? Best to attend Saturdays when staff demonstrates colonial crafts, (candles, weaving, paper cut art - called "scherenschnitte") or tending to the animals. Special events and exhibits representing Pennsylvania German culture and early American farm life take place throughout the year.

BERK'S COUNTY HERITAGE CENTER

Wyomissing - Red Bridge Road (off Route 183) 19610. Phone: (610) 374-8839. **Web: www.berksparkandrec.org/heritage/** *Hours: Tuesday-Saturday, Holidays 10:00am-4:00pm, Sunday Noon-5:00pm (May - October). Admission: $3.00-$5.00 (age 7+) per museum. Discount combo prices.*

The Gruber Wagon Works survives as one of the most complete examples of an integrated rural manufactory of its kind in the nation. Wagon wheels were constructed in the bench shop, and wooden parts of the wagon were made from patterns in the wood shop. Wheels were "tired" and wagons were "ironed" and assembled in the blacksmith shop. The distinctive striping and scrollwork were applied by hand in the paint shop.

C. Howard Hiester Canal Center: Canals saw their rise and fall in the 19th century. They offered means of bulk transportation and travel in the era prior to railroads when the only alternative to walking was the horse and wagon. Red Bridge (longest covered bridge in the state).

SUGGESTED LODGING AND DINING

FULTON STEAMBOAT INN - **Strasburg**. (US30 & SR896). Phone: (717) 299-9999 or (800) 922-2229. **Web: www.fultonsteamboatinn.com**. From the first "Welcome Aboard" to the last splash in the pool – your kids will think it's cool to overnight in a steamboat. They have an indoor pool, jacuzzi, playground (really fun, outside) and an observation deck that looks onto the pond and walking trail. This hotel is right in the middle of Dutch Country – easy to "pop" in and out of all day. Check out all of the ship's wheels and Victorian flare – esp. the lobby. After you spend the night sleeping on a steamboat, enjoy a meal in a room full of steamboat antiques. The outside of this Inn looks just like a steamboat complete with wheels and smoke stacks. As you hear occasional seagulls sounds, select from Steamboat or Mid-Ship Specialties for breakfast, lunch or dinner.

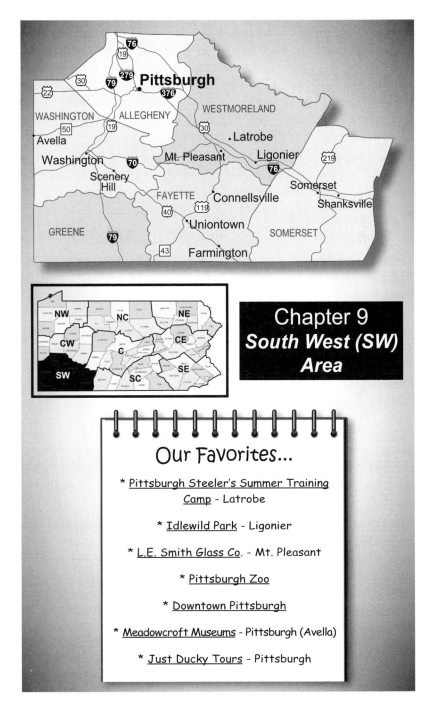

Pittsburgh

WESTMORELAND

WASHINGTON ALLEGHENY

Avella

Washington

Scenery
Hill

FAYETTE

GREENE

. Latrobe

Ligonier

Mt. Pleasant

Connellsville

Somerset

Shanksville

Uniontown

SOMERSET

Farmington

NW
NC
NE
CW
C
CE
SW
SC
SE

Chapter 9
South West (SW) Area

Our Favorites...

* <u>Pittsburgh Steeler's Summer Training Camp</u> - Latrobe

* <u>Idlewild Park</u> - Ligonier

* <u>L.E. Smith Glass Co.</u> - Mt. Pleasant

* <u>Pittsburgh Zoo</u>

* <u>Downtown Pittsburgh</u>

* <u>Meadowcroft Museums</u> - Pittsburgh (Avella)

* <u>Just Ducky Tours</u> - Pittsburgh

NEMACOLIN CASTLE

Brownsville - Front Street - US 40 east 15417. ***Web:*** *www.nemacolincastle.org Phone: (724) 785-6882. Hours: Tuesday-Sunday 11:00am-5:00pm (Summer). Weekends only (Mid-March - May, September - Mid-October). Admission: $6.00 adult, $3.00 child (12 and under).*

Previously known as Nemacolin Towers, the tudor style building dates back to the 1790s. The castle was built by Jacob Bowman who was appointed by George Washington as Brownsville's first postmaster. The Bowman family were businessmen and bank founders. It looks like a castle because of the turret towers and battlements. Tour 20 rooms of formal Victorian plus the oldest part that was the original trading post Bowman set up.

SEVEN SPRINGS MOUNTAIN RESORT

Champion - RR#1 Box 110 (I-76 exit 9 or 10, follow Rte. 31 or 711) 15622. Phone: (814) 352-7777, (800) 452-2223 (continental US). Snow Report: (800) 523-7777. ***Web:*** *www.7springs.com*

Longest Run: 1.2 miles; 30 Slopes & Trails. Pennsylvania's largest ski and year-round resort. Be sure to get all of the latest details by calling or visiting their website. The "resort cam" shows live pictures that are updated every 5 minutes. Tons of lodging & restaurants, indoor bowling, roller skating, swimming & mini-golf. Outdoor summer alpine slide, craft days, outdoor pool, horseback riding and tennis.

LIVING TREASURES ANIMAL PARK

Donegal - SR 711 (south of rte. 31) 15628. ***Web:*** *www.ltanimalpark.com Phone: (724) 593-8300. Hours: Daily 10:00am-8:00pm (Summer). Daily 10:00am-6:00pm (April, May, September, October). Admission: $7.50 adult, $7.00 senior, $5.50 child (3-11).*

Watch kangaroos, tigers and wolves and ride the miniature horses. Kids love the petting area (babies, reindeer, camels) and feeding areas (bears, otters, monkeys, goats, sheep, & llamas). Cups of animal feed are available in the gift shop or at coin-operated food dispensers throughout the park. The Laurel Highlands location has several new additions each year including Black Leopards and Dingos. But the "biggest" addition is their Grizzly Bear family or baby camels!

ROUND HILL EXHIBIT FARM

Elizabeth - 651 Round Hill Road (SR51 & SR48 to Round Hill Road) 15037. Phone: (412) 384-4701. Web: www.county.allegheny.pa.us/parks/rhfac.asp Hours: Daily 8:00am-DUSK. Admission: FREE

A small scale working farm dating back to the late 1700s. A brick farmhouse with barns and fields including dairy and beef cattle, pigs, chicken, sheep, horses, and a duck pond. Be ready to watch the cows being milked daily at 8:30am and 4:30pm. You can tour the grounds, play with the animals, plan a picnic, romp and play on the soccer fields, and walk the trails.

FORT NECESSITY NATIONAL BATTLEFIELD

Farmington - 1 Washington Parkway - US40 15437. Web: www.nps.gov/fone Phone: (724) 329-5805. Hours: 8:00am-Sunset (park), Visitor's Center 9:00am-5:00pm, Closed many holidays. Admission: $5.00 adult, Children FREE (15 and under) Miscellaneous: Visitor's Center with slide show, exhibits, store. Picnic areas.

Commemoraing the 1754 battle - George Washington's first battle of the French and Indian War, The Visitor Center is the best place to begin your visit. The twenty-minute movie "Road of Necessity" introduces the park story. Begin at Jumonville Glen - the site where the first skirmish occurred with the French. Washington feared they would return with backup forces, so, he had this fort built quickly, out of "necessity". See the reconstructed fort - 53 feet in diameter, the gate is only 3.5 feet wide. Tours of the Mount Washington Tavern are available when staffing permits. The Tavern is a museum of life along the National Road and operated from 1828 to 1855. Talks, tours, and historic weapons demonstrations are offered during the summer months.

LAUREL CAVERNS

Farmington - 200 Caverns Park Road (Chestnut Ridge in Laurel Highlands, off US 40) 15437. Phone: (800) 515-4150 or (724) 438-3003. Web: www.laurelcaverns.com Hours: Daily 9:00am-5:00pm (May-October). Weekends only (November, March, April). Admission: $7.00-$10.00 (age 6+). Miscellaneous: Visitors center, picnic areas.

Pennsylvania's largest cave 2.3 miles. - well-lit tours of the "Grand Canyon" or Spelunking - 3 hour tour for those in your family looking for a strenuous adventure. Kavernputt is so unique (additional activity fee required). A ten thousand square foot simulated cave is an eighteen hole golf course. The course is handicapped accessible with each hole conveying some unique aspect of caves.

NEMACOLIN WOODLANDS RESORT SKI AREA

Farmington - *1001 LaFayette Drive 15437. Phone: (800) 422-2736. Snow Report: (724) 329-8555. Web: www.nemacolin.com*

Mystic Mountain Skiing Area. Longest Run: .5 miles; 7 Slopes & Trails. A selection of resort lodging and activity packages are available year round with 5 swimming pools, mini-golf, trails and Equestrian Center, to name a few.

FRIENDSHIP HILL NATIONAL HISTORIC SITE

Farmington - *223 New Geneva Road (US 119 to PA 166) 15474. Phone: (724) 725-9190. Web: www.nps.gov/frhi Hours: Daily 9:00am-5:00pm (spring thru early fall). Winter hours are Friday-Sunday only. Closed Christmas day only. Admission: FREE*

Visit the home of Albert Gallatin (a famous local financier, scholar and diplomat of the early republic). "A country, like a household, should live within its means and avoid debt", says Albert Gallatin. Albert Gallatin is best remembered for his thirteen year tenure as Secretary of the Treasury during the Jefferson and Madison administrations. In that time he reduced the national debt, purchased the Louisiana Territory and funded the Lewis & Clark exploration. Gallatin's accomplishments and contributions are highlighted in his restored country estate, Friendship Hill. Ranger guided tours (summer) and self-guided Audio tours (rest of year).

ACT 1 STAGE

Greensburg - *951 Old Salem Road (Civic Theatre) 15601. Phone: (724) 836-PLAY. Web: www.act1.org/stage.htm*

Children's Theatre, produced during the summer at the Palace by the youth program, ACT I STAGE!. Their productions are really playful and clever.

WESTMORELAND MUSEUM OF AMERICAN ART

Greensburg - *221 North Main Street (downtown) 15601. Phone: (724) 837-1500. Web: www.wmuseumaa.org Hours: Wednesday-Sunday 11:00am-5:00pm. Thursday 11:00am-9:00pm. Admission: Suggested donation $3.00.*

"Arty-Facts" educational programs for children. Kidspace interactive area - Exhibitions include artwork from the permanent collection on display together with accompanying hands-on activities and a well-stocked reading corner. Regional industry, rural and cityscapes, toys of yesteryear, historical heroes.

BUSHY RUN BATTLEFIELD

Harrison City - Bushy Run Road (off US22 to Bus66 to SR993) 15636. Phone: (724) 527-5584. Web: www.bushyrunbattlefield.com/WelcomePage.html Hours: Wednesday-Saturday 9:00am-5:00pm, Sunday Noon-5:00pm. (April-October). Admission: $2.00-$3.00 (age 6+). Miscellaneous: Visitor Center.

The battle that opened Western Pennsylvania to settlement - Pontiac's War in 1763. Native American forces lead by Chief Pontiac had occupied nearby forts. The British finally stopped advancements at Bushy Run - this reopened supply routes. Kids will either be scared or say "cool" when they see a life-size mannequin of an Indian Warrior dressed for battle with war paint from head to toe. In this same area, children can take turns dressing up like a British soldier (check out all the buttons!). Learn what "lock, stock, and barrel" means or discover all the different ways they used nature to provide basic needs (ex. Flour bags - fortification and wounds, or trees for gun stock, food, and dyes). View the electronic map of the battle - then walk outside to markers of the actual battlefield ground.

HIDDEN VALLEY SKI

Hidden Valley - One Craighead Drive (PA Route 31) 15502. Phone: (814) 443-2600. Snow Report: (800) 443-7544. Web: www.hiddenvalleyresort.com

Longest Run: 1 mile; 17 Slopes & Trails. Sleigh rides, Children's Snow Play area, Snowtubing and snowboarding. Year-round sports and recreation at Hidden Valley Resort from golf, outdoor swimming, indoor swimming, and mountain biking in the spring, summer and fall. Lodging in condos w/ kitchens.

PITTSBURGH STEELERS SUMMER TRAINING CAMP

Latrobe - US30 at Fraser Purchase Road (St. Vincent College) 15650. Phone: (724) 323-1200. Web: www.steelers.com Hours: Daily practice - get a schedule at the field. (Mid-July - August). Admission: FREE.

Since 1967, this has been the site of the NFL - Pittsburgh Steelers pre-season training camp. Young fans can root for their favorite team member in a much smaller and more intimate setting. Children can also learn that the glamour and the glory of the NFL only comes from hard, focused work each day on the practice field. If you're lucky, you might have a chance to get some autographs. Be sure to bring a pen (a Sharpie® is best), paper, old program, or Steeler's memorbilia for the players to sign! A wonderful children's area offers face painting with Steeler's logos, photo boards and 3-D player props, plus kicking, passing, and running games. From our experience, it's tough to see the practice, and get autographs on the same visit. If you

William & Daniel watching the pros at work...

want autographs, stay up on the hill near the dorms by the entrance to the camp. The practices take place on the lower fields and the coaches usually enter from the dorm driveway farthest from the entrance. What fun!

KEYSTONE STATE PARK

Latrobe (Derry) - *RD 2, Box 101 (on SR 1018, the park is three miles from SR 981/ SR 22) 15627.* ***Web: www.dcnr.state.pa.us/stateparks/parks/keystone.aspx*** *Phone: (724) 668-2939.*

Camping, modern cabins, trails of all sorts, a lake, and a swimming beach provide an ideal setting for a summer outing. The park offers a variety of trails open year-round for hiking, cross-country skiing and snowshoeing. All trails have easy access with parking available at the trailheads. Visitor Center, Year-round Education & Interpretation Center, Boat Rentals, Horseback Riding, Sledding, Fishing.

COMPASS INN MUSEUM

Laughlintown - *PO Box 167 (US30 East, 3 miles east of Fort Ligonier) 15655. Phone: (724) 238-4983.* ***Web: www.compassinn.com*** *Hours: Tuesday-Saturday 11:00am-4:00pm, Sunday & Holidays 1:00-5:00pm. (Mid April -October) Admission: $7.00 adult, $4.00 child (6-17).*

A great chance to see a restored 1799 stagecoach stop that was a typical roadside inn - complete with cramped sleeping quarters. In the reconstructed cookhouse, you'll learn what terms like "uppercrust" (the bottom of the bread

was sooty from the stove - so the upper crust was much better) mean. The bottom of the bread was "caked" with soot. "Let them eat cake" had a meaning of "Let them eat dirt". Also view the contents of The Barn & Blacksmith Shop.

FORBES STATE FOREST

Laughlintown - PO Box 519 (Del. Rt. 30E) 15655. Phone: (412) 238-9533. **Web:** *www.dcnr.state.pa.us/forestry/stateforests/forests/forbes/forbes.htm*

Fishing, Camping, Trails, Winter Sports.

BLUE HOLE DIVISION - a deep hole with water appearing blue, located on Blue Hole Creek and Cole Run Falls is located a few yards west of the Cole Run Road.

BRADDOCK DIVISION - Pine Knob is an observation point overlooking Uniontown. Cabin Hollow Rocks is an interesting rock formation. Wharton Furnace was one of the last active iron furnaces in Fayette County. Old Water-Powered Grist Mill and Ponderfield Fire Tower.

LINN RUN DIVISION - Grove Run Spring is a walled, much used, spring. Adams Falls is a miniature water fall. Rock formations and Bluestone Quarry (stone from this quarry was used to pave the streets of Pittsburgh).

KOOSER DIVISION- Beck Springs, Old Sawmill Site, & Kooser Fire Tower, Old Logging Railroad Grades & Bridges remain throughout the area.

NEGRO MOUNTAIN DIVISION- many rock formations and Tarkiln is a kiln used to extract tar from the knots of pitch pine.

FORT LIGONIER

Ligonier - 216 South Market Street (US30 & SR 711) 15658. Phone: (724) 238-9701. **Web:** *www.fortligonier.org Hours: Monday-Saturday 10:00am-4:30pm, Sunday Noon-4:30pm (May-October). Admission: $7.00 adult, $5.50 senior, $4.00 child (6-14). Miscellaneous: Fort Ligonier Days in October - reenactments in summer. Quaint town shops within walking distance - some are toy stores!*

Built by the British during the French and Indian War (1758), it was a vital link to the supply line to the West. You'll be able to view gun batteries, the very visibly and painful sharp wooden pickets of re-trenchment, the quarter master's store, a home, hospital (saws made from bone), and the commissary. Because you're free to roam in and out of buildings within the fort, it's ideal for antsy or playful children. The Museum displaying models and realistic dioramas, as well as a new audiovisual presentation about General Washington, serves as your gateway to the Fort complex.

We got the "point" here...

IDLEWILD PARK & SOAK ZONE

Ligonier - Route 30 East, PO Box C (I-80 to I-76, exit 9, Donegal to 711, Left at Route 30) 15658. Phone: (724) 238-3666 or (800) 4 FUNDAY. **Web: www.idlewild.com**

Hours: Opens at 10:00am (Memorial Day Weekend - Labor Day). Admission: $17.00-$26.00 GENERAL (Children age 2 and under FREE). Miscellaneous: Goofy golf, rental boats and pony rides extra.

Now, I know we boast about few amusement parks but our recent visit back (after 30 years) to Idlewild and

Storybook Forest was too fun! Story Book Forest is timeless. You can still meet Goldilocks, Snow White, the Old Woman in the Shoe, and even get a lollypop from the Goodship Lollypop captain. Ride a real trolley into the Neighborhood of Make-Believe. Ask everyone on your trip to a Hug n' Song event at the castle. This village is like being zapped into a giant TV set!

Some other featured spots include:

MISTER ROGER'S NEIGHBORHOOD OF MAKE BELIEVE - ride as a real trolley introduces you to X the Owl , King Friday the XIII and other neighbors.

JUMPIN' JUNGLE - crawl, climb, swing, and bounce.

SOAK ZONE - water slides, pool, Little Squirts Kiddie area.

HOOTIN HOLLER - mining town with Cowboy shows, Old West games and food, Confusion Hill and Loyalhanna Railroad.

OLDE IDLEWILD - roller coasters, merry-go-round, and Raccoon Lagoon kiddie rides (largest kiddie area in the US!)

School-aged kids can ride most every ride in the park and waterpark and families can bring in picnic baskets and grill. If you don't want all that fuss, they offer reasonable prices at Hootin' Holler' and the food is varied and good. Well before or after you eat, try a ride on the "Howler" replica tornado ride around a funnel cloud. There's entertainment from foot stompin', hand clappin' music and dancing to street actors. Every part of the park is clean and easy to manage, even with younger kids. Look for discount days each month or get a membership. Still a great place for old-fashioned family amusement.

FALLINGWATER

Mill Run - Route 381, PO Box R (I-76 exit 9, to SR31 East) 15464. Phone: (724) 329-8501. Web: www.paconserve.org/index-fw1.asp   Hours: Tuesday-Sunday, 10:00am-4:00pm. (mid-March thru Thanksgiving). December weekends only. Closed January and February Admission: $10.00-$16.00 per person. Miscellaneous: For the safety and comfort of all visitors, children must be 6 years old to accompany adults on regular Fallingwater tours; 9 years old for the in-depth tour. Children 9 and under may remain at the supervised Child Care Center where they can enjoy indoor and outdoor games and toys related to architecture and nature. The fee is $2.00 per child per hour. Children's tours for ages 5 and up are available by advance reservation. Falling Water restaurant. Want to see more, visit nearby Kentucky Knob, in Ohiopyle.

One of the most famous houses in America - and a memorable experience that is sure to delight all ages. (See miscellaneous above for age restrictions). The Edgar Kaufmann family used to vacation on this exact spot in the woods during the summer months and loved to picnic by this waterfall. They loved it so much that they commissioned Frank Lloyd Wright (the famous architect) to build a home that would allow them to live on this spot, but not take away from its natural beauty. Wright commented, "I wanted you to live with the waterfall, not just look at it." The home is built from several cantilevers (stacked like Legos) that hang over the waterfall (actually - the stream goes right through the inside of

the home is one with the waterfall...

the house!). Boulders were used as flooring and windows and walls on the first floor. Closer cave-like spaces were used as bedrooms. This visit is sure to make a lasting impression!

L.E. SMITH GLASS COMPANY

Mt. Pleasant - 1900 Liberty Street (I-70 to SR 119 south, then off SR31 - follow signs) 15666. Phone: (800) 537-6484. Web: www.lesmithglass.com   Admission: FREE.

The oldest industry in America - making glassware by hand, started in the early 1600s. This company makes glass pictures, goblets, plates, figurines, and even exclusives patterns for famous people. Your guide starts the tour explaining the glass-making process from the beginning when glass powder (sand, cullet, color) are heated to 2000+ degrees F. in a furnace. Once melted, the molten glass is pulled on a stick and then molded or pressed, fire- glazed and then cooled in a Lehr which uniformly reduces the temperature to prevent shattering. They were making pedestal cake servers the day we were there. They still use many old-time tools and techniques - for example, to frost glass, they dip it in acid. Their warehouse discount prices are great! Fascinating, almost unbelievable, work conditions create an interest for kids.

OHIO PYLE STATE PARK

Ohiopyle - PO Box 105 Rt. 381 North, Off Rt. 40 15470. Phone: (412) 329-8591. Web: www.dcnr.state.pa.us/stateparks/parks/ohiopyle.aspx Miscellaneous: Suggested Whitewater Raft Companies in the area: Laurel Highlands River Tours, 800-4-RAFTIN. Mountain Streams and Trails Outfitters, 800-RAFT-NOW.

Wilderness Voyageurs, 800-272-4141. White Water Adventurers, 800-WWA-RAFT.

More than 14 miles of the Youghiogheny River Gorge churns though the heart of Ohiopyle. The famous Lower Yough, below the scenic Ohiopyle Falls, provides some of the best whitewater boating in the Eastern US. You can also hike or bike the 28-mile Youghiogheny River Trail. Ferncliff Peninsula Park - trails, flowers, trees, birds and wildlife abound. Sit in the creek bed and ride the water through two natural waterslides in Meadow Run. Parking is available adjacent to the SR 381 bridge. Visitor Center, Boat Rentals, Mountain Biking, Fishing, Trails, Winter Sports.

PITTSBURGH SPORTS

Pittsburgh -

PITTSBURGH STEELERS FOOTBALL - Phone: (412) 323-1200 or www.steelers.com. NFL Professional football team and 5-time Super Bowl Champs! Home games played at the new Heinz Field. Heinz Field's horseshoe shape allows for a beautiful view of the city's unique skyline and the fountain at the Point while watching a University of Pitt (Saturday) or Steelers (Sunday/Monday) home game.

PITTSBURGH PIRATES BASEBALL - (412) 321-BUCS or (800) BUY-BUCS or **www.pirateball.com**. PNC Park. National League Professional Baseball (April-September).

PITTSBURGH PENGUINS HOCKEY - Phone: (412) 642-PENS. **www.pittsburghpenguins.com**. Mellon Arena. National Hockey League (October-early April). Look for Family Programs where kids get admission for around $10.00 with paid adult.

SAND CASTLE

Pittsburgh - 1000 Sandcastle Drive (I-376 exit 5, west Route 837) 15120. Phone: (412) 462-6666. ***Web: www.sandcastlewaterpark.com*** *Hours: Daily (June-Labor Day); June 11:00am-6:00pm, July & August 11:00am-7:00pm. Admission: ~$25.00 general, Junior Whitewater Pass (46 inches and under) is about half price, ~$18.00 senior (65+). Parking $5.00. Tidal Wave Café buffet can be added for discount combo pricing.*

15 water slides including "Cliffhangers" pond slide and Two shotgun slides (patron rides on her/his back to a surprise ending - it drops in a free fall to the water below), giant Lazy River, Wet Willie's waterplay, Japanese tidal wave, kiddie and adult pools, Boardwalk and the world's largest hot tub. Riverplex Amphitheater.

PITTSBURGH ZOO & PPG AQUARIUM

Pittsburgh - One Wild Place (In Highland Park, SR 28 North to exit 6, follow signs) 15206. Phone: (412) 665-3640 or 1-800-4-PGH-ZOO. ***Web: www.pittsburghzoo.com*** *Hours: Daily 10:00am-6:00pm (Summer), 9:00am-5:00pm (fall/spring). Reduced hours in winter. Zoo is open year-round except Thanksgiving, Christmas, and New Year's Days. Admission: $10.00 adult, $9.00 senior (60+), $8.00 child (2-13). Parking Free. Reduced fees in the winter. Miscellaneous: Train, boat or carousel rides $2.00. Food available. Fun "incline" escalator takes you up the hill to the zoo.*

Over 4000 creatures both great and small. Natural settings with themes like: Tropical Forest, Asian Forest (Siberian Tigers), African Savanna (elephants), Water's Edge and newer PPG Aquarium - wonderful use of glass that allows you to feel you can almost "touch" the fish. Tunnels, too!

Pittsburgh Zoo & PPG Aquarium *(cont.)*

WATER'S EDGE - Stories woven by Inuit natives who live side by side with these magnificent creatures provide the introduction to the bears and their environment. Paw prints lead to the polar bear den for a nose-to-snout

encounter when the bears lounge in this temperature-controlled climate. Two large viewing windows intensify the excitement of seeing the young brother bears as they splash in their freshwater waterfall and play in their dig yard. The paw prints continue to lead visitors down a nature trail to Pier Town, a replica of an Alaskan fishing village, complete with a cannery, a bait and tackle shop, and a sustainable seafood market. Wow!

Mr. Polar Bear having a little swim time...

KIDS KINGDOM - Where kids can act like animals! This interactive facility is complete with playground equipment that replicates animal motions and behaviors so kids can play like the animals play. It's also full of hands-on animal experiences, like the walk-through Deer Yard, where kids can actually touch a white-tailed deer or the walk-through Kangaroo Yard where Australian gray kangaroos get so close, kids can reach out and touch them! There's also a friendly Goat Yard, the meerkat exhibit through a see-through tunnel, beaver and otter exhibits and a fabulous sea lion pool featuring several of these playful marine mammals. Swing-like spiders, Turtle Race, Penguin Slide, or climb through Mole Tunnel (big hits with the kiddies!).

FRICK ART & HISTORICAL CENTER

Pittsburgh - 7227 Reynolds Street (I-376, Exit # 9) 15208. Phone: (412) 371-0600. Web: http://frickart.org/home/ Hours: Tuesday-Sunday 10:00am-5:00pm. Reservations suggested holiday weekends. Admission: FREE. Clayton is $10.00-$12.00. Reduced for Family Days tours.

Henry Clay Frick's (industrialist & art collector) mansion (Clayton) with original possessions, gardens, art museum and children's playhouse (now the Visitor's Center). Check out the floorboards that were once the bowling alley (playhouse). Kids will love the pretend food displayed in the dining rooms and Helen's bedroom. Family Days (ages 6-12) teaches about late 1800s life in Pittsburgh with a hands-on activity (dress up or craft) after the shortened tour with teen docents.

DUQUESNE INCLINE

Pittsburgh - *1220 Grandview Avenue (use either West Carson Street, or the Station Square access road which parallels the Monongahela and Ohio rivers) 15211. Phone: (412) 381-1665. Web: http://trfn.clpgh.org/incline Hours: Monday-Saturday 5:30am-12:45am. Sundays and Major Holidays 7:00am-12:45am. Admission: $1.00-$2.00 (age 6+) - Fares are each way. Seniors are FREE.*

One of the few remaining cable cars still in use. Look for the red lights heading up the hill and the wood carved, paneled and trimmed cars. The cars climb and descend 400 ft at a 30 degree angle. The Upper Station, on Grandview Avenue, includes a new platform for the public to view the Incline's historic hoisting equipment, as well as displays regarding the history of the Incline and the City of Pittsburgh, and pictures of other cable and rail cars from around the world. The observation platform outside has the best view of the city.

...the famous incline hard at work...

CARNEGIE SCIENCE CENTER

Pittsburgh - *One Allegheny Avenue (near Stadium - off I-279 or I-376) 15212. Phone: (412) 237-3400. Web: www.carnegiesciencecenter.org Hours: Sunday-Friday 10:00am-5:00pm, Saturday 10:00am-7:00pm. Admission: $14.00 adult, $10.00 senior (62+), $10.00 child (3-18). General admission includes exhibits, UPMC SportsWorks, Buhl Planetarium and USS Requin. Omnimax & Laser Fantasy Show extra. Miscellaneous: Discovery Store. Restaurant café.*

Over 250 hands-on exhibits! Here's a menu of what you can expect at this fun-filled science center:

EXPLORATION STATION & JUNIOR STATION - Habitats and live animals, structures & building, magnets and electric. Launching air rockets; Playing the laser harp and the PVC pipe organ; or Engineering dams, locks, channels and flood plains to control the flow of a river.

OMNIMAX THEATER - Movies that literally make you a PART of the action.

INTERACTIVE PLANETARIUM - Keeps you on "an edge". Also features laser light shows.

WW II SUBMARINE - Climb aboard the authentic USS Reguin. See demonstrations on dives, power generators, even touch a real torpedo!

Carnegie Science Center (cont.)

SCIQUEST LIVE SCIENCE DEMONSTRATIONS or KITCHEN CHEMISTRY - Push a button to create a 4 ft. tornado or learn cooking chemistry (in a themed classroom setting). Lots of waves and air here!

SEASCAPE - A large coral reef aquarium and water play table.

SPORTWORKS - Best Virtual Sports Facility we've seen for kids! Experience virtual reality basketball and pitching cage. Cruise down Olympic bobsleds, hang glide the Grand Canyon or mini-golf Math. 60 + interactives - all included in admission price. This place is family-interactive and lets each family member "show off" their skills. Plan to spend half your time in here!

MINIATURE RAILROAD & VILLAGE - 2300 square feet of a re-created village connecting the history and culture of southwestern PA between late 1800s and the 1930s.

HEINZ FIELD TOURS

Pittsburgh - 400 Stadium Circle (Heinz Field) 15212. Phone: Heinz Field Tour Hotline (412) 697-7150. **Web: http://news.steelers.com/heinzfield/** *Admission: $6.00 adult, $4.00 senior (55+), $3.00 child (18 and under). Various weekdays and some Saturdays (April-October - see website for details). Miscellaneous: McDonald's Steelers KidZONE Show - Show taping takes place at Heinz Field in the Coca-Cola Great Hall on select Tuesdays early Fall.* Heinz Field is not only the home of the Pittsburgh Steelers and the University of Pittsburgh Panthers football teams but a proud icon in downtown Pittsburgh. Tours of Heinz Field consist of the Coca-Cola Great Hall, club, suite and service levels, press box, warning track, south plaza and much more.

NATIONAL AVIARY

Pittsburgh - Allegheny Commons West (off I-279 North Shore exit - follow signs) 15212. Phone: (412) 323-7235. **Web: www.aviary.org** *Hours: Daily 9:00am-5:00pm (everyday but Christmas). Admission: $8.00 adult, $7.00 senior (60+), $6.50 child (2-12). Miscellaneous: Get up-close-and-personal with African Penguin "Stanley" or resident owls daily right before or after lunchtime.*

See 220 species of birds live in natural habitats like rainforests, deserts, and marshes. The tropical areas have rare, exotic birds in free-flight atriums. Favorites to look for are the live Toucan (so animated, it appears mechanical!), a real cuckoo bird (that sings a loud, sweet sound), and the funny billed marsh birds (boat and spoon shaped, for example). The

Tropical Rainstorm at 12:30pm daily in the Wetlands of the Americas 200,000 cubic foot walk-through exhibit is so-o-o cool! Don't you just love the birds flying overhead…especially entertaining during feeding times (early afternoons).

PHOTO ANTIQUITIES

Pittsburgh - *531 East Ohio Street 15212. Web: www.photoantiquities.com Phone: (412) 231-7881. Hours: Monday-Saturday 10:00am-4:00pm, except Tuesdays, Sundays and holidays. Admission: $3.00-$6.50 (age 5+).*

Photo Antiquities Museum of Photographic History offers a history lesson on photography. The Museum, designed in the Victorian style with period music playing in the background, lends to the feeling of being in the 19th century. Photo and paper processes, antique cameras, vintage historical print exhibits. Follow the history of photography with a guided tour, from the Daguerreotype c. 1839 (the first commercially viable photographic image produced onto a silver coated copper plate) to present day digital photography.

PITTSBURGH CHILDREN'S MUSEUM

Pittsburgh - *10 Children's Way - Allegheny Square (off I-279, follow signs - just blocks from the stadium) 15212. Phone: (412) 322-5058. Web: www.pittsburghkids.org Hours: Monday-Saturday 10:00am-5:00pm, Sunday Noon-5:00pm. (Closed Monday during the school year). Admission: $9.00 adult, $8.00 senior (55+) or child (2-18). Parking is $5.00. Miscellaneous: Open until 8:00pm on Fridays. Pecaboo Café. Workshops on Saturdays and some Friday evenings. Oh Baby! Area for infants/toddlers. Changing Lower Level Gallery. Surprises in Store Gift Shop.*

The expanded Museum offers exhibits based on the philosophy of "Play with Real Stuff." Children can tinker under

© Albert VecerkaEsto

Waterplay fun…

the hood of a MINI Cooper and pound nails with a hammer in the Garage Workshop, build a boat and sail it down the rapids on a 53-foot waterway in Waterplay, stage their own performances with costumes and makeup in the Theater and much more. Many of the new exhibits are interactive art. Here are some favorites:

GARDEN OF GIZMOS - an interactive exhibit that combines beauty, interesting motion, fascinating physical phenomenon and an enchanting look at plants over time. Watch the seasons pass in a few minutes as a circle of 16 video monitors displays a time-lapse, panoramic view of the great outdoors. Make bouncy "springs" dance, sway with the palms, crank out the groundhogs, open a peacock's elaborate tail, make a circle of birds flap and turn overhead, or inspire a flock of doves to "do the wave".

BACKYARD - exhibits include Allegheny Waterworks, a fountain made from historical artifacts where children control the water flow; Animated Earth, vats of bubbling "mud" where children get their hands dirty in fun, creative ways; Musical Swing Set, where swinging inspires a symphony of sound; and Poodle Sphinx, a 25-foot pink poodle.

MISTER ROGERS' NEIGHBORHOOD - a life-sized recreation of the television show's set where children can find many activities that encourage them to explore, imagine and create. Loved Mr. Rogers Neighborhood? The Neighborhood features water exhibits, a video welcome from the beloved Fred Rogers, a closet of cardigans and sneakers to play pretend, a replica trolley and replica home.

Isn't it neat how you can climb the ropes in a dome of the former planetarium and launch your parachute? Look for Al, Mo & Oh... The Three That Got Away fish sculpture on the way in.

RODEF SHALOM BIBLICAL BOTANICAL GARDENS

Pittsburgh - 4905 Fifth Avenue 15213. Web: www.biblicalgardenpittsburgh.org Phone: (412) 621-6566. Hours: Sunday-Thursday 10:00am-2:00pm. Also from 7:00-9:00pm on Wednesday and from Noon-1:00pm Saturday. (June - mid-September).

The garden was established in 1987. It is the largest of its kind in North America (1/3 acre) and the only one with an ongoing program of research and publication. Visit the land of the Bible in a setting of a waterfall, a desert, a stream, the Jordan, which meanders through the garden from Lake Galilee to the Dead Sea. All plants are labeled with biblical verses accompanying them. See wheat, barley, millet and many herbs grown by the ancient Israelites along with olives, dates, pomegranates, figs, cedars. Biblical names given to local plants show the affection of each generation for the Bible. Free Admission.

SOLDIERS AND SAILORS MEMORIAL MUSEUM

Pittsburgh - 4141 Fifth Ave. 15213. Web: www.soldiersandsailorshall.org/index.html Phone: (412) 621-4254.   Hours: Monday-Saturday 10:00am-4:00pm. Admission: Small fee.

Soldiers & Sailors National Military Museum & Memorial is one of the country's largest museums dedicated to honoring & remembering our Veterans. The museum houses exhibits that span from the Civil War to present day conflicts that tell the stories of ordinary citizens called upon to do extraordinary duties for the United States of America. Also African-American and Revolutionary War films.

ALLEGHENY OBSERVATORY

Pittsburgh - Riverview Park (US19 in Riverview Park off Perrysville Avenue) 15214. Phone: (412) 321-2400. Web: www.pitt.edu/~aobsvtry/ Hours: Thursday-Friday (by appointment - evenings - April - October). Thursday night tours are held from May 1st through the third week of August and the Friday night tours are held from April 1st through November 1st. Admission: FREE

One of the foremost observatories in the world. A short slide or film presentation is shown followed by a walking tour of the building finally ending up at the 13" Fitz-Clark refractor. If it's a clear night you would be shown whatever celestial objects are within range of the telescope that night. Dress for the temperature outside.

GATEWAY CLIPPER FLEET

Pittsburgh - 9 Station Square Dock - Downtown (I-376 exit Smithfield Street) 15219. Phone: (412) 355-7980. Web: www.gatewayclipper.com   Admission: $9.00-$11.00 adult, $5.00-$7.50 child signtseeing. Add $8.00-$20.00 for lunch or dinner cruises. Miscellaneous: On board gift shops and snacks available.

A "Pittsburgh River Tradition" has sightseeing cruises sailing the three rivers. They are the largest and most successful sightseeing vessels in the America. There are several different boats in their fleet (all climate controlled) and many targeted toward ages 12 and under. These include Sunday Fun Cruises (w/ DJ

Dance), Good Ship Lollipop Cruise (meet Lolly the Clown), Lock N Dam Adventure Cruises and 2 hour Sunset Cruises. Other mascots who frequent kids' cruises are Deckster Duck, and River Rover.

JUST DUCKY TOURS

Pittsburgh - Station Square - Downtown (I-376 exit Smithfield Street, next to Hard Rock Cafe) 15219. Phone: (412) 402-DUCK. **Web: www.justduckytours.com** *Hours: Daily (mid-April - October). November weekends. Admission: $19.00 adult, $18.00 senior/student, $15.00 child (3-12), $5.00 child (2 and under).*

Venture aboard these funny, fully restored WW II Land and Water Vehicles! On land they use wheels and conventional steering. On water they use a propeller and a rudder. By land - narrated tours include Pennsylvania and Lake Erie Railroad, Penn Station, South End and many historical downtown buildings. Learn Pittsburghese and about many movies made here. By water - see the Allegheny

River and Golden Triangle or the Monongahela.

...part bus...part boat...SPLASH!

Kids may get the chance to be captain of the boat for awhile (they get a sticker to prove it!). You'll quack, sing and laugh a ton. Have fun!

MONONGAHELA INCLINE

Pittsburgh - Carson Street at Station Square   15219. Phone: (412) 442-2000. Hours: Monday-Saturday 5:30am-12:45am, Sunday & Holidays 7:00am-12:45am. Admission: Small fare each way.

The first US incline...boasting a 35 degree climbing angle and 358 foot elevation, this incline transports tourists and commuters daily from downtown to Mt. Washington. A special note to point out to the kids is that this engineering feat was designed in 1870 - before electric streetcars and the automobile! The trick is that one car climbs while the other descends

...the view at night

- look for the green and yellow lights highlighting the track.

FORT PITT MUSEUM & POINT STATE PARK

Pittsburgh - *101 Commonwealth Place (off I-376, I-279, SR8, or SR51 on the forks of downtown, Ohio River) 15222. Web: www.fortpittmuseum.com/WelcomePage.html Phone: (412) 281-9284. Hours: Wednesday-Sunday 9:00am-5:00pm. Admission: $5.00 adult, $4.00 senior (60+), $2.00 child (6-17). Miscellaneous: Blockhouse welcome center and gift shop (free to visit). Living history re-enactments (Summer-Sunday afternoons).*

This was the site of the largest British post in North America until they were forced to leave during the American Revolution. The fort played a pivotal role in the French and Indian War. Exhibits re-create the story of war, trade, and the founding of Pittsburgh. Listen to a taped explanation of the fort while viewing a scale model of Fort Pitt. There's also an 18th century trading post. Located at the tip of Pittsburgh's Golden Triangle, POINT STATE PARK has a fabulous water fountain, paved promenades along the riverfront & overlooks with dramatic views of the city, busy waterways, impressive hillside scenery (**www.dcnr.state.pa.us/stateparks/parks/point.htm** or 412-471-0235).

HEINZ PITTSBURGH REGIONAL HISTORY CENTER

Pittsburgh - *1212 Smallman Street (in the Strip District, off I-579 and I-376) 15222. Phone: (412) 454-6000. Web: www.pghhistory.org Hours: Daily 10:00am-5:00pm. Closed Easter, Thanksgiving, Christmas, New Years. Admission: $7.50 adult, $6.00 senior (62+), $5.00 student w/ id, $3.50 child (6-18). Miscellaneous: Museum shop, café.*

The initiative of this museum is to preserve Western Pennsylvania history through intriguing exhibits such as:

POINTS IN TIME - Emphasis is placed on Steelworkers who were immigrants. Meet Mary, the mother of 5 children and married to a steelworker. Or, an African American journey to Freedom.

GREAT HALL - 1949 restored trolley with audio and a Conestoga wagon. ISALY's Dairy (Klondikes!) and a greeting from a robot that speaks fluent Pittsburghese.

WESTERN PENNSYLVANIA SPORTS MUSEUM - which includes exhibits dedicated to high school, collegiate, and professional sports in the Pittsburgh region (*go Steelers!*). The space promises to "get you in the

 game" with more than 70 hands-on interactive exhibits, a two-story video theatre and 20 audio-visual programs for visitors of all ages. The Interactive Football Exhibit, Make Your Own Medal, and Franco Harris' Immaculate Reception Shoes are the highlights for kids.

HEINZ 57 DISCOVERY AREA – Tells a story of 8 real kids from the area – a steel worker, a servant, and an over-privileged child. Children even as young as 12-14 were laborers – learn how some of them did their jobs (ex. packing pickles for Heinz or ironing clothes for pennies).

LEWIS AND CLARK - Rediscovering Lewis & Clark: A Journey with the Rooney Family on the Corps of Discovery Trail.

People with a heritage from Pittsburgh should be very proud and touched by this emotional history center!

SOCIETY FOR CONTEMPORARY CRAFTS

Pittsburgh - 2100 Smallman Street (Strip District) 15222. Phone: (412) 261-7003. Web: www.contemporarycraft.org Hours: Tuesday-Saturday 9:00am-5:00pm.

Visitors discover latest trends in the gallery, the store and the children's studio. Weekends for Families include demos, performances and workshops related to current exhibits. Because families are one of their primary audiences, they have developed the Drop In Studio, a free hands-on activity area for children and adults. The space, which is open during all public hours, allows visitors to participate in a hands-on art activity that has been developed by artists to tie-in to the special exhibitions

BEECHWOOD FARM NATURE PRESERVE

Pittsburgh - 614 Dorseyville Road (SR8 & SR28) 15238. Phone: (412) 963-6100. Web: www.aswp.org Hours: Tuesday-Saturday, 9:00am-5:00pm. Sunday, 1:00-5:00pm. Free admission.

Headquarters of the Audubon Society of Western Pennsylvania. Acres of fields, woodlands, ponds, and trails. Beechwood's 134 acres contain more than five miles of walking trails, which are open to the public from dawn to dusk everyday, year-round. The Bird observation room, Discovery Room & Outdoor Discovery field programs are favorites for kids.

MEADOWCROFT ROCKSHELTER AND MUSEUM OF RURAL LIFE

Pittsburgh (Avella) - *401 Meadowcroft Road (I-79 - Exit 11 Bridgeville to SR50 West) 15312. Phone: (724) 587-3412.* **Web: http://meadowcroft.pghhistory.org/** *Hours: Wednesday-Saturday Noon-5:00pm, Sunday 1:00-5:00pm (Memorial Day-Labor Day). Weekends only (May, September, October). Open some weekends in November and December for special events. Admission: $6.50 adult, $3.50 (6-16) Rural Life Museum. Additional fee for tours of the Rockshelter. Miscellaneous: Visitors Center and Café. Best during festivals for" hands on history" personalized sessions.*

Re-live rugged rural life from 200 years ago as you walk the dirt and stone roads of this reconstructed village. By touring a settler log house, schoolhouse, country store, barn and blacksmith shop - you'll be introduced to inhabitants like the Native Americans, frontier settlers, farmers, lumbermen,

coal miners, and conservationists who have worked the land. Get involved by taking a real school lesson (with slate and chalk) in a 1 room schoolhouse. Shear sheep and then spin and weave wool.

Meadowcroft Rockshelter has provided archaeologists with a rare glimpse into the lives of the first people to arrive in the New World. Visitors may go inside the open excavation and see evidence of tools and campfires made by these first Americans thousands of years ago. Discover how these ancient people survived - from what they ate to the weapons they relied on everyday - and, actually practice using a Native American "atlatl" (spear throwing). The grounds of this living history museum are on an archeological prehistoric dig site.

WILLOWBROOK SKI AREA

Pittsburgh (Belle Vernon) - *RD #2   15012. Phone: (724) 872-7272 or (724) 929-2294. Web: http://pittsburgh.about.com/library/blwillowbrook.htm*

With one slope for beginners and another for intermediates, the resort is perfect for learning new skills or brushing up on old ones. Snowboarding and Children's Programs. Longest Run: 1500 ft.; 2 Slopes & Trails.

LITTLE LAKE THEATRE COMPANY

Pittsburgh (Canonsburg) - 500 Lakeside Drive, South 15317. Phone: (724) 745-6300. Web: www.littlelaketheatre.org

Plays for the entire family for 50 years. Looking Glass Theatres, Fall Family Matinees.

PITTSBURGH'S PENNSYLVANIA MOTOR SPEEDWAY

Pittsburgh (Carnegie) - (US 22/30, Noblestown Exit) 15106. Phone: (724) 853-RACE. Web: www.ppms.com

Auto Racing every Saturday Night, April through mid-September featuring the Super Late Models, Advance Auto Parts Crate Late Models, Pure Stocks, E-Mods, Amateur Stocks, Young Guns, and Demos on Dirt's Monster Half Mile. Visit their Sister Track Motordrome Speedway on Friday Evenings for exciting NASCAR Dodge Weekly Series Action. Their slogan: "We'll sell you the whole seat, but you'll only need the edge!"

BOYCE PARK SKI AREA

Pittsburgh (Monroeville) - 675 Old Frankstown Road (near U.S. 22 and right off of I-76) 15639. Web: www.county.allegheny.pa.us/parks/fees/ski.asp Phone: (724) 733-4656. Snow Report: (724) 733-4665.

This ski area may be tiny and run by a county park, but lift tickets are inexpensive ($9 weekdays and $13 weekends). The park offers nine runs including moguls, halfpipe, Nastar timing runs with gates, jumps and night skiing. Lodge with a roaring fireplace, hot food and drinks. There's also a fitness center, roller skating, swimming, outdoor hot tubs, snow tubing, sleigh rides and even bowling.

CARNEGIE MUSEUM OF ART

Pittsburgh (Oakland) - 4400 Forbes Avenue (connected to Natural History Museum) 15213. Phone: (412) 622-3131. Web: www.cmoa.org Hours: Tuesday-Saturday 10:00am-5:00pm, Sunday Noon-5:00pm. Admission: $6.00-$10.00 (age 3+). Admission includes Carnegie Museum of Natural History. Miscellaneous: ARTventures: family art activities Every Saturday 12:30-4:30 p.m., ongoing. Ages 4 and up with an adult. Café open for lunch.

Paintings, sculpture, film and video projections reflect values and ideas from cultures long ago and today. Hall of Sculpture. Hall of Architecture. Add this museum to your visit to the Museum of Natural History (included).

CARNEGIE MUSEUM OF NATURAL HISTORY

Pittsburgh (Oakland) - 4400 Forbes Avenue (I-579 to Oakland/Monroeville exit to Blvd. Of the Allies OR I-376E to Forbes Ave exit 2a) 15213. Phone: (412) 622-3131. Web: www.carnegiemnh.org Hours: Tuesday-Saturday 10:00am-5:00pm, Sunday Noon-5:00pm. Admission: $10.00 adult, $7.00 senior, $6.00 child (3-18). Admission includes same-day access to both Carnegie Museum of Natural History and Carnegie Museum of Art. Miscellaneous: Store, café. Earth Theater - 210 degree wrap around screen featuring tornadoes or meteors or dinos (extra small admission). Family Programs on weekends.

See a world famous dinosaur collection with a T-Rex and 9 other species plus a PaleoLab and Bonehunters Quarry (Dino Hall fossil digs). In the Stratavator,

a simulated elevator ride takes you 16,000 feet down into the Earth below the museum. Visitors enter the elevator cab, and meet their tour guide, a miner, seen through the cab's "window"—a video screen. The stratavator stops at the museum's basement storage rooms, a coal mine, a limestone cave, and other geological features. As the cab vibrates, rock strata whiz by between stops. (This is a "hot" one

...all aboard, the "Stratavator"

for the kids!) American Indians and the Natural World examine the belief systems, philosophies, and practical knowledge that guide Indian people. Polar World Dioramas illustrate the Arctic environment and the traditional

...digging for clues...

Inuit way of life. Scenes depict kayak hunting, ice fishing, and a life-size recreation of an Inuit snowhouse. Additional sites include Egyptian mummies and a crawl-thru Egyptian tomb; a Discovery Room (hands-on); Hall of Botany; and the Hall of Minerals and Gems (fluorescent minerals, crystals). Watch, around every corner you may be greeted by a giant surprise!

PHIPPS CONSERVATORY

Pittsburgh (Oakland) - One Schenley Park (I-376 East, take the Forbes Ave./Oakland exit 2a). 15213. Phone: (412) 622-6914. Web: www.phipps.conservatory.org Hours: Daily 9:30am-5:00pm, Hours extended to 9:00pm on Friday. Admission: $6.00-$9.00 (age 2+).

A historic landmark 13 room Victorian glass house featuring tropical and desert motifs plus one of the nation's finest Bonsai collections. Feel the heat in the desert or smell the wafting fragrance in the Orchid Room. Discovery Garden - outdoor hands-on learning for children (boxwood maze, sensory garden). Summer-Butterfly Forest.

PITTSBURGH PLAYHOUSE JR.

Pittsburgh (Oakland) - 222 Craft Avenue 15213. Phone: (412) 621-4445. Web: www.pointpark.edu/default.aspx?id=2319

Over 50 years of children's classics and new works like Snow White or Winnie-the-Pooh (November - May)

NATIONALITY CLASSROOMS

Pittsburgh (Oakland) - 1209 Cathedral of Learning (I-376 west to exit 7A, University of Pittsburgh) 15260. Phone: (412) 624-6000. Web: www.pitt.edu/~natrooms/ Hours: Monday-Saturday 9:00am-2:30pm, Sunday 11:00am-2:30pm. Admission: $3.00 adult, $2.00 senior (60+), $1.00 child (8-18). Miscellaneous: While on campus, musically inclined may want to visit the Stephen Foster Memorial Museum (ex. Foster's piano, musical instruments and compositions. (412) 624-4100 or www.pitt.edu/~amerimus/museum.htm.)

"Tour the World in 90 Minutes!" - Visit 24 classrooms depicting heritages of different ethnic communities. In these rooms, themes are rendered in wood and glass, iron and stone, fabric, color, and words. Inspiration flows from such varied sources as Athens in the time of Pericles, a palace hall in Beijing's Forbidden City, an ancient monastic Indian university, flowers that grow in Czech and Slovak valleys, a 6th-century oratory from Ireland's Golden Age, an Asante temple courtyard in Ghana, London's House of Commons, and the intimate hearth-centered life of America's early New Englanders. See authentic examples of cultural architecture and décor from Africa, Asia, Middle East, and Eastern and Western Europe including: Ukrainian Room – wood carvings on beams and doors, hand painted pottery and tile. German - stained glass fairy tales. African - Sankofa birds.

KENNYWOOD PARK

Pittsburgh (West Mifflin) - *4800 Kennywood Blvd. (I-376, Exit 9) 15122. Phone: (412) 461-0500. Web: www.kennywood.com Hours: Monday-Sunday 11:00am-after dark (Mid-May - Labor Day). Open some weekends in early May & early September. Admission: $15.00-$19.00 general (Junior and senior passes). All day general passes available ~$31.00. Parking is free.*

A traditional amusement park -- and a National historic landmark. The park features thirty-one major rides, including three water rides, three classic wood coasters, the Phantom's Revenge steel coaster, and a one-of-a-kind indoor, dark coaster, the Exterminator. Kiddieland offers 14 "just for kids" rides. Home of the world's fastest coaster, live shows, arcades, mini-golf, paddle boats, and Lost Kennywood Lagoon area.

LINN RUN STATE PARK

Rector - *Linn Run Road (US 30 east & PA Rte. 81 south) 15677. Phone: (412) 238-6623. Web: www.dcnr.state.pa.us/STATEPARKS/PARKS/linnrun.aspx*

The varied topography and mixed hardwood and evergreen forest make this park a scenic place for picnicking, hiking and cabin rentals. Grove and Rock runs join to make Linn Run, an excellent trout stream which has a waterfall, Adams Falls. Boat Rentals, Mountain Biking, Sledding, Campsites and Rustic Cabins.

LAUREL RIDGE STATE PARK

Rockwood - *1117 Jim Mountain Road 15557. Phone: (724) 455-3744. Web: www.dcnr.state.pa.us/stateparks/parks/laurelridge.aspx*

Laurel Ridge State Park stretches along the Laurel Mountains from the Yougiogheny River at Ohiopyle to the Conemaugh Gorge near Johnstown. Most visitors come to hike the 70 miles of the Laurel Highland trails. Snowmobiling and cross-country skiing on trails in winter.

WESTERWALD POTTERY

Scenery Hill - *40 Pottery Lane (US 40 - 7.5 miles east of I-79) 15360. Phone: (724) 945-6000. Web: www.westerwaldpottery.com Hours: Monday-Friday 8:00am-5:00pm. Admission: FREE. Miscellaneous: Gift shop. Discounted pieces outside.*

Potters making their signature country-style decorative wares are simply amazing to watch! See a pre-measured lump of clay get hand thrown on a wheel and shaped before your eyes. They make pots, plates, mugs, and cute (and useful) apple bakers. The Westerwald signature is on every piece and they specialize in personalized giftware. You'll even get to see the drying (hardening kilns bricked up for 3 days) and the artists who glaze and paint each piece by hand. The blue and gray stoneware is a reproduction quality of those made in Germany's Westerwald region (thus the company name) as early as the 16th century. Look for a specialized name piece as a souvenir.

WEST OVERTON MUSEUMS

Scottdale - Overholt Drive (West Overton Village - SR819) 15683. Phone: (724) 887-7910. Web: http://fay-west.com/westoverton/ Hours: Tuesday-Saturday 10:00am-4:00pm, Sunday 1:00-5:00pm (Mid-May - September). Admission: $4.00-$7.00 (age 7+).

A 19th Century industrial village with a museum, barns, and a gristmill. Visitors to West Overton Museums may view the film, Pillars of Fire, which illustrates the process of turning coal into coke; visit the Overholt Homestead and Gift Shop; tour two floors of the Overholt Mill/Distillery, which contains a large collection of household, farm and industrial tools; visit the birthplace of Henry Clay Frick (millionaire by age 30 with steel coke business); and tour the wash house and smokehouse.

FLIGHT 93 MEMORIAL CHAPEL & IMPACT SITE

Shanksville - Boulevard of Heroes, P.O. Box 134 (Boulevard of Heroes) 15560. Phone: (814) 444-8339 or 444-1935. Web: www.flt93memorialchapel.org Hours: Friday-Monday 10:00am-3:00pm. Miscellaneous: To continue journey to IMPACT SITE from FLIGHT 93 MEMORIAL CHAPEL - Continue 3 more miles to Stop sign in Shanksville. (Continuing Boulevard of Heroes) U.S. POST OFFICE, Shanksville, Immediately on right before Stop sign. LEFT one block, onto Lambertsville Road (Continuing Boulevard of Heroes). 2.5 miles on Lambertsville Road to Lambertsville (Continuing Boulevard of Heroes). To Right onto Skyline Drive up and over the rise to IMPACT SITE.

Just three miles from the actual crash site, the non-denominational chapel is dedicated as a spiritual memorial and perpetual tribute in honor of the heroes of Flight 93 and all others who perished Sept. 11, 2001. The chapel is open to people of all faiths and is available for individual faith groups to worship together under the direction of their respective religious leaders. Everything about the design of the chapel is reminiscent of the story of Flight 93 and so the visual experience keeps bringing the visitor's thoughts back to that place and time.

KOOSER STATE PARK

Somerset - 943 Glades Pike (PA Route 31) 15501. Phone: (814) 445-8673 or (888) PA-Parks. Web: www.dcnr.state.pa.us/stateparks/parks/kooser.aspx

Kooser State Park is bound by Forbes State Forest on two sides and is an ideal spot to start an overnight backpacking trip on the 70-mile Laurel Highlands Hiking Trail. The early settlers told of an American Indian battle that was fought nearby and a number of war arrows and spearheads have been found in the area. Beach, Campsites, Rustic Cabins, Fishing.

LAUREL HILL STATE PARK

Somerset - 1454 Laurel Hill Park Road (Pennsylvania Turnpike Exit 110 (Somerset), drive west on PA Rte. 31) 15501. Web: www.dcnr.state.pa.us/stateparks/parks/ laurelhill.aspx Phone: (814) 445-7725.

The 63-acre Laurel Hill Lake is a focal point of the park. A beautiful stand of old growth hemlocks lies along the Hemlock Trail. Remains of a logging railroad, like a wooden cross-tie or a rusty rail spike, can be seen along the Tramroad Trail. Beach, Year-round Education & Interpretation Center, Boat Rentals, Campsites, Fishing, and Trails. Some feel this park is best in the winter with abundant snowfalls and winter sport recreation opportunities in abundance.

SOMERSET HISTORICAL CENTER

Somerset - 10649 Somerset Pike (SR601 and SR985) 15501. Phone: (814) 445-6077. Web: www.somersetcounty.com/historicalcenter Hours: Tuesday-Saturday 9:00am-5:00pm, Sunday Noon-5:00pm (May-October). Admission: $2.00-$4.00 (age 5+). Miscellaneous: 12 minute film about the history of the mountain barrier area.

This center interprets daily rural life in southwestern Pennsylvania from 1750 - 1950. Isolated because of the Allegheny Mountains, they had to produce necessities from home - maple sugar, ginseng, and furs were traded - food was produced on the farm. With the Industrial Revolution came advances in farming (hand labor to machines and commercial crops). The site includes a log house, a smokehouse, a log barn, a covered bridge, a maple sugar camp, a general store, and various machines (corn husker & shredder, reaper, buggy). Pioneer and agricultural demonstrations daily.

TOUR-ED MINE AND MUSEUM

Tarentum - 748 Bull Creek Road (SR28 north, exit 14 - Allegheny Valley Expressway) 15084. Phone: (724) 224-4720. Web: www.tour-edmine.com Hours: Wednesday-Monday, 10:00am-4:00pm. (Memorial Day-Labor Day). Admission: $6.50-$8.00. Miscellaneous: Cool temperatures below - about 50 degrees F. - A jacket or sweater is suggested. Gift shop.

Wearing required hard hats and ducking down a little, you'll board a modernized mining car as you travel 1/2 mile underground into an actual coal mine. Original mines began in 1800 when labor was all done by hand. See demonstrations of this plus setting up a new mine area (installing the roof supports to prevent cave-ins), and the most modern mining - a continuous miner (robotic). Above ground, you can take a stroll to the past again as you view company stores, housing, strip mines, and a sawmill.

SEARIGHT TOLL HOUSE MUSEUM

Uniontown - US40 west 15401. Phone: (724) 439-4422. Hours: Tuesday-Saturday 10:00am-4:00pm, Sunday 2:00-6:00pm (Mid-May - Mid-October). Admission is $1.00 for adults and children are free.

In 1806, the National Road began construction connecting the East and West. Searight Tollhouse received its name from its location near the village of Searight, named for its most prominent citizen, William Searight. Searight owned a prosperous tavern on the National Road, the ruins of which may still be seen today. The National Road tollhouse is kept as it once was, with a toll keeper's office, kitchen, and living room.

PENNSYLVANIA TROLLEY MUSEUM

Washington - One Museum Road (I-79 to Meadowlands, exit 8) 15301. Phone: (877) PA-TROLLEY. Web: www.pa-trolley.org Hours: Daily 11:00am-5:00pm (Memorial Day-Labor Day), Long Weekends & Holidays (April, May, September-December). Admission: $7.00 adult, $6.00 senior (65+), $4.00 child (3-15). Additional $1.00-$3.00 for tours of Trolley Display Buildings. Miscellaneous: Museum store. In cooler weather, heated trolleys are running. Trolley theatre videos. Air conditioned museum.

Because the kids will be heavy with anticipation once they see the rail yard full of trolleys - plan on taking a ride right away! The trolleys are run on four miles of Pennsylvania rail and each ride takes approximately 30 minutes. Along the rail, you'll learn the history of the vehicle that you are riding on and why it's so special. As you complete your guided or self-guided tour, you'll get to meet CAR #832 - "The Streetcar Named Desire" used in the stage play by Tennessee Williams. Be sure to peek in the car shop where volunteers are restoring cars for future use.

...famous streetcars...

WASHINGTON COUNTY MUSEUM

Washington - *49 East Maiden Street (Route 40 - downtown) 15301. Phone: (412) 225-6740.* **Web: www.wchspa.org/html/house.htm** *Hours: Tuesday - Friday 11:00am-4:00pm and reserved group tours on Saturdays (March-December). Admission: $2.00-$4.00.*

The stately stone house, located in downtown Washington, Pennsylvania, was built in 1812 by John Julius LeMoyne, the father of Francis Julius LeMoyne. Both father and son were practicing physicians, but it was the courageous Francis Julius LeMoyne who, despite the strict Fugitive Slave Law of 1850, risked his personal freedom and fortune to do what he knew was morally right — take a stand against the institution of slavery. This successful 19th Century doctor, reformer and builder of the first crematory in the western hemisphere, opened his home and properties as stops along the Underground Railroad. Dr. LeMoyne was also a leader in herbal health remedies. See the beds under which runaway slaves hid and the beehive in the herb garden on the roof.

GREENE COUNTY MUSEUM

Waynesburg - *PO Box 127 (I-79, exit 3 to SR21) 15370. Phone: (724) 627-3204.* **Web: www.greenepa.net/~museum** *Hours: Wednesday-Friday 10:00am-4:00pm, Saturday & Sunday Noon-4:00pm (May - August). Thursday-Sunday Noon-4:00pm (September, October). Admission: $2.00-$4.00. Miscellaneous: The Historical Society also maintains the Young Foundry and Machine Shop - Century old, belt driven machine shop and foundry with 25 fully operational machines.*

Colonial to Victorian... displays of local artifacts dating from the early native Monongahela culture to the early 20th Century. One of the rooms is devoted to an exhibit of early watches and clocks. The early watch and clockmaker was a talented craftsman, capable of very precise work. He was also the village jeweler. "Monongahela Culture" is the name for prehistoric Indians from the area. Look at the way they constructed their houses, the types of pottery they made and used, the stone materials they used for their tools, weapons, and cultivation of crops. Also on display are quilts, period clothing, early glassware & pottery, and an extraordinary birdhouse that stands over six feet tall and contains 104 rooms. A fun and informative worksheet is available for an interactive view of the exhibit. A fun project for families.

GEORGE WESTINGHOUSE MUSEUM

Wilmerding - Castle Main - 325 Commerce Street (US30 to SR148 - Fifth Avenue - Left on Herman Avenue, Left on Commerce) 15148. www.georgewestinghouse.com Phone: (412) 823-0500. Hours: Monday-Friday 10:00am-4:00pm, Saturday 11:00am-3:00pm. Closed holidays. Admission: Donation.

A tribute to George Westinghouse - the inventor and entrepreneur - plus key people who worked for his companies. The small museum is broken down into four rooms - The Family Room (personal & home belongings), the Inventions and Room of Achievement (highlights of 361 patents, the first radio broadcast in the country - KDKA in Pittsburgh!, time capsules) and the Appliance Room. Highlights for kids are the Spencer switch display where two  metals put together in a disc, react differently to temperature. As they heat, they jump away from the hot plate, and as they cool, they freely jump back. The principle was used for discs to regulate an iron's temperature. The kids are greeted by "Saranade" - the first electronic doll, in the Appliance Room, along with other "Every House Needs Westinghouse" inventions. These include washers, dryers, irons, waffle grills, radios, and home entertainment centers.

RYERSON STATION STATE PARK

Wind Ridge - 361 Bristoria Road (both sides of Bristoria Road, just off of PA Route 21) 15380. Web: www.dcnr.state.pa.us/stateparks/parks/ryersonstation.aspx Phone: (724) 428-4254 or (888) PA-Parks.

Pool, Visitor Center, Boat Rentals, Sledding, Campsites, Fishing, and Winter Sports. The trails invite you to explore the park on foot during spring, summer, fall and on cross-country skis in winter. The trails traverse many habitats, like forests, wet valley bottoms, evergreen plantations and fields. There are several opportunities to observe the beauty of Duke Lake.

SUGGESTED LODGING AND DINING

DISALVO'S STATION RESTAURANT - **Latrobe**. 325 McKinley Avenue (Latrobe Train Station - downtown Amtrak station), Phone: (724) 539-0500 or **http://disalvosrestaurant.com**. An early 1900 train station that has been restored and decorated with railroad memorabilia. Ride from Pittsburgh on Amtrak to get here (adds to the railroad experience). When walking into the restaurant, you'll enter through a tunnel that trains pass over often. Feel and hear the rumble! Once through the tunnel, you may be seated in the atrium (formerly the train yard) with fountains, greenery and a full-size railroad dining car. Most families are seated in the original main concourse room with a continuously running model train above. A children's menu is offered. Hours: Tuesday-Sunday, Lunch and Dinner. Early Bird specials 4:00-6:30pm ($6.95). Reservations strongly suggested. Moderate to fine dining.

RADISSON HOTEL / MONROEVILLE - **Pittsburgh**. (412) 373-7300. Has a combo indoor/outdoor pool. Near the zoo.

RAMADA INN HISTORIC LIGONIER - **Ligonier**. 216 West Loyalhanna Street, entrance off US 30. (724) 238-9545 or **www.ramadainnligonier.com** The closest family-friendly lodging to IDLEWILD. Cozy doubles to spacious kings or suites at reasonable prices. Enjoy breakfast or dinner at the casual Bistro, see the sites, or relax by the outdoor heated pool. Walking distance to quaint shops and eateries or Fort Ligonier.

Chapter 10

Seasonal &
Special Events

JANUARY

ICE HARVEST FESTIVAL

NE – **Tobyhanna**, Mill Pond #1. 570-894-8205. Commemorating the ice business that was prominent in Pennsylvania until electric refrigerators arrived in the 1930s. Those attending the one-day festival at Millpond #1 can help the local experts cut blocks of ice using traditional saws, then transport the ice using a tractor or mules up a hill to the icehouse, which holds 50 tons. The ice is used throughout the summer to fill the coolers of fishermen and picnickers. FREE for spectators. Admission for Steamtown excursions. (mid-January weekend)

ENDLESS MOUNTAINS WINTERFEST / SLED DOG RACES

NE - **Estella**. Camp Brule. (570) 836-5431. Sled dog teams compete for cash prizes. Mid-distance and sprint races. Food, displays. Admission. (Last weekend in January or first weekend in February)

PENNSYLVANIA FARM SHOW

SC – **Harrisburg**, Farm Show Complex. **www.agriculture.state.pa.us/ farmshow/** (717) 787-5373. The largest indoor agricultural event in America. The Farm Show Complex houses 16 acres under roof, spread throughout 7 buildings. America's Top Rodeo/Livestock Events. FREE. (second week of January)

FIRE & ICE FESTIVAL

SW – **Somerset**. Uptown. **www.somersetborough.com**. (814) 443-1748. Ice sculptures, carving, food and winter events. (mid-January weekend)

BATTLE OF THE BULGE RE-ENACTMENT

SW – **Waynesburg**. Lebanon City. (724) 627-8545 or **www.wwiifederation.org**. World's largest WW II re-enactment with battle demos, equipment displays and many veteran reunions. (last weekend in January)

FEBRUARY

GROUNDHOG DAY

CW - **Punxsutawney**. (800) 752-PHIL. Join thousands of Phil's faithful followers for his annual prediction. Fun for everyone. Hours vary. **www.groundhog.org**. (morning of February 2)

GREATER PHILADELPHIA SCOTTISH AND IRISH MUSIC FESTIVAL AND FAIR

SE - **King of Prussia**. Valley Forge Convention Center. (610) 825-7268 or **www.eohebrides.com/events/index.cfm**. Scottish and Irish musical entertainment with Highland and step dancing, bands, singers, storytellers, exhibits, craft vendors Scottish and Irish foods and fraternal organizations. Admission. (mid-February weekend)

FIRE & ICE FESTIVAL

SE – **Lititz**, throughout town. **www.lititzwomeninbusiness.com**. The "ice" of this family festival is in ice sculptures in downtown Lititz, and the "fire" is in a chili cook-off on Saturday! Enjoy Friday night block party, on-site ice carvings, an art show and auction, fire eating, magicians, jugglers, clowns, an igloo/ice fort contest and much more. (mid-February long weekend)

MARCH / APRIL

MAPLE SUGARING

Actual tapping of trees. Syrup making. Demonstrations of coopering and sugaring off in a realistic sugar camp. Pancakes and syrup served.

C – **State College (Charter Oak)**. Shavers Creek Environmental Center, Stone Valley Rec Area. (814) 863-2000.

CE - **Swiftwater**. Delaware State Forest, Messing Nature Center. (570) 895-9000. (March)

CW – **Slippery Rock**. Jennings Environmental Education Center. (724) 794-6011. (Mid-March)

NE - **Troy**. Endless Mountains. Mt. Pisgah State Park. (570) 297-2791. (Last weekend in April)

NW – **Edinboro**. Hurry Hill Maple Syrup Farm. (814) 734-1350. Tours by appointment.

NW – **Erie**. Asbury Woods Nature Center. (814) 835-5356 or **www.ashburywoods.org**. (end of March weekend)

NW – **Spartansburg**. Firth Maple Products. **www.firthmapleproducts.com** or (814) 654-7265.

SC – **Harrisburg**. Fort Hunter Mansion & Park. (717) 599-5751. FREE. (early March)

SE – **Downingtown**. Springton Manor Farm. (610) 942-2450.

SE – **Media**. Tyler Arboretum. **www.tylerarboretum.org**. (610) 566-5431 or (mid-February)

SE – **Philadelphia**. Andorra Natural Area in Fairmount Park. (215) 685-9285. (Late February – Early March)

SW – **Meyersdale**. US 219 Meyers Ave. Historic Bldgs. (814) 634-0213 or **www.pamaplefestival.com**. War encampment, too. (second & third weekend in March)

ST. PATRICK'S DAY

NE – **Scranton (Moosic)**. Lackawanna County Stadium or Downtown Scranton. (800) 22-WELCOME.

NW – **Meadville**. Downtown. (814) 333-1258.

SW – **Pittsburgh**. Downtown. (412) 621-0600.

EASTER EGG HUNTS

NW - **Erie**. Erie Zoo. (814) 864-4091.

SC – **Gettysburg**. www.BoydsBearCountry.com

SE – **Philadelphia**. Elmwood Park Zoo. (610) 277-DUCK.

EASTER BUNNY TRAIN OR BOAT RIDES

Candy treats with the Easter Bunny riding along. Admission. (Easter Weekend)

NE - **Honesdale** Train Station. Stourbridge Line. (570) 253-1960 or **www.waynecountycc.com/train.php**. 1 1/2 hours. Mr. Mouse, too! Entertainment.

NW – **Titusville**. OC & T Railroad. Perry Street Station. (814) 676-1733. Departure 2:00pm. (Weekend before Easter)

SC - **Middletown**. Race Street Station. (717) 944-4435 or **www.mhrailroad.com**. Live music. (Easter weekend and weekend before)

SE – **Kempton**. WK&S Steam Railroad. **www.kemptontrain.com**.

SE – **Strasburg** Railroad. **www.strasburgrailroad.com** or (717) 687-7522.

SW–**Pittsburgh**. Gateway Clipper. (412) 355-7980 or **www.gatewayclipper.com**. Easter crafts, DJ Dance Party.

SW – **Washington**. Pennsylvania Trolley Museum. (877) PA-TROLLEY.

CHARTER DAY - MARCH

Commemorates the original charter given to William Penn for the land that is today the Commonwealth of Pennsylvania. FREE admission to all Pennsylvania State Museums.

NW – **Erie**. Maritime Museum. (814) 452-BRIG.

NW - **Titusville**. Drake Well Museum. (814) 827-2797. (Afternoon)

SE – **Chadds Ford**. (610) 459-3342. Tours of historic homes and living history demos.

SE - **Horsham**. Graeme Park. (215) 646-1595. (Afternoon)

SE – **Lancaster**. Landis Valley Museum. (717) 569-0401.

SE – **Strasburg**. Railroad Museum of PA. (717) 687-8628.

For updates & travel games visit: **www.KidsLoveTravel.com**

REVOLUTIONARY ROCKFORD

SE - **Lancaster**. Historic Rockford Plantation. (717) 392-7223. Gigantic Revolutionary War Encampment featuring over 1000 costumed re-enactors. Enjoy 18th century music and demonstrations at the historic home of Edward Hand, George Washington's Adjutant. Admission. (early April weekend)

MAY

CIVIL WAR ENCAMPMENT

C - **Boalsburg**. Pennsylvania Military Museum Parade Grounds. (814) 466-6263 **www.boalsburgcentral.com/specialevents.html**. Northern and Southern military units encamped throughout the area. Daily living history demonstrations. Live fire artillery demonstrations. Day-long festivities in nearby Boalsburg. Did you know that this is the birthplace of Memorial Day? Parking fee only. (Memorial Day Weekend)

GREEK FESTIVAL

CE – **Stroudsburg**, Holy Cross Greek Orthodox Church, 135 Stokes Ave. (570) 421-5734. Listen to the Greek music, watch the dancing exhibitions or enjoy the exhibits and church tours, but we challenge you to leave without buying some outstanding homemade Greek cuisine. FREE. (first long weekend in May)

AMBRIDGE NATIONALITY DAYS

CW - **Ambridge**. Merchant Street from 4th to 8th Street. (724) 266-3040 or **www.nationalitydays.org**. A celebration of ethnic pride offering tasty foods from all over the world plus entertainment, crafts, and special children's attractions. (Mid-month, Thursday-Sunday in May)

BLOSSBURG COAL FESTIVAL

NC - **Blossburg**. Island Park. **www.blossburg.org/coalfest/** or (717) 638-2527. Crafts, coal museum, carnival, car show, general store. Parade Saturday morning. No Admission. (Memorial Day weekend in May)

HIGHLAND GAMES & SCOTTISH FESTIVAL

NW – **Edinboro** University. **www.usscots.com/events/usa/pennsylvania.html**. (814) 732-2745 or   Highland dance, pipe band competition, music, sheep-herding, medieval camp, kids games & crafts. (mid-May weekend)

APPLE BLOSSOM FESTIVAL

SC – **Arendtsville**, Adams County. South Mountain Fairgrounds. (717) 677-7444 or (717) 374-6274. Live entertainment, orchard tours, scenic train rides, delicious apple foods, plus! (first weekend of May)

May *(cont.)*

NATIONAL ROAD FESTIVAL

SC - 26 Municipalities. **www.washpatourism.org/nrfestival.html**. or (800) 925-7669. 90 miles of fun, food, entertainment, crafts, wagon train re-enactments, historic tourism. Family reunions on the road commissioned by Jefferson that opened travel to the West. (Mid-month in May)

MERCER MUSEUM FOLKFEST

SE - **Doylestown**. Mercer Museum. (215) 345-0210. Traditional artisans make the skills and trades of early America come to life during this nationally acclaimed festival. Entertainment, militia encampment, and full picnic fare. Admission. **www.buckscountyhistorical.org/folkfest/index.html**. (Mothers Day weekend - May)

RHUBARB FESTIVAL

SE – **Intercourse**. (800) 732-3538. Kitchen Kettle Village. Annual festival that teaches us that rhubarb (a red-stalked vegetable) is no longer just for pies. You won't believe the colorful menus of rhubarb-inspired foods, baked goods and beverages, and the Rhubarb Jams made special at festival time. Kids can play games (even build mini-racecars – The Rhubarb Race Car Derby). Food and games. FREE. (third Friday/Saturday in May)

PHILADELPHIA INTERNATIONAL CHILDREN'S FESTIVAL

SE – **Philadelphia**. University of Penn. Annenberg Center for the Performing Arts. (215) 898-3900 or **www.PENNPresents.org**. Performances throughout each day…you pick and choose from international acts like a circus from Finland, a dance company form the Ivory Coast, comedy from Denmark, fairy tales from England or folk singers from the USA. The Playworks area is where international artisans teach their art and help kids create versions of crafts such as African drums, Hmong tapestry, egg painting, dream catchers and Peruvian sundials. Stageworks is where emerging regional performers can share their talent. Admission/packages. (first week of May)

INTERNATIONAL CHILDREN'S FESTIVAL

SW - **Pittsburgh**. Allegheny Center, North Shore. (412) 321-5520 or **www.pghkids.org/festival.htm**. Indoor main stage performances by world class professional theater companies along with outdoor stages, strolling performers, workshops, and recreational, educational, and cultural activities. Admission. (second week of May)

ST. NICHOLAS GREEK ORTHODOX CATHEDRAL GREEK
FOOD FESTIVAL

SW - **Pittsburgh (Oakland)**. St. Nicholas Cathedral Community Center, 419 S. Dithridge St. (412) 682-3866 or **www.stnickspgh.org/greekfood_info.asp**. People from all over enjoy authentic Greek cuisine. (first full week of May)

MAY/JUNE

STRAWBERRY FESTIVALS

Sample strawberry treats like fresh strawberry shortcakes and strawberry ice cream or sundaes. From great beverages and tempting sweets to colorful side dishes and barbecued meats grilled with berry sauces. Entertainment, demonstrations, contests and prizes. Kids' activities.

SC - **McConnellsburg**. McConnell Park. (717) 485-4064.

SE – **Intercourse**. Kitchen Kettle. **www.kitchenkettle.com** (mid-June)

SE – **Lahaska**. Peddlers Village (Rte. 202 & Rte. 263). (215) 794-4000 or **www.peddlersvillage.com**. (first weekend in May)

SW - **Finleyville**. Trax Farms. (724) 835-3246. Watch them make strawberry jam. Pick your own. (second weekend of June)

INDIAN POW WOWS

Native American singing and dancing. Arts and crafts. Native food storytelling and much more! (June, July, August, September - Summer)

CE – **Lehighton**. Lenape Tears Pow Wow. McCall's Farm, Rte. 443. (610) 681-3709 or (570) 929-3102. (last weekend in September & first weekend in October)

NE - **Forksville**. Sullivan County Fairgrounds. Rte. 154. Eastern Delaware Nations' Pow Wow. (570) 924-9082. (second weekend of June)

NE – **Hawley**. Triple W Riding Stables. (570) 226-2620. Horseback Western riding and live country music too. (mid-June & early September)

NW – **Erie**. Rte. 430 & Williams exit. (814) 459-8509. Woodland Indian Veterans Memorial Festival. (early June weekend)

SE - **Media**. Ridley Creek State Park. (610) 566-1725. Native Americans of the Delaware Valley present a Pow Wow at Colonial Pennsylvania Plantation. Admission. (second weekend in September)

JUNE

HARRISBURG PIPES AND DRUMS FESTIVAL

C – **Harrisburg**, Ft. Hunter Park. (717) 731-6289. **www.PennScots.Org**. Event is free to the public and offers bagpipe bands, Scottish Country dance, Celtic food and gift vendors. FREE. (last Saturday in June)

RAYSTOWN REGATTA

C - **Huntingdon** - Seven Points Recreation Area. 16652. (800) 269-4684 or (888) RAYS-TOWN. **www.raystown.org**. Boat racing, concerts, kids' activities, area Pow Wows, & fireworks. (June weekend)

MIFFLINBURG BUGGY DAYS

C - **Mifflinburg** - SR45 - Downtown. (570) 966-1355. Explore the actual home, carriage house, and workshop of the Heiss Coach Works, the only operation rescued from almost 50 different buggy works in the area (early 1900's). It looks as it did before the Heiss family left. Working demonstrations and buggy rides. **www.mifflinburgpa.com/cal_summer.htm** (first weekend in June)

CANAL FESTIVAL

CE - **Easton**. Hugh Moore Park. (610) 559-6613. Annual canal festival featuring canal boat rides, 19th century living history encampments and reenactments, Locktender's House tours, continuous music and entertainment, food. Parking $5.00. (last Sunday of June)

PATCH TOWN DAYS

CE - **Hazelton**.   Eckley Miners Village. (570) 636-2070. Family-oriented living history festival featuring street fair, coal mining and dance troups, wagon rides, huge craft show with period demos, children's activities, and ethnic food. Admission. (third weekend of June)

STREET ROD NATIONALS - EAST

SC – **York**. Expo Center. (717) 848-4000. **www.nsra-usa.com/east.htm**. Over 4500 pre-1949 street rods, games, live entertainment, food. Admission. (first full weekend in June).

STAHL'S POTTERY FESTIVAL

SC - **Zionsville**.   Stahl's Pottery, 6826 Corning Road. (610) 965-5019. **www.stahlspottery.org**. Tour historic, early 20th century wood-fired kiln and pottery site. Potting techniques demonstrated. Over 15 contemporary potters display and sell their wares. Light lunch available. FREE. (third Saturday of June)

KUTZTOWN PA – GERMAN FESTIVAL

SE – **Kutztown**. Fairgrounds. **www.kutztownfestival.com**. An annual celebration of the Pennsylvania Dutch lifestyle with demonstrating craftsmen, entertainment, food, nature center, antique farm museum and much more. Delightful baby farm animals, puppets, make-and- take crafts, hay stacks and mazes, story time, singalongs, and hands on fun. Admission. (last Saturday, June thru the first Saturday, July)

CELTIC FLING & HIGHLAND GAMES

SE – **Manheim**, Mount Hope Estate & Winery. 83 Mansion House Road, Route 72 & PA Turnpike Exit 20. **www.parenfaire.com**. Held on the festival grounds of the PA Renaissance Faire turns Amish Country into the Celtic Capital of the US! This Irish and Scottish heritage celebration covers the Faire's 35 acres in kilts, cabers and Celts with each day featuring musical sets, competitions and demonstrations. $10-$25 admission (age 5+). (third weekend in June)

CHERRY FAIR

SE - **Schaefferstown**. Alexander Schaeffer Farm Museum. (717) 949-2244. **www.hsimuseum.org**. Celebrating Cherry Season with food, games, traditional period craftsmen, musical entertainment, cherry quilt raffle, and homemade cherry pies, fritters, and ice cream. FREE. (last Saturday of June)

JULY

JULY 4TH CELEBRATIONS

Parades, music, food, fireworks & contests.

C - **Martinsburg**. Morrison's Cove Memorial Park. (814) 793-2176. Rides, too! (Weeklong)

CW - **New Wilmington**. Westminster College. Lawn of Brittain Lake. (412) 946-7354. (July 3rd)

NC - **Galeton**. (814)435-2321. Firemen's competition. (July 3rd and 4th)

NE – **Milford**. **www.pikechamber.com**.

NW – **Edinboro**. Lakeside Association. (814) 734-3184.

NW – **Erie**. Mercyhurst College. (814) 824-2000.

NW - **Sharon**. Three by the River. (412) 981-3123. Small Ships Revue (anything that floats) regatta. (July 3rd)

SC - **York**. Fairgrounds. (800) 372-7374.

SE - **Doylestown**. Fonthill Museum. (215)348-9461. **www.mercermuseum.org**. Town ball game, Pony rides, contests. Admission.

July 4th Celebrations *(cont.)*

SE – Kutztown. Fairgrounds & Railroad Station. **www.kutztownfestival.com**. (610) 683-1597. Pennsylvania Dutch culture and food. Folk artists, children's activities, farmyard zoo. Meet Uncle Sam with patriotic sing-a-longs on the railroad . Admission. (week of July 4th)

SE – Lititz. Spring Park. **www.lititzspringspark.org**. Oldest continuous community-wide celebration in the U.S., since 1818.

SE – Philadelphia. Welcome America Festival. **www.americasbirthday.com**. Top name musical groups and dramatic readings by famous actors. FREE.

SW - Avella. Meadowcroft Museum of Rural Life. (724) 587-3412. Historical patriotic activities. Admission.

SW - Latrobe. Downtown. (724) 537-8417.

SW – Pittsburgh. Point State Park. (412) 255-8983.

REVOLUTIONARY WAR DAYS

C - Altoona. Fort Roberdeau Historic Site. **www.fortroberdeau.org/events/**. Experience danger on the 1778 frontier when British Rangers and Iroquois attack patriots and ruin bullet-making at General Roberdeau's lead mine fort. Admission. (second weekend in July)

CENTRAL PENNSYLVANIA FESTIVAL OF THE ARTS

C - State College - (Downtown & PSU Campus). **www.arts-festival.com**. The first day is usually Children and Youth Day featuring art creations of local kids ages 8-18. Art and mask parade with costumed characters, storytelling, marionettes, and concerts. (second Full Week of July, Monday - Friday)

BLUEBERRY FESTIVAL

CE - Bethlehem. Burnside Plantation, **www.historicbethlehem.org**. Schoenersville Road. Enjoy blueberry delights galore on a 250 year old restored Moravian farm. Crafts, demonstrations, children's activities, and special tours are featured. Admission. (third weekend of July)

INTERNATIONAL BASEBALL INVITATIONAL

CW - Freeport. (724) 353-9426 **www.fortheloveofthegame.org**. They come from around the world (15 to 19 year-olds, that is) to compete. Also, Pittsburgh Pirates Alumni participate in an "Old Timers" game mid-week. Fireworks. FREE. (late July weekend)

FIREWORKS CAPITAL OF AMERICA FIREWORKS FESTIVAL

CW – **New Castle**. Downtown area. (724) 654-8408. Children's activities, street dancing, musical entertainment, "Ducky Derby", Ice Cream Social, plus a Fireworks Spectacular. No Admission. (second Saturday of July)

BARK PEELER'S CONVENTION

NC - **Galeton**. Pennsylvania Lumber Museum. (814) 435-2652 or **www.lumbermuseum.org/bark.htm**. Annual woods festival. Events include crafts, music, saw milling, woodhick demonstrations. Contests: birling, fiddling, tobacco spitting, frog jumping. Admission (weekend before or after July 4th)

ARMED FORCES SHOW

NE – **Scranton / Wilkes-Barre**. Wilkes-Barre/Scranton International Airport. (877) 2-FLYAVP. Best Air Show in the East. World-class aerobatics. Top Gun fighter demonstrations. Parachuting, Vintage Warbirds and classics. Over 100 aircraft and exhibits on display. Admission. (second weekend of July)

GREEK FESTIVAL

NW - **Erie**. Assumption Greek Orthodox Church, 4376 West Lake Road. (814) 838-8808. **www.greek-fest.com**. Greek food and pastries, Greek music and dancing. FREE parking and church tours. (weekend after July 4th)

PIONEER AND ARTS FESTIVAL

NW - **Jamestown**. Pymatuning State Park. (724) 932-3141. Displays, demonstrations, arts and crafts, Indian dancers, frontier activities, encampment, historical program, tour of the Gatehouse, food and live entertainment. No Admission. (last weekend in July)

BATTLE OF GETTYSBURG

SC – **Gettysburg** Battlefield. **www.gettysburgreenactment.com**. (717) 338-1525. Reenactments, events at Yingling Farm (site of film) include camps, gallant stands and charges. (long week of July 4th)

CIVIL WAR ENCAMPMENT

SE - Berks County. Berks County Heritage Center. (610) 374-8839. The year is 1863, and Pennsylvania Federal Regiment try to enlist new recruits and demonstrate military life. Free. (second weekend in July)

July *(cont.)*

SCOTTISH HERITAGE FESTIVAL

SE - Horsham. Graeme Park. (215) 343-0965. Explore the Scottish Heritage of the Keith and Graeme families through music, dance, exhibits, food and more. See Scottish games and crafts. Admission. (third Sunday of July)

PITTSBURGH THREE RIVERS REGATTA

SW – Pittsburgh. Point State Park. (412) 338-8765. **www.pghregatta.com**. Downtown rivers and shores host the world's largest inland regatta. Air shows, powerboat races, hot air balloon races, fireworks and water-skiing demos. FREE. (first week in July including July 4th)

VINTAGE GRAND PRIX

SW – Pittsburgh. Schenley Park. **www.pittsburghvintagegrandprix.com** (412) 471-7847. Racing and car shows. Run by volunteers with proceeds benefiting mentally retarded and autistic children and adults. (third weekend in July)

AUGUST

ALL-AMERICAN AMATEUR BASEBALL ASSOCIATION TOURNAMENT (AAABA)

C - Johnstown - Point Stadium. **www.johnstownpa.com/aaaba** or (814) 536-7993. Major League Scouts are in attendance to watch sixteen teams of 18-20 year-olds compete for the championship. Also, visit the AAABA Hall of Fame featuring tournament legends who made it to the "big leagues". (first weekend in August)

AG PROGRESS DAYS

C - Rock Springs. Larson Ag Research Center - SR45, (814) 865-2081 or (800) PSU-1010 or **http://apd.cas.psu.edu**. Ag museum (open mid-April to Mid-October). One of the largest agricultural shows in the country features a petting zoo, live animal expos, games and food, and farming technology demos. Kids Climb a 25 foot tree, fishing center, corn maze and ImAGination Station with other fun things for kids. FREE (Tuesday – Thursday, mid-August)

MUSIK FEST

CE - Bethlehem. **www.musikfest.org**. More than 650 FREE performances indoor and outdoors. All styles of music, children's activities, fireworks, international foods. (second weekend of August)

CIVIL WAR ENCAMPMENT

CE – **Hazleton**. Eckley Miners Village. **www.eckleyminers.org/aug.htm**. (570) 636-2070. Living history event. Civil War re-enactors display authentic camp life, cavalry drill demonstrations, and cannon firings. Period music, wagon rides, house tours, town ballgame, and period church service. Admission. (third weekend in August)

POCONO STATE CRAFT FESTIVAL

CE – **Shawnee on Delaware**. Sun Mountain Recreation area, Hollow Road. (570) 476-4460. **www.poconocrafts.com**. Craft demonstrations, musical entertainment and an interactive children's play area are among the activities held under tents at this lakeside center. Admission (12+). (late August)

CROOK FARM COUNTY FAIR

NC – **Bradford**. (814) 362-6730. 1800s restored buildings including a farmhouse, one-room schoolhouse, blacksmith's shop, carpenter's shack, a barn and candle-making shop. Carnival, entertainment, tours, old-fashioned cooking and craft demonstrations. Admission. (mid-August weekend)

CHERRY SPRINGS WOODSMAN SHOW

NC - **Galeton**. Cherry Springs State Park. **www.woodsmenshow.com**. (814) 435-2907. Lumberjack competition and horse pulling contest. Entertainment, displays, food. No Admission. (first weekend of August)

MT. JEWETT SWEDISH FESTIVAL

NC - **Mt. Jewett**. (814) 778-5441. A community-wide festival celebrating Swedish heritage. Highlights include a parade, fireworks, Swedish smorgasbord. Entertainment for all ages. (third weekend of August)

WAYNE COUNTY FAIR

NE – **Honesdale**. Rte. 191. (570) 253-3240. County Farm Museum. (first full week in August)

OIL FESTIVAL

NW - **Titusville**. Throughout town. (814) 897-2797. Heritage festival celebrating the history of oil. Festival includes sporting events, concerts, parades, children's events, historic tours, and a stagecoach robbery. FREE. (early August)

August *(cont.)*

HANS HERR HERITAGE DAY

SE - **Lancaster** - US222 to 1849 Hans Herr Drive, 17584. (717) 464-4438 or **www.hansherr.org/heritageday.htm**. House Tours. (April - early December). Tour the oldest Mennonite meeting house in America. Site includes stone house, farm, orchard, and picnic areas plus a Visitor's Center. During this farm festival see demonstrations of 18th and 20th Century farm activity. Wagon rides, food. Admission (first Saturday in August)

PENNSYLVANIA RENAISSANCE FAIRE

SE - **Manheim**. Mount Hope Estate, 83 Mansion House Road. (717) 665-7021 or **www.parenfaire.com**. The Faire, with a cast of hundreds of colorfully costumed merriemakers, is a rollicking recreation of a 16th Century country festival celebrating a visit by Her Majesty, Queen Elizabeth I, "God Save The Queen!" Hundreds of costumed merrymakers create a fantasy of bygone days and knights. Shows include jousting, cuttings from Shakespeare's immortal plays, Commedia Del Arte, puppet shows, sword swallowing, juggling, rope walking, and much more. Strolling minstrels and memorable street characters delight visitors hither and yon about the Shire. Admission. (weekends, mid-August thru mid-October)

ANNIVERSARY OF THE BATTLE OF BUSHY RUN

SW - **Harrison City**. Bushy Run Battlefield. (412) 527-5584. Live re-enactment of the Battle of Bushy Run, 1763. Period British and Native American campsites, and a variety of other programs. Admission. (first weekend in August)

PONY LEAGUE WORLD SERIES BASEBALL

SW – **Washington**. Lew Hays Pony Field. 15301. (800) 531-4114 or (724) 222-9315. **www.ponyworldseries.com**. The world's best 13 and 14 year-old Pony League players meet. (third week of August)

SEPTEMBER

WOODHICK WEEKEND

C - **Penfield**. Parker Dam State Park. (814) 765-0630. A hands-on competition in old logging events to see who is the best woodhick of the year. X-cut sawing, log rolling, shoe pitching, seed spitting, and more. FREE. (Sunday of Labor Day Weekend)

CELTIC CLASSIC HIGHLAND GAMES & FESTIVAL

CE - **Bethlehem**. Historic Downtown Area. **www.celticfest.org**. (610) 868-9599. Exciting and educational weekend celebrating the cultures of Ireland, Scotland, and Wales. Music, dance, bag piping, athletic competition, children's activities, and authentic vendors. FREE. (last weekend of September)

CIDER AND SAUERKRAUT FESTIVAL

CW – Butler Heritage Center. Cooper Cabin Pioneer Homestead. Applebutter making, cider pressing, sauerkraut making, lap hoop quilting demonstrations, and tours of the cabin. Hot dogs with chili or sauerkraut, chips, beverages, & baked goods will be available for purchase. **www.butlercountyhistoricalsociety-pa.org**. Admission. (last full weekend in September)

HERITAGE FESTIVAL

CW – **Portersville**, McConnells Mill State Park. The festival celebrates the operational era of the Old Mill (1852-1928). Visitors can witness artisans and craftspeople making art and try old time games and crafts. Other activities include mill tours, corn grinding demonstrations, musical entertainment, a Civil War encampment and food vendors. **www.dcnr.state.pa.us/stateparks/parks/mcconnellsmill.aspx**. (third or fourth weekend in September)

KINZUA BRIDGE "FESTIVAL OF THE ARTS"

NC - **Mt. Jewett**. Kinzua Bridge State Park. (814) 887-3235. Features local arts & crafts, vendors, & food concessions. Native American village & crafts, live family-oriented entertainment, children's games, antique cars. No Admission. (third weekend of September)

LA FESTA ITALIANA

NE - **Scranton**. Courthouse Square. (570) 346-6384. **www.lafestaitaliana.org**. Italian style festival features delicious ethnic food, crafts and live entertainment to suit young & old. Great fun for the whole family. FREE. (Labor Day weekend)

CIVIL WAR REMEMBERED

SC – **Middletown**. M&H Railroad. **www.middletownboro.com/calendar/civilwar.asp**. (717) 944-4435. Reenactment with skirmishes along the tracks & during the ride. Trains leave two times/day. Admission. (last weekend in September)

BATTLE OF BRANDYWINE

SE – **Chadds Ford**, Brandywine Battlefield Park. Annual re-enactment of the Battle of Brandywine, the largest single day battle of the American War for Independence. **www.ushistory.org/brandywine**. Admission. (weekend nearest September 11)

September *(cont.)*

POLISH AMERICAN FESTIVAL

SE - **Doylestown**. National Shrine of Our Lady of Czestochowa. Ferry Road. **www.czestochowa.us**. Polish folk song dance ensembles, polka bands, entertainment shows, Polish and American foods, and amusements. Admission. (1st two weekends of September)

SCARECROW COMPETITION & DISPLAY

SE - **Lahaska**. Peddler's Village. (215) 794-4000, Unusual and delightful bird-chasing creations compete for over $1400 in prizes. Vote for your favorite traditional, contemporary, whirl-a-gig and amateur. Displayed throughout the village. Pumpkin painting, square dancing. Make one workshop. (Mid-September to Mid-October)

HIGHLAND GAMES

SW - **Ligonier**. Idlewild Park. **www.ligoniergames.org** or (412) 851-9900. Scottish Fair. Massed bagpipe bands on parade, Highland dancing, athletics, Scottish breed dog exhibit, genealogy services. children's games. Admission. (second weekend of September)

MT. PLEASANT GLASS & ETHNIC FESTIVAL

SW - **Mt. Pleasant**. Washington Street & Veterans Park. (724) 547-7738. **www.mtpleasantglassandethnicfestival.com**. Over 100 arts, crafts and ethnic food booths. Two stages of national and regional entertainment. Parade, contests, rides and glass blowing demonstrations. FREE. (last weekend of September)

PITTSBURGH IRISH FESTIVAL

SW - **Pittsburgh**. Amphitheater, Station Square. (412) 422-5642. **www.pghirishfest.org**. Entertainment, food, marketplace, cultural and educational children's activities, bingo, Irish dogs, customs. Admission. (second weekend of September)

COVERED BRIDGE FESTIVAL

SW - **Washington**. (800) 531-4114. Enjoy the rich heritage of Washington and Green Counties' 9 different covered bridges during this festival. Old time fiddlers, country style foods, petting zoo, wagon rides. No Admission. (third weekend of September)

SEPTEMBER / OCTOBER

FALL PLAYLANDS

Petting zoo, refreshments, pumpkin patch, corn maze, pony or wagon rides.

CE – **Allentown**. Game Preserve. **www.gamepreserve.org**. Hay play area. Admission.

CE - **Breinigsville**. Grim's Corny Maze. **www.grimsgreenhouse.com**. (610) 395-5655. 4-acre maze. Straw maze and corn box. Free. (Weekends, last week of August - last week of October)

CE - **Catawissa**. Pumpkin Fall Festival. Rohrbach's Farm Market. (570) 356-7654 or **www.rohrbachfarm.com**. Flashlight nights too. (Corn Maze begins Labor Day weekend. Pumpkin Patch weekends in October)

CW – **Butler**. Schramm's Farm Market, 291 Crisswell Road. (724) 282-3714. **www.schrammfarms.com**.

CW – **Valencia**. Harvest Valley Farms, 125 Ida Lane (off Rte. 8). (724) 443-5869 or **www.harvestvalleyfarms.com**. Entertainment on weekends. (weekends, end of September thru October)

NE - **Uniondale**. Fall Festival. Elk Mountain Ski Resort. (717) 679-4400. Scenic chair lift rides, entertainment. (second weekend in October)

NW - **Cambridge Springs**. Pumpkinville. Finney's Farm. Rte. 99 South. (814) 398-4590. Pumpkin characters out in the field.

SC – **Gettysburg**. The Maize, Rte. 30 & Rte. 94. (717) 624-9435 or **www.cornfieldmaze.com**. Ten acre labyrinth maze of corn.

SC - **New Park**. Maize Quest. Maple Lawn Farm. (717) 382-4846. **www.cornmaze.com**. 10 acres of corn maze with fountains and bridges. Admission.

SE - **Monocacy**. UFO Corn Maze. SR 724. (610) UFO MAZE. Enter the largest UFO ever spotted, explore Area 51, see crop circles. Then, can U Find Out? Admission. (Friday-Sunday and weekdays starting mid-October)

SE - **Ronks**. Amazing Maize Maze. Cherry Crest Farm. (717) 687-6843 or **www.cherrycrestfarm.com**. Different design each year. (i.e. Noah's Ark). Also 4 smaller mazes and hay jump on property. Admission.

SW - **Champion**. Autumnfest. Seven Spring Mountains Resort. (800) 452-2223. Scenic chair lift rides, Alpine slide, open-spit cooked foods. (last weekend in September, all October weekends)

September / October - Fall Playlands *(cont.)*

SW - **Clinton**. Hozak Farms. (724) 899-2400. **www.hozakfarms.com**. Admission. (October weekends)

SW – **Clinton**. Janoski's Farm, 1714 Rte. 30. (724) 899-3438. Pumpkinland. (October weekends)

SW – **McMurray**. Simmons Farms, 170 Simmons Road. (724) 941-1490. **www.simmonsfarm.com**. (daily)

SW – **Monongahela**. Triple B Farms, 823 Berry Lane. (724) 258-3557 or **www.triplebfarms.com**. Maize Quest.

SW – **Ohio Township**. Reilly's Farm, 1120 Roosevelt Road. (412) 364-8662. Craft activities. (weekends in October)

FALL HARVEST FESTIVALS

Tractor pulls, antique steam engines, parades, food (made with steam), threshing, baling, cider and apple butter making, hayrides, children's activities, petting zoo & fall crafts.

C - **Centre Hall**. Nittany Antique Steam Engine Days. Penn's Cave Grounds. (814) 364-1664. Admission. (first week of September)

CE - **Stroudsburg**. Harvest Festival. Quiet Valley Living Historical Farm. (570) 992-6161. Admission. (second weekend in October)

CW – **New Wilmington**. Apple Castle (Rte. 18). (724) 652-3221. Bag your own apples, focus on apples. (second Saturday in October)

CW - **Portersville**. Fall Fling. NW PA Steam Engine & Old Equipment Show Grounds. (724) 452-9545. Admission. (first weekend in October)

NE - **Forksville**. Endless Mountains Flaming Foliage Show. Sullivan County Fairgrounds. (570) 247-7625. (first or second weekend in October)

NE - **Hawley**. Harvest Hoedown. Keystone Street & Main. (570) 226-3191. FREE. (first Saturday in October)

SC - **Harrisburg** - Fort Hunter Day. (717) 599-5751. (third Sunday in September)

SC - **McConnellsburg**. Fall Folk Festival. Fulton County Fairgrounds. (717) 485-4064. Admission. (third weekend in October)

SC – **Williams Grove**. Williams Grove Historical Steam Engine Association Show. (717) 766-4001. (week of Labor Day)

SE - **Harleysville**. Apple Butter Frolic. Indian Creek Haven Farm. (215) 256-3020. Admission. (first Saturday in October)

SE - **Lancaster**. Harvest Days. Landis Valley Museum. (717) 569-0401. Admission. (second weekend in October)

SE - **Schaefferstown**. Harvest Fair. Alexander Schaeffer Farm Museum. (717) 949-2244. Admission. (2nd weekend in September)

SW - **Avella**. Rural Heritage Days. Meadowcroft Museum of Rural Life. (724) 587-3412. Admission. (third weekend in October)

SW - **Somerset**. Farmers Jubilee. New Centerville area. (814) 926-3142. Admission. (weekend after Labor Day)

SW – **Waynesburg**. Greene County Museum. **www.greenepa.net/~mus7eum**. Admission. (second weekend in October)

OCTOBER

PUMPKIN FESTIVALS

Pumpkin painting and carving, pie-eating contests. Pumpkin patch (wagon rides out there). Refreshments.

CE – **Forest Inn**. Country Junction (US 209). (610) 377-5050. Petting zoo. (October weekends)

CE – **Kunkletown**. Old Homestead Tree Farm (US 209). (610) 381-2582. (October weekends)

CW - **Volant**. Main Street. (724) 533-2252. (second Saturday)

NW - **Conneaut Lake Park**. (800) 332-2338. (second weekend)

SC – **Bedford**. Old Bedford Village. **www.oldbedfordvillage.com**. (third weekend)

SE - **Chadds Ford**. (610) 388-7376. (last weekend)

SE - **Doylestown**. Fonthill Park. (215) 345-6644. Admission. (last weekend)

SE - **Lancaster**. Landis Valley Museum. **www.landisvalleymuseum.org**. (717) 569-0401. (last weekend)

SE – **Langhorne**. Cornell Pumpkin Festival. (215) 357-4005.

OCTOBERFESTS

German music, dance, foods & cultural exhibits. "Um-pah-pah" bands & cloggers.

CE – **Pocono Lake**. The Edelweiss (PA 940). (570) 646-3938. (Labor Day weekend)

CE – **Tannersville**. Camelback Ski Area. (570) 629-1661. Pumpkin painting and hayrides. FREE. (late October)

Octoberfests *(cont.)*

CW - **Ambridge**. Old Economy Village. Erntefest. (724) 266-4500. Admission. (last Saturday in September or first Saturday in October)

CW – **Enon Valley**. Rec Center (PA 108). (877) 767-5732.

NW – **Erie**. St. Nick's Picnic Grove. (814) 891-7669 or **www.dank-erie.org**.

SE – **Doylestown**. Township Central Park. (215) 348-9915 (first weekend in October)

SE – **Manheim**. Salunga Exit off Rte 283. (717) 898-8451. (late September/ early October weekends)

PUMPKIN PATCH TROLLEY

C – **Rockhill Furnace** Trolley. **www.rockhilltrolley.org**. Visit the Pumpkin Patch while riding aboard a historic trolley. All children 12 years and under receive a free pumpkin with their paid fare. All riders are welcome to ride as often as they like all day long. Admission. (weekends in October)

TIME OF THANKSGIVING FESTIVAL

CE – **Allentown**. Lenape Museum of Indian Culture. **www.lenape.org**. Drums, dancers, singing, music, native lifeways demos (flint knapping, basketry, cookery), and kids crafts. Admission. (third weekend in October)

APPLE HARVEST FESTIVAL

CE - **Catawissa**. Krum's Orchards. (570) 356-2339 or **www.krumorchards.com**. Hayrides, entertainment, apple cider, baked goods, farm tours, Apple Dumpling Special, caramel apples, scarecrow making, apple butter, barbecue, etc. (Saturdays in October)

COVERED BRIDGE AND ARTS FESTIVAL

CE - **Elysburg & Forks**. Knoebels Amusement & Twin Bridges Park. (570)784-8279 or **www.cmtpa.org/festival.html**. Crafters, demonstrations, entertainment, and food. For the children, face painting, clowns, and a selection of rides will be open in the park. End your day with a bus tour of several covered bridges including the nation's only twin covered bridges. FREE. (first weekend in October)

FALL FOLIAGE FESTIVAL

CE - **Jim Thorpe**. ASA Packer Park. (888) JIM - THORPE. Crafts, ethnic food, bands, and 3-hour train or whitewater excursions. Last Dam Release of season – rushing whitewater against background of peak fall colors. Tour the Old Jail and Home. (weekends in October)

TIMBER & TETHER FESTIVAL

CE - **Shawnee on Delaware**. Shawnee Inn & Golf Resort. (570) 421-1500. http://shawneemt.com. More than 25 hot air balloons aglow, daytime and night. Crafters, food, music, amusement rides, children's shows, animals, and pony/ mule rides. Eastern Ironjack Competition. Birling, pole climbing, buck sawing, skunk races, pony rides, chair lift rides, chainsaw carving and more! Fall foliage in full bloom. Admission. (second full weekend in October)

AMERICAN FUR TRADE RENDEZVOUS

CE – **Wind Gap**, Jacobsburg Environmental Education Park, 610-746- 2801. Annual pre-1840s era living history encampment at Boulton, one of Jacobsburg Environmental Education Center's three historical gun and iron making communities. See what living on America's eastern frontier was really like! Complete with knife and tomahawk throwing competitions, blackpowder shooting, primitive fishing and archery, hearth cooking, and all the sights, sounds and smells of real history! Crafts and trade goods will be available for sale. The Pennsylvania Longrifle Museum at the 1812 Henry Homestead will be open all day each day, and scheduled tours will be offered of the 1834 John Joseph Henry House Museum both days. Admission fee of $3.00 for adults. (last weekend in October)

NATIONAL APPLE HARVEST FESTIVAL

SC - **Arendtsville** and Adams County. South Mountain Fairgrounds. www.appleharvest.com. An Old time festival of apple products, live country music, hundreds of arts and crafters, antique autos and tractors, steam engines, orchard tours and food. Gettysburg Scenic Railway train ride thru apple countryside. Admission. (first and second weekend in October)

HERSHEYPARK IN THE DARK BALLOONFEST

SC - **Hershey**. (800) HERSHEY or **www.hersheypa.com**. See 50 colorful and unusually shaped hot air balloons at the annual Balloonfest. Includes several launches, balloon glows, rides, entertainment, crafts and food. Fall harvest foods, storytelling, Frightlights Laser Show, flashlight tours of nocturnal zoo animals & costumes everywhere. Parking and rides fee. (last two weekends in October)

OLD FASHIONED CIDER SQUEEZE

SC – **Newport**. Little Buffalo State Park. (717) 567-9255. Apple butter cooked in large copper kettles. At Shoaff's Mill, apples are ground and pressed. Corn is also ground and sold. Tasty foods. (third weekend in October)

October *(cont.)*

FALL APPLE FESTIVAL

SE – **Audubon**, Mill Grove. 610-666-5593. Activities include apple pressing, apple butter making, scarecrow making contest (pre-registration required), and more. Featuring music. FREE. (first Saturday in October)

1777 ENCAMPMENT RE-ENACTMENT

SE - **Fort Washington**. (215) 646-1595. Admission. (late October, early November)

HARVEST MOON TRAIN

SE – **Kempton**, WK&S Railroad. (610) 756-6469. **www.kemptontrain.com**. Autumn moonlight train ride with musicians and light refreshments. Admission. (third weekend in October)

HAY CREEK APPLE FESTIVAL

SE - **Morgantown**. Historic Joanne Furnace. **www.haycreek.org**. (610) 286-0388. Homemade apple specialties. Scarecrows, pumpkin paintings, hay and pony rides. FREE. (second Saturday in October)

BATTLE OF GERMANTOWN RE-ENACTMENT

SE - **Philadelphia** - Germantown Avenue on Market Square, (215) 848-1777 or **www.cliveden.org**. This historic district is home to Cliveden (family homestead with original furnishings and bullet marks still visible) plus a museum with an overview of America's first German settlement. This land was the scene of a Revolutionary Battle of Germantown, the birthplace of writer Louisa May Alcott, and the site of the Underground Railroad. What some kids may feel are normally boring museums, become more interesting during a festival as history is relived. (first Saturday in October)

FALL FARM DAYS & APPLE FEST

SE – **Lancaster**. **www.AmishFarmAndHouse.com**. Fall celebration of the harvest, especially the apple harvest. See cider being pressed, apple "schnitzing", taste historic apple varieties. Games for children. Corn maze, buggy rides and wood carving. Admission. (first long weekend in October)

FORT LIGONIER DAYS

SW – **Ligonier, Midtown**. (724) 238-4200. Commemorates the key battle of the French and Indian War. (second weekend of October)

PUMPKIN PATCH TROLLEY

SW - **Washington**. PA Trolley Museum. **www.pa-trolley.org**. (724) 228-9256. Ride orange-colored trolleys and the kids get to pick a pumpkin, too! (second or third weekend in October)

NOVEMBER

ANNIVERSARY OF LINCOLN'S GETTYSBURG ADDRESS

SC - **Gettysburg**. Daytime, Gettysburg National Cemetery. (717) 334-1124. The annual observance of President Abraham Lincoln's famous address with brief memorial services and noted speakers. (one day in the third week, as announced, in November)

PEDDLER'S VILLAGE ANNUAL APPLE FESTIVAL

SE - **Lahaska**. Peddler's Village. (215) 794-4000. Live music, marionettes, pie-eating contests. Apples served up in fritters, pastries, butter, dipped in chocolate and caramel, or enjoyed plain. (first weekend in November)

NOVEMBER / DECEMBER

HERSHEYPARK CHRISTMAS CANDYLANE

SC - **Hershey**. Hersheypark. **www.hersheypa.com** or (717) 534-3090. More than 1,000,000 lights, unique shops, holiday entertainment, great food and rides. Look for Santa and his live reindeer! Admission for rides, park entrance free. Lodging packages. Breakfast with Santa. (mid-November - New Year's weekend)

HOLLY DAYS

SE – **Intercourse**, **www.KitchenKettle.com**. Rte. 340. Strolling entertainers, cider, crafts. (weekends Thanksgiving thru December)

WINTER WONDERLAND

SE – **Lancaster**. Dutch Wonderland. **www.dutchwonderland.com**. (866) Fun-At-DW. Selected rides and attractions open. Santa. Decorate cookies. Storytelling by the Princess of DW. FREE (rides & crafts, pay as you go). (late November-December)

TAFFY PARTIES

SW – **Pittsburgh (Avella)**. Meadowcroft Museum. (724) 587-3412. Taffy pulling party in log house, holiday programs in one-room schoolhouse. Make an ornament. (mid-November and early December weekend)

November *(cont.)*

PITTSBURGH MODEL RAILROAD MUSEUM

SW – **Pittsburgh (Gibsonia)** - 5507 Lakeside Drive (I-79N exit Wexford to Rte. 910east & Hardt Road). (724) 444-6944 **www.wpmrm.org**. Holiday Miniature railroad displays the transportation systems in Pittsburgh during the 1950s. Accent on coal, steel, and steam production in use. Admission. (Friday evenings & weekends, mid-November - early January)

LIGHT UP NIGHTS & PITTSBURGH SPARKLES

SW - Pittsburgh. Downtown area. **www.downtownpittsburgh.com**. (412) 566-4190. Celebrate the holiday season in downtown Pittsburgh! Over 1,000 displays, performances, activities & events - many free! Wintergarden Santa Display & outdoor Ice Rink at PPG Center. Nativity Scene at US Steel. Boat rides (**www.gatewayclipper.com**). Holly Trolley; Polar Express and Mini RR & village (Science Center). Includes Parade, fireworks and carriage rides. Go to the website for details! (every Saturday from third week November - first week of January)

FESTIVAL OF LIGHTS

Glistening lights. Visit with Santa. Hot chocolate. Freshly baked cookies. Toy/gift shops. Weekend entertainment. Admission. (Evenings - late November through New Year's Day unless noted otherwise)

C - **Altoona**. Lights on the Lake. Lakemont Park. I-99 Frankstown Rd. Exit. **www.lakemontparkfun.com** or (814) 949-7275. Model train display.

CE - **Allentown**. Lights in the Parkway. (610) 437-7616.

CW – **New Castle**. Cascade of Lights. **www.newcastlepa.org**.

NE – **Scranton**. Montage Mountain. Road. Holiday Lights Spectacular. (570) 344-3990.

NW - **Erie**. Zoolumination. Erie Zoo. (814) 864-4091. Walk-thru. (mid - to - late December only)

SC - **York**. Christmas Magic. Rocky Ridge County Park. (717) 840-7440. Walk-thru.

SE - **Bernville**. Koziar's Christmas Village. Off SR 183. (610) 488-1110. Top 10 PA Travel Attractions. Walk-thru.

SW - **Greensburg**. Overly's Country Christmas. Westmoreland Fairgrounds. (800) 9-Overly or **www.overlys.com**. Mini railroad display. Talking & dancing trees. Train ride. (mid-November thru early January)

SW - Indiana. "It's A Wonderful Life". Blue Spruce Park. (724) 463-7505. Jimmy Stewart's home town. See "Blue the Spruce Ness Monster". Sleigh and pony rides. Drive-thru.

TRAIN RIDES WITH SANTA

Sing songs and eat treats as you ride the train with Santa aboard. Admission. (Thanksgiving - December weekends)

C – **Altoona (Roaring Spring)**. Train Station. Heads to Martinsburg and returns. (888) 4-ALTOONA or **www.railroadcity.com**. Children under age of 12 receive fruit and candy treat bag from Santa. Admission. (third Saturday in November & various in December)

C – **Bellefonte** Historical Railroad. (810) 355-0311. Holiday excursions thru Victorian Christmas. (first weekend in December)

C – **Rockhill Furnace**. Rockhill Trolley Museum. **www.rockhilltrolley.org**. Polar Express & Santa. (Thanksgiving weekend and first weekend in December)

CE - Jim Thorpe. (570) 325-4371. Heated cars. Model train display and horse-drawn trolley ride, too. (first two weekends)

NE - Honesdale. Stourbridge Line Rail. **www.hawleywinterfest.com**. (800) 433-9008. Mrs. Claus and Rudolph, too! Stop at Winterfest in Hawley. (first two weekends in December)

NE - Scranton. Steamtown National Historic Site. (888) 693-9391. Face painting, live music. Polar Express. (first & third weekends in December)

NW - Titusville. OC&T Railroad. Perry Street Station. (814) 676-1733. (second weekend in December)

SC – **Gettysburg** Scenic Railway. (717) 334-6932 or **www.gettysburgrail.com**.

SC - Middletown. Race Street Station. (717)944-4435. **www.mhrailroad.com**. Santa Express or The Polar Express. (Saturdays in December)

SE – **Kempton**. WK&S Railroad. (610) 756-6469. **www.kemptontrain.com**. Frosty and elves too. (first weekend in December)

SE – **New Hope** & Ivyland Railroad. **www.newhoperailroad.com**. (215) 862-2322 or North Pole Express.

SE – **Strasburg** Railroad. (717) 687-7522 or **www.railroad.com**. (two weekends before Christmas)

SE - West Chester. Brandywine Service Railroad. (610) 430-2233. (Thanksgiving - Christmas)

SW - Washington. PA Trolley Museum. (724) 228-9256. Toy train lay-out.

DECEMBER

"THE NUTCRACKER" AND CHRISTMAS MUSICALS

C – **State College**. Ballet Theatre of Central PA. (814) 234-4961.

CE – **Avoca**. NE PA Philharmonic. Kirby Center & Scranton Cultural Center. Home for the Holidays. (570) 457-8301.

CW – **New Castle**. Parou Ballet Company. (412) 652-1762.

NW – **Erie**. Ballet Theater Company. Warner Theatre. (814) 871-4356 or **www.lakeerieballet.com**. (weekend before Christmas)

NW - **Franklin**. A Christmas Carol and Handels Messiah. Barrow Theatre. (814) 437-3440.

SC - **Chambersburg**. A Christmas Carol. Caledonia Theatre Company. Capitol Theatre. (717) 352-2164. (Month-long)

SC - **Hershey**. Christmas in Chocolate Town. Dinner with chocolate desserts plus Holiday Musical Review. Hershey Lodge. **www.holidaysinhershey.com**. (800) HERSHEY.

SE - **Lancaster**. American Music Theatre. (800) 648-4102.

SE – **Lancaster**. Dutch Apple Theatre. (717) 898-1900 or **www.dutchapple.com**. (December, except Mondays)

SE - **West Chester**. Brandywine Ballet Company. (610) 696-2711.

SE – **Philadelphia** Orchestra. Handels Messiah & Winter Wonderland. **www.philorch.org**.

SE – **Strasburg**. Sight & Sound Theatre. **www.bibleonstage.com**. (717) 687-7800. (early November thru early January)

SW – **Pittsburgh**. Pittsburgh Ballet Theatre, Benedum Center. The new Nutcracker. (412) 456-6666 or **www.pbf.org**. (evenings and some matinees in December)

SW - **Pittsburgh**. Pittsburgh Pops and Mendelsohn Choir. Heinz Hall. (412) 392-4900.

CHRISTMAS OPEN HOUSES

Tours of decorated, historical buildings. Refreshments and musical entertainment. Admission.

C - **Altoona**. Baker Mansion Museum. (814) 942-3916. Admission. (Thanksgiving weekend & first 2 weekends in December)

C – **Bellefonte**. Talleyrand Park, Centre Furnace Museum. (814) 355-0311 or **www.bellefonte.org**. Gingerbread house contest, mini-trains, buggy rides & Victorian tea parties.

CE - **Bethlehem**. (800) 360-8687. Admission. (Thanksgiving weekend thru weekend after New Year's)

CE - **Hazelton**. Eckleys Miners Village. (570) 636-2070. Wagon rides, arts & crafts, and storytelling. (Thanksgiving weekend)

CE – **Stroudsburg**. Quiet Valley Old Time Christmas Farm. (570) 992-6161. Led by lantern lights. (first two weekends in December)

CW - **Ambridge**. Old Economy Village. (724) 266-4500. Traditional craft activities. (1st weekend in December)

CW - **Butler**. Butler County Shaw House. (724) 283-8116.

CW - **Clarion**. Sutton-Ditz House Museum. (814) 226-4450. (day after Thanksgiving)

CW – **Harmony**. Museum Complex, Main & Mercer Sts. (888) 821-4822.

NE – **Milford**. Grey Towers. (570) 296-9630. **www.fs.fed.us/na/gt**. Home of Gifford Pinchot, the founder of USDA Forest Service.

SC - **Bedford**. Old Bedford Village. **www.oldbedfordvillage.com**. Reenactors. (first & second weekend in December)

SC - **Gettysburg**. Downtown. (717) 334-6274. Admission. (first & second weekend in December)

SC - **Harrisburg**. Fort Hunter Mansion. (717) 599-5751. Admission. (December 1st-23rd)

SE – **Chadds Ford**. Brandywine River Museum (US 1 & SR 100). Model railroad, Victorian dollhouse and whimsical "critter" ornaments. (610) 388-2700. (Thanksgiving weekend thru weekend after New Years)

SE – **Doylestown**. Fonthill Museum & Tile Works. (215) 348-9461. **www.mercermuseum.org**. Dolls, toys, crafts. (weekends in December)

SE – **Elverson**. Hopewell Furnace Iron Plantation. (610) 582-8773. (first Saturday in December)

SE – **Ephrata** Cloister. (717) 733-6600. (late December)

SE - **Fort Washington/Fort Mifflin**. Hope Lodge. **www.ushistory.org/hope**. (610) 834-1550. (first weekend in December)

SE – **Hilltown**. Pearl S. Buck House. Green Hills Farm. (215) 249-0100. (Tuesday – Saturday)

December - Christmas Open Houses *(cont.)*

SE – **Lancaster**. Hans Herr House. (717) 469-4438.

SE - **Lancaster**. Landis Valley Museum. **www.landisvalleymuseum.org**. Lunch & dinner tours. (first & second Wednesday - Saturday in December)

SE - **Lancaster**. Wheatland. (717) 382-8721. (first & last week in December)

SE - **Morrisville**. Pennsbury Manor. (215) 946-0400. (second weekend in December)

SE - **Kennett Square**. Longwood Gardens. (610) 398-1000. (Thanksgiving thru early January)

SE - **Strasburg**. Railroad Museum of Pennsylvania. (717) 687-8628. (second Sunday in December)

SW - **Brownsville**. Nemacolin Castle. Candlelight tours. (724) 785-6882. (Friday after Thanksgiving and December weekends)

SW – **Finleyville**. Trax Farms. (412) 835-3246 or **www.traxfarms.com**. Lunch/ breakfast with Santa. (weekends after Thanksgiving)

SW - **Indiana**. Jimmy Stewart Museum. It's a Wonderful Life Festival. (800) 83-JIMMY. (Thanksgiving weekend thru December)

SW - **Laughlintown**. Compass Inn Museum. **www.compassinn.com**. (724) 238-4983. Admission. (first Saturday in November thru second Saturday in December - weekends only)

SW - **Pittsburgh**. Cathedral of Learning Nationality Rooms. (412) 624-6000. Admission. (Month of December)

SW – **Pittsburgh**. Hartwood Acres (north of downtown). (412) 767-9200. Estate tours. (mid-November thru December)

SW - **Pittsburgh**. The Henry Clay Frick Estate. Pittsburgh (412) 371-0600. Reservations suggested. (3rd Thursday in November – early January, Tuesday – Sunday)

SW – **Pittsburgh**. Phipps Conservatory. (412) 622-6914. Candlelight paths. (evenings mid-December thru December)

SW - **Washington**. LeMoyne House. (412) 225-6740. (first & second weekend in December)

SW – **Waynesburg**. Greene County Museum. **www.greenepa.net/~museum**. FREE. (December weekends)

FESTIVAL OF TREES

Indoor display of 50+ artificial decorated trees. Gift shop. Snacks. Entertainment. Santa & Christmas/Winter characters. Arts & crafts.

C - State College. Penn State Ag Arena. (800) 350-5084. (second week of December)

CW – Beaver Falls. Beaver County, Brady's Run Park Lodge (Rte. 51). (724) 775-4510. Mini-railroad. Small admission. (Thanksgiving weekend and first weekend in December)

NE - Scranton. Electric City Trolley Station. (570) 963-6590. Admission. (mid-December through New Year's weekend)

SE – West Chester. Chester County History Center. **www.chesterhistorical.org**. Doll Tea Parties, Santa visits. Admission. (mid-November thru mid-December)

DECEMBER

SNOWLAND

NE - Poconos. Great Wolf Lodge. **www.greatwolflodge.com**. The lodge is decorated in a winter scene. It snows 3x daily, hot cocoa and live music, clock tower sing along, Rowdy the Reindeer Storytime. Attend the North Pole University for Elves. Admission (includes lodging and indoor waterpark passes). (month-long in December)

SANTA AT THE ZOO

SE – Philadelphia Zoo. (215) 243-5254 or **www.phillyzoo.org**. Food, arts & crafts, games, face painting, Santa & Mrs. Claus, sing-alongs, storytime and sweets. (weekend in December before Christmas)

KIDS HOLIDAY CRAWL

SW - Pittsburgh. Presented by the Pittsburgh Cultural Trust. **www.pgharts.org/ education/gallerycrawl.aspx**. The Cultural District is crawling with fun activities for the whole family from cookie decorating and caroling to card-making and storytelling. Join friends at SPACE, the Pittsburgh Ballet Theatre, Pittsburgh Opera, Three Rivers Arts Festival and the African American Cultural Center as they celebrate the holiday season at over 10 venues throughout the Cultural District. Children can sit on Santa's lap, create crafts with the Pittsburgh Children's Museum and the Jewish Community Center of Greater Pittsburgh, meet the Radio City Rockettes and so much more. (first Saturday in December)

December *(cont.)*

SANTA FAMILY FUN CRUISES

SW - **Pittsburgh**.   Gateway Clipper Fleet. **www.gatewayclipper.com**. (412) 355-7980. Two hours of DJ Dance Party with costumed mascots, visit from Santa with treat, and make your own ornaments. Admission. (weekends in December)

NEW YEAR'S EVE - FIRST NIGHT

An alcohol-free, family-oriented celebration for New Year's Eve. Music, dance, theatre, comedy, poetry. Giant ice sculptures. Fireworks. Arts and crafts, storytellers and puppets. Admission.

C - **State College**. Downtown and Penn State Campus. (800) 358-5466.

NW - **Erie**. Downtown.

NW – **Oil City**. (800) 483-6264.

SC - **Harrisburg**. Downtown. (717) 255-3020.

SC – **Lancaster**. Downtown. **www.cityoflancasterpa.com**.

SE – **Newtown**. (215) 860-0819.

SW - **Pittsburgh**. Downtown. (412) 392-4533.

SW – **Pittsburgh**. Phipps Conservatory. (412) 622-6914. Garden circus from 6:00-9:00pm.

Activity Index

AMUSEMENTS

C - Altoona, *Lakemont Park*, 3

C - Raystown Lake (Entriken), *Lake Raystown Resort*, 13

C - Tipton, *Delgrosso's Amusement Park*, 19

CE- Allentown, *Dorney Park And Wildwater Kingdom*, 24

CE- Easton, *Bushkill Park*, 28

CE- Elysburg, *Knoebel's Amusement Resort*, 31

CE- Poconos (Scotrun), *Great Wolf Lodge/Indoor Waterpark*, 34

CE- Poconos (Shawnee-on-Delaware), *Shawnee Place Children's Play And Water Park*, 35

CE- Tannersville, *Camel Beach Water Park (Camelback Ski Area)*, 36

NE- Beach Lake, *Carousel Water And Fun Park*, 60

NW- Conneaut Lake, *Conneaut Lake Park*, 72

NW- Erie, *Waldameer Park And Water World*, 75

NW- Erie, *Splash Lagoon*, 79

SC- Bedford (Schellsburgh), *Gravity Hill*, 89

SC- Hershey, *Hersheypark*, 106

SE- Breinigsville, *Terry Hill Waterpark*, 118

SE- Lancaster, *Dutch Wonderland Family Amusement Park*, 129

SE- Philadelphia, *Science Park*, 140

SE- Philadelphia (Langhorne), *Sesame Place*, 153

SE- Shartlesville, *Roadside America*, 156

SE- Strasburg, *Choo Choo Barn, Traintown USA*, 157

SW- Ligonier, *Idlewild Pk/Soak Zone*, 172

SW- Pittsburgh, *Sand Castle*, 175

SW- Pittsburgh (West Mifflin), *Kennywood Park*, 189

ANIMALS & FARMS

CE- Allentown (Schnecksville), *Lehigh Valley Zoo*, 24

CE- Poconos (Marshalls Creek), *Pocono Snake & Animal Farm*, 34

CW- Cooksburg, *Double Diamond Deer Ranch*, 41

CW- Moraine, *Living Treasures Animal Park*, 42

CW- Punxsutawney, *Punxsutawney Groundhog Zoo*, 43

NC- Williamsport (Allenwood), *Reptiland, Clyde Peeling's*, 56

NE- Hamlin (Lake Ariel), *Claws And Paws Animal Park*, 61

NW- Edinboro, *Wooden Nickel Buffalo Farm*, 73

NW- Erie, *Erie Zoo*, 78

NW- Jamestown, *Pymatuning Deer Park*, 82

SC- Brogue, *Hope Acres Farm, Home Of The Brown Cow*, 90

SC- Gettysburg, *Land Of Little Horses*, 96

SC- Halifax, *Lake Tobias Wildlife Park*, 97

SC- Hershey, *Zoo America North American Wildlife Park*, 107

SE- Kempton, *Hawk Mountain*, 125

SE- Kutztown, *Rodale Institute Farm*, 126

SE- Norristown, *Elmwood Park Zoo*, 135

SE- Philadelphia, *Philadelphia Zoo*, 140

SE- Worcester, *Peter Wentz Farmstead*, 163

SW- Donegal, *Living Treasures Animal Park*, 166

SW- Elizabeth, *Round Hill Exhibit Farm*, 167

SW- Pittsburgh, *Pittsburgh Zoo & PPG Aquarium*, 175

SW- Pittsburgh, *National Aviary*, 178

SW- Pittsburgh, *Beechwood Farm Nature Preserve*, 184

For updates & travel games visit: **www.KidsLoveTravel.com**

HISTORY

HISTORY *(cont.)*

For updates & travel games visit: **www.KidsLoveTravel.com**

SCIENCE *(cont.)*

SE- Philadelphia, *Academy Of Natural Sciences*, 138

SE- Philadelphia, *Franklin Institute Science Museum*, 138

SE- Philadelphia, *Insectarium*, 151

SW- Farmington, *Laurel Caverns*, 167

SW- Pittsburgh, *Carnegie Science Center*, 177

SW- Pittsburgh, *Allegheny Observatory*, 181

SW- Pittsburgh (Oakland), *Carnegie Museum Of Natural History*, 187

SPORTS

C - Altoona, *Altoona Curve Baseball Club*, 2

C - Boalsburg, *Tussey Mountain Ski,* 6

C - Claysburg, *Blue Knob All Seasons Resort / Ski Area*, 6

C - Johnstown, *Johnstown Chiefs Hockey*, 8

C - Johnstown, *Johnstown Riverhawks*, 8

CE- Analomink, *Alpine Mountain*, 25

CE- Lake Harmony, *Split Rock Resort Ski Area*, 32

CE- Minersville, *Big Diamond Raceway*, 33

CE- Palmerton, *Blue Mountain Ski*, 33

CE- Poconos (Blakeslee), *Jack Frost Mountain & Big Boulder Ski,* 34

CE- Poconos (Shawnee-on-Delaware), *Shawnee Mountain Ski Area*, 35

NC- Coudersport, *Ski Denton*, 48

NC- Hughesville, *Crystal Lake Ski Center*, 51

NC- Morris, *Ski Sawmill Mountain Resort*, 53

NC- Williamsport, South, *Little League Museum*, 57

NE- Bushkill, *Fernwood Resort*, 61

NE- Poconos (Long Pond), *Pocono Raceway*, 65

NE- Poconos (Tafton), *Tanglwood Ski Area*, 65

NE- Scranton, *Montage Ski Area*, 68

NE- Scranton, *Red Barons Baseball*, 68

NE- Union Dale, *Elk Mountain Ski Area*, 69

NE- Wilkes-Barre, *Wilkes-Barre/ Scranton Penguins Hockey*, 69

NW- Cambridge Springs, *Mountain View Ski Area*, 72

NW- Erie, *Erie Otters Hockey*, 74

NW- Erie, *Erie Sea Wolves*, 74

SC- Carroll Valley, *Ski Liberty*, 90

SC- Harrisburg, *Harrisburg Senators Baseball*, 102

SC- Hershey, *Hershey Bears Hockey*, 104

SC- Lewisberry, *Ski Roundtop*, 108

SC- Mercersburg, *Whitetail Ski Resort And Mountain Biking Center*, 109

SE- Lancaster, *Lancaster Barnstormers Professional Baseball*, 130

SE- Philadelphia, *Philadelphia Sports*, 136

SE- Reading, *Reading Phillies Baseball*, 155

SW- Champion, *Seven Springs Mountain Resort*, 166

SW- Farmington, *Nemacolin Woodlands Resort Ski Area*, 168

SW- Hidden Valley, *Hidden Valley Ski*, 169

SW- Latrobe, *Pittsburgh Steelers Summer Training Camp*, 174

SW- Pittsburgh, *Pittsburgh Sports*, 174

SW- Pittsburgh (Belle Vernon), *Willowbrook Ski Area*, 185

SW- Pittsburgh (Carnegie), *Pittsburgh's Pennsylvania Motor Speedway*, 186

SW- Pittsburgh (Monroeville), *Boyce Park Ski Area*, 186

For updates & travel games visit: **www.KidsLoveTravel.com**

TOURS *(cont.)*